"The in-depth stories throughout *Personalized* provide a compelling account of how personalization is transforming every sector today. At a time when there is so much talk about AI driving efficiencies, Abraham and Edelman have provided a prescient handbook filled with practical advice on how to use AI to turbocharge growth by keeping the consumer at the center."

—ABHISHEK DALMIA, Chief Strategy and Transformation Officer, VF

"Abraham and Edelman demystify what's required to build best-in-class personalization systems—and it does not require a large, expensive team of machine-learning engineers and developers. The concepts of 'smart integration' and 'modularity' are spot-on and create the flexibility that brands will need."

—JON FRANCIS, Chief Data and Analytics Officer, General Motors

"*Personalized* is full of pragmatic and timely advice on making 1:1 personalization happen. Senior executives will learn from its fresh perspective on critical areas like sophisticated creative testing, leveraging new technologies, such as CDPs and gen AI, managing risk, and evolving corporate roles, while practitioners will benefit from the book's many thoughtful exercises."

—VINEET MEHRA, Chief Marketing Officer, Chime

PERSONALIZED

PERSONALIZED

CUSTOMER STRATEGY IN THE AGE OF AI

Mark Abraham
David C. Edelman

HARVARD BUSINESS REVIEW PRESS
BOSTON, MASSACHUSETTS

Copyright 2024 The Boston Consulting Group, Inc.

Printed in the United States of America

10 9 8 7 6 5 4 3 2 1

The web addresses referenced in this book were live and correct at the time of the book's publication but may be subject to change.

Library of Congress Cataloging-in-Publication Data

Names: Abraham, Mark (Partner at BCG), author. | Edelman, David C. (David Carl), 1961– author.
Title: Personalized : customer strategy in the age of AI / Mark Abraham and David C. Edelman.
Description: Boston, Massachusetts : Harvard Business Review Press, [2024] | Includes index.
Identifiers: LCCN 2024002911 (print) | LCCN 2024002912 (ebook) | ISBN 9781647826277 (hardcover) | ISBN 9781647826284 (epub)
Subjects: LCSH: Customer relations. | Artificial intelligence.
Classification: LCC HF5415.5 .A27 2024 (print) | LCC HF5415.5 (ebook) | DDC 658.8/12—dc23/eng/20240514
LC record available at https://lccn.loc.gov/2024002911
LC ebook record available at https://lccn.loc.gov/2024002912

ISBN: 978-1-64782-627-7
eISBN: 978-1-64782-628-4

*To my sons, Benji and Noah, and my loving partner, Jason,
for their patience and support during the creation of this book.*

Mark Abraham

*To my wife, Miriam, for her patience, support, and encouragement
through the years, especially lately to pursue writing this book.*

David C. Edelman

Contents

Preface

Companies have been chasing the promise of personalization for decades, with most falling short of delivering the hoped-for impact for customers and the business. But in the age of AI, personalization leaders are redefining what's possible and building market-leading positions as a result.

At its best, personalization feels almost magical. Spotify knows exactly the right music to play for your mood while you're cooking dinner. Uber senses you're on a business trip in New York and automatically fills in the destination from your calendar. Your mortgage application takes only minutes, not hours, because your bank's website prefills all the information it already has about you.

But more often we see examples of personalization gone awry. Consider a "personalized" email addressed to Abraham Mark, not Mark Abraham . . . three times in a month. Or a brand continuously targeting a middle-aged man with ads for women's yoga clothes, all because of a gift purchased for someone else. Or a piece of direct mail advertising a model of hot tub that the recipient already purchased a month earlier from the same company. These are just a few examples from our own recent experience, and there are many more every day.

Many companies invest millions in technology, data, and AI in launching ambitious personalization initiatives, only to see progress falter. We know this all too well. Between the two of us, we've spent fifty years thinking about and working on personalization.

Way back in 1989, David published "Segment-of-One Marketing," a seminal BCG Perspective about using a company's proprietary database of customer preferences to tailor the customer experience. It was a novel concept that foreshadowed everything from the birth of Spotify and advanced loyalty programs to apps that recommend the right cosmetics (now augmented by generative AI) and smart retail "clienteling." In the decades that followed, we both advised many companies on this idea, and saw progress on many fronts.

But it wasn't until the early 2010s, with the rise of smartphones, content management systems, AI, and other new technologies, that companies were able to carry out the segment-of-one approach in earnest. In 2015, this led to Mark founding BCG's personalization business, bringing together teams of change management and strategy consultants as well as hands-on data scientists, data engineers, and human-centered designers to help companies realize their ambitions.

This book distills the learnings from our work accelerating the personalization, retail media, and AI efforts of hundreds of iconic brands, including the likes of Starbucks, Home Depot, and Google.[1] We draw on Mark's launching a personalization software-as-a-service company and building Fabriq, BCG's own AI platform for personalization, endeavors that have given him firsthand experience with the technology and operations requirements for delivering impact with personalization across a variety of sectors. We complement this with David's insights from his time as chief marketing officer at Aetna, where he transformed the customer experience, from his work advising companies on integrating AI into their operations, and from his work with more than two dozen early-stage companies.

There is an urgent need for a book to guide business leaders on how to build and scale great personalized experiences for their customers. To be sure, there's no shortage of articles on the subject. But there is also no widely accepted definition of personalization. Most books on the topic address only one aspect of it, like content personalization, or the data and AI requirements. The unprecedented and enthusiastic reception of our 2022 *Harvard Business Review* article "Customer Experience in the Age of AI" made clear that readers were keen to get a holistic perspective on personalization.

Throughout these pages, we go well beyond what has been written before, applying a practitioner's lens to over a hundred in-depth interviews conducted for this book and dozens of examples from companies that have given us an insider's view through our work together. We want to equip you with a clear understanding of what personalization is and how to get it done, end to end, from the strategic role of executive leadership to the tactics needed deep in the company's operations.

In the last few years, it has become clear to us that personalization is a do-or-die aspect of corporate strategy. The nature of competition has changed. Data is now plentiful. The shift to digital channels took a quantum leap forward in the early 2020s, spawning millions of new direct customer relationships and a wealth of data about behavior and preferences. With the advent of generative AI, customers can increasingly call on virtual assistants for most of their needs, raising the bar for the level of personalization other channels must offer to stay relevant. Technology is more accessible; many more off-the-shelf tools are available for companies—even ones with more limited budgets—to use, if they can smartly integrate them.

Making Personalization Personal

We know from our work and personal experiences that personalization can create a superior customer experience even in commoditized industries, and can be a powerful competitive advantage even for small players. David's purchase of solar panels provides an illustrative example of what it feels like for the customer when companies get personalization right.

A few years ago, my town of Lexington, Massachusetts, introduced a substantial rebate to homeowners for installing solar panels. Solar installers then bombarded residents with emails, digital ads, local newspaper ads, kiosks at town fairs, mailbox flyers, even targeted direct mail. My wife and I had already been considering solar, but the marketing barrage—everything to everyone all at once—was overwhelming.

One direct-mail piece, however, caught my eye. It was from a company called Sungevity, and was addressed to me personally. On the outer envelope a message noted "We've checked out your house and determined that you could convert at least 25 percent of your energy consumption to solar. A personal URL inside will explain it all." I opened the envelope, entered the URL on my laptop, and was immediately taken to an aerial Google Earth image of my house with solar panels superimposed on the roof. Beside the image was running text explaining how many panels could fit on my roof and how much energy they would likely generate over the course of a year, given our house's location, orientation, tree cover, and roof pitch. Using our house's square footage (pulled from Zillow), Sungevity then estimated our annual energy consumption and calculated a ballpark percentage of our household energy use that could shift to solar.

So far, they had my attention.

A link on the image connected me to a live rep who greeted me by name, saying how excited he was to show me how solar could save me 25 percent on my energy bills. The rep already had all the information from my Google Earth image, so I was the one asking most of the questions. As the discussion progressed, the rep pulled up several lease or buy options, each tailored to my circumstances.

The economics of solar panel usage are incredibly complicated, given the incentive structures, local differences in energy prices, the ability to sell excess power back to the grid, and the inevitable fluctuations in the amount of sunshine over the course of a year. That's not counting the likelihood of servicing necessitated by damage (hail and squirrels being two of the most common sources). The math was laid out cleanly, showing a guaranteed minimum savings. All of the information was downloadable and easy to import into a spreadsheet. The rep even sent me the email addresses of three neighbors who could serve as references.

The data made sense and the referrals were quite positive, so I picked a lease option. I set a follow-up appointment with the same rep, who then sent me the digital paperwork to sign, all of which was prefilled with the needed information. From that point on, the process unfolded through an app: scheduling an initial visit to verify the site details and create an installation plan, tracking every aspect of the installation, and then once the panels were installed, tracking our solar energy production, paying bills, receiving alerts to problems (such as a squirrel-induced outage), and connecting for any service issues. I even became a reference, and connected my sister to the company. (She, too, had panels installed.)

My customer journey was remarkable. Even more remarkable was the contrast between my journey—tailored to a "tee"—and the fact that what I was buying was essentially a commodity. At any given moment, the material costs of solar panels are fairly standard. Local installers (who subcontract out to a master brand) work for several companies. Leases are set and managed by a bank that works with several brands. And the rebates are available to all buyers.

Sungevity, however, saw a clear opportunity to innovate the soup-to-nuts experience in a wholly personalized way. (The company is now part of Pineapple Energy.) The personalization is what caught my eye initially; but it's also what propelled me through an essentially seamless experience, one that flowed easily from one step to the next, and that also vastly simplified the underlying complexities. It was fast, highly automated, and focused on making me feel in control.

Also important was that all of the personal information that Sungevity had gathered was channeled to all of the parties that needed it in order to serve me: the rep, the installers, the leasing company, the service suppliers. Sungevity orchestrated a personalized value proposition for what is fundamentally a commodity item, albeit one whose implementation is complex. Today, a growing number of companies are doing just what Sungevity did: rooting the value they provide in the personalization they deliver.

Competing on Personalization

This book is a call to action. As the Sungevity example shows, personalization elevates companies above the rest and has emerged as the new basis of competition, as first-movers build a competitive moat of customer insights that is hard for competitors to replicate. The advances in personalization capability have been so sweeping that they are calling into question long-held tenets about economies of scale as a key to creating competitive advantage. New competitors are building end-to-end businesses based on scale in information about customers and the breadth of their relationship with each customer, and less so on scale in manufacturing. Moreover, personalization goes well beyond marketing. It is becoming embedded into every aspect of customer service and operations.

Every company can do—*needs* to do—considerably more to make its customers' lives easier by more effectively using what it already knows about them. If you work for a typical company, you and your teams may be thinking, "We already do personalization." Most organizations have had personalization initiatives for years. But spend a day in your own customer's shoes: ask your customers about your website and app, the last phone interactions they had with your call center or the most recent emails they received from you. More likely than not, the experience wasn't as seamless or productive for them as it could have been. Our work with the Personalization Index shows this. Meanwhile, our new global consumer research with thousands of customers confirms the near-universal consumer acceptance of personalization. But it also shows that a significant majority of consumers have had recent personalized experiences that were either inaccurate or felt invasive. Every customer-obsessed leader should be thinking, "We have so much more to do!"

While no one is doing personalization perfectly, we all have a lot to learn from the personalization leaders. It's important to look at leaders across industries, in both the business-to-consumer and business-to-business sectors, at companies large and small, and at innovators across continents, to truly understand the playbook for success. Reflecting on our work and discussions with all the personalization leaders featured in this book, we are excited for the future of personalization. Indeed, that future is already here.

Personalization at the Core of Your Strategy

Our extensive research on personalization leaders, along with our work with hundreds of companies, shows definitively that companies that create a competitive advantage from personalization do so by *putting personalization at the center of their enterprise strategy.* Unlike the average company, the vast majority of personalization leaders—80 percent—consider personalization to be a CEO-sponsored initiative, and they've appointed a dedicated personalization "owner" who reports to the CEO. Such owners may not control all the personalization levers enterprise-wide, but they are charged with the leadership and cross-functional orchestration that can activate personalization at scale. They have a mandate to drive change and are held to a set of measurable targets. This accountability is shared with the functional and business leadership that needs to work to embed personalization into key processes. This book serves as a guide full of stories, facts, and arguments to build a case for change and for taking action, across the enterprise.

Personalization is hard, but the payoffs are substantial. Our playbook for personalization at scale is achievable for a broad range of companies, not just the big digital natives. Our research shows the payoff: *an almost $2 trillion prize in accelerated growth awaits personalization leaders this decade.*

Skeptics might point to the risks involved, as customer data, algorithms that use that data, and personalized outreaches to individuals proliferate, sometimes without proper permissioning or in violation of individual privacy. They get even more agitated by the potential for generative AI to exacerbate those risks, as access to tools expands. We recognize the reality of those risks, and we raise many more. But we also see leaders explicitly managing those risks in a strategic manner, through careful guardrails, audit processes, technology and cybersecurity investments, and other mechanisms we'll describe. A strategy based on personalization hinges on the trust that you build with your customers, and personalization leaders put the development and preservation of that trust on the same level as the performance gains they aim to achieve.

So, before you claim, "We are already doing personalization," think again. Most likely, you are not—at least not in the way you could be. Not in the way your customers deserve. And not in a way that will build real competitive advantage. There is much more to do, and no time to waste.

Because the personalization field is constantly evolving, as we continue to learn through our work, and from the experiences of leading practitioners and companies, we'll be sharing more details about our research, best practices, case studies, interviews, tools, and tips in our online hub at www.personalizedthebook.com. Additional perspectives are also available at http://on.bcg.com/personalized.

PERSONALIZED

Chapter 1

The Personalization Advantage

Personalization has become an overused buzzword. Every company claims to be doing it. But are they? What exactly is personalization?

Some might define personalization as "something built or delivered for me, just the way I want it." It would entail providing the customer with choices from a range of parameters, letting them select what they want, and then delivering it. Companies have been doing this for a long time: offering the choice of fabric for a sofa, the specifications of a PC, the choice of a seat at an event, and so on. It may come in the form of price differences for various options or the physical production of something to the customer's specifications. But this isn't *personalization*; it is simply *customization*.

To be sure, we've seen enormous advances in the customization of physical and digital goods through robotics, 3D printing, and open-source componentization. While these refinements are certainly related to personalization—entire books have been written on this progress—these are not examples of personalization.

Nor is personalization a matter of adding a "Hi, Jordan" greeting at the beginning of an email or a simple "Others who bought this also bought . . ." recommendation to an online shopping site search. Some companies see their segmented marketing efforts as personalization. It seems everything is being labelled as personalization, and these are just a few examples of overstatement.

Well, then what is personalization? It's what happens when you're searching on a website and are shown items based not just on what others who searched for that term would like but on what *you* would like, based on your context, search history, and any items you recently bought. It's when you phone a call center and the agent has all the information about you and your history with the company at their fingertips (based on the number you are calling from) and can get right to solving your problem. It's when your favorite sales associate in a store greets you by name, remembers your last purchases and tastes, and creates a tailored shopping experience to delight you. And more to the point, it's when every sales associate in that store does that with every one of their regular customers.

Personalization is creating experiences at scale that get fine-tuned with each successive interaction, empowering customers to get what they want—better, faster, cheaper, or more easily. The difference lies in the way personalized communications build on everything the company learns about the customer over time. In our experience across industries and consumer contexts, this is what makes personalization truly effective.

It's about speed

At its core, personalization is about speed. Speed in getting to know the customer throughout the customer journey, and speed in constantly improving the experience based on that knowledge. BCG has long championed the importance of "time-based competition," the concept of competing on the basis of speed. In personalization, it is foundational.

Netflix has revolutionized the way we watch television, by building a learning loop for personalization, surfacing massive amounts of content to its base of around 250 million subscribers. For example, it has created more than a million personalized versions of TV-series trailers, using the data on viewers' reactions to personalize the recommendations viewers see next. What Netflix has done in movies (and Spotify in music streaming) is now playing out in categories as varied as fashion, grocery, air travel, hospitality, home goods, coffee, home security, insurance, and countless others.

It's about scale

Personalization introduces a new way to achieve scale. We have long advocated for building economies of scale, especially in the physical aspects of competition: supply chains, production, distribution. But personalization changes the nature of scale in the customer experience, from the mass production of goods to the mass delivery of 1:1 experiences built on accumulated intelligence.

Personalization at scale and the ongoing cycle of activities that power it create a competitive moat that is very hard to replicate. It is no coincidence that companies across a wide swath of categories, including home improvement (such as Home Depot), banking (JPMorgan Chase), restaurants (Starbucks), grocery (Kroger), and apparel (Nike), have publicly announced that personalized and seamless omnichannel experiences are central to their corporate strategy.[1]

Business is now effectively at the point where competitive advantage will be based on a company's ability to capture, analyze, and utilize customer data on a gargantuan scale—and on how it uses that data to understand, shape, personalize, and optimize the customer's journey.

In short, competitive advantage from personalization (P) is a function of scale, or the volume of interactions from which the company can learn (n), times the speed of learning (v), which has an exponential impact (in our experience, doubling the number of experiments more than doubles the quality of the learnings). For the mathematically inclined, the main idea of this book can be distilled into a simple equation:

$$P = n \times v^2$$

As we detail later in this chapter, the size of this competitive advantage from personalization (P) can be quantified at the company, as well as the industry, level. We estimate that by the end of this decade, personalization leaders across industries will capture almost $2 trillion in incremental growth.

The Case for Personalization, throughout the Customer Journey

In a world where consumers are expecting more products, services, and support to be accessible instantly, seamlessly, and the way they want, personalization has become a strategic imperative. Rather than just treating it as a marketing challenge, leading companies are putting personalization at the center of their enterprise strategy. They are embedding it *throughout* the customer journey, launching cross-functional efforts that span operations, marketing, technology, analytics, and beyond.

Fundamentally, personalization is about enabling consumers to get what they want. For this book, we surveyed more than five thousand consumers from ten countries: Australia, Brazil, China, France, Germany, India, Japan, South Africa, the United States, and the United Kingdom. Our findings clearly show that personalization is critical at every point in the customer journey, although consumers consider it even more important in the early and later stages of their journeys than at the moment of first purchase, where simple recommendations (e.g., "customers like you also bought . . .") are already commonplace (see figure 1-1).

But the ability to personalize, as well as which aspects of the customer journey to focus on, will vary, based on the nature of the sector and the way a company competes.

- If you are a retailer or otherwise sell goods, your personalization actions may start at prepurchase consideration. But you can actually engage customers personally in their everyday lives, even in low-frequency categories. For example, people may buy clothes only twice a year, but they make wardrobe choices every day.

- If you are selling an experience (say, travel or dining), personalization should begin from the moment the customer starts thinking about the experience and continue through to the experience itself, and beyond.

- If you are selling an ongoing service relationship (e.g., as a telco, bank, or health insurer), your personalization efforts should take place across all customer interactions, on a continuous basis.

- In B2B industries, if you are selling a business outcome, personalization should happen as soon as you begin driving the transaction and continue throughout the relationship to ensure the client's success, even as individuals change within companies.

Our consumer research also confirmed that personalization is widely accepted globally (see figure 1-2). In India, whose Aadhaar program assigns a unique, biometrically verifiable identification number to every citizen, public trust in personalization is near universal.

FIGURE 1-1

Personalization is critical throughout the customer journey

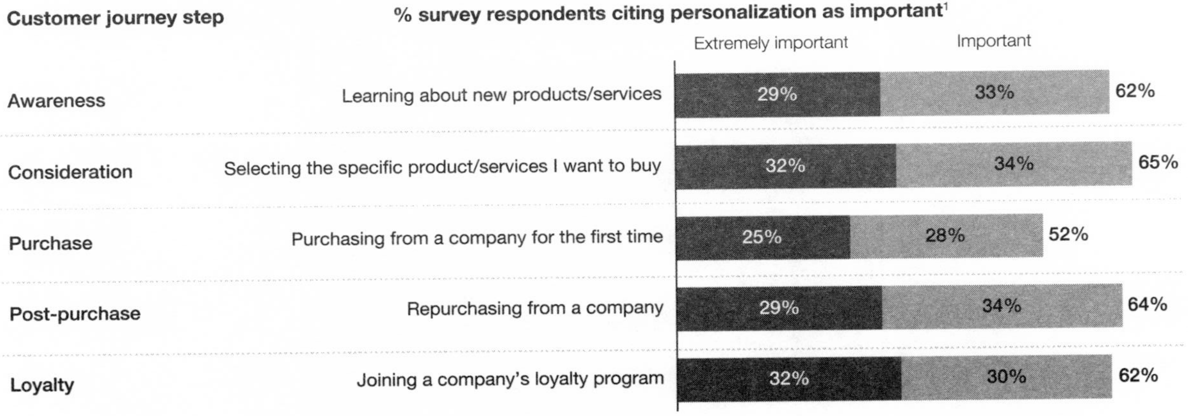

Customer journey step	% survey respondents citing personalization as important[1]	Extremely important	Important
Awareness	Learning about new products/services	29%	33% (62%)
Consideration	Selecting the specific product/services I want to buy	32%	34% (65%)
Purchase	Purchasing from a company for the first time	25%	28% (52%)
Post-purchase	Repurchasing from a company	29%	34% (64%)
Loyalty	Joining a company's loyalty program	32%	30% (62%)

1. Survey question: In general, how important is it for companies to use your data and past behavior to customize your customer experience during the following activities?

Note: Total numbers may not match sums due to rounding.

Source: 2023 BCG Customer Personalization Survey (n = 5,000).

FIGURE 1-2

Acceptance of personalization, by country

Percentage of customers comfortable with companies using publicly available information to create a customized experience[1]

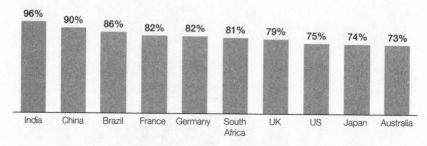

1. Survey question: How comfortable are you with companies using publicly available information about you to create a customized experience (for example, if publicly available, age, gender, marital status, social media activity, home address, zip code, income)? Select all that apply.
Source: 2023 BCG Customer Personalization Survey (n = 5,000).

Despite its widespread acceptance, personalization is not measuring up. In the second quarter of 2023, 66 percent of consumers across the ten markets surveyed reported that a company's communication was either inaccurate or felt invasive. Interestingly, the percentage was even higher in markets where acceptance is higher, such as India and Brazil.

In our decade of helping companies with their personalization efforts, we've talked to thousands of our clients' customers. One customer summed up our research findings well: "I may not have chosen to live in a world where brands have this much data about me, but they do. So now they need to put it to good use, responsibly, to make my life easier and better."[2]

Personalization, done right, goes beyond pushing customers to buy specific products. It's about making customers' lives easier. Personalization distinctively meets customer expectations. But at its most impactful, it can anticipate a customer's needs even before the customer expresses them. We're speaking of a proactive process, something altogether different from the sea of targeted, but not contextually relevant, marketing messages that get lost in the noise. This process, moreover, extends well beyond the marketing function; it must be embedded in customer strategy, the digital experience, operations, customer service, employee training, the supply chain, and inventory management.

The Five Promises of Personalization

This book seeks to demystify delivering personalization at scale. We have distilled the formula for success into what we call the Five Promises of Personalization, promises the company makes to the customer and needs to live up to (see figure 1-3). In the age of AI, we make the case that every one of these promises must be delivered by bringing together both a human touch and the right technology.

Empower Me

Empower Me is the overarching, and most important, Promise of Personalization. It represents your effort to put the customer in the driver's seat of the relationship. Each customer has a particular set of needs to address, now and in the future, that can be the basis of an enduring relationship. You want to help them achieve a goal, whether it's inspiring them early in their journey with different choices, educating them about the products they are considering, making it easy to find what they want,

FIGURE 1-3

The Five Promises of Personalization

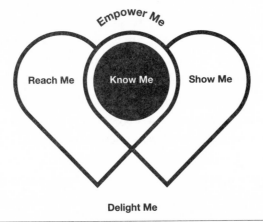

helping them nab a great deal as they consider a purchase, or making a return seamless.

To empower your customers, you must first determine which parts of the customer journey are most critical for personalization. Which experiences can you personalize that will help customers achieve their desired goal? Too often, companies concentrate on the moment of purchase, with add-to-cart recommendations; or on retargeting (finding them in a paid digital channel and serving them relevant ads). To truly live up to this first Promise of Personalization, think instead about the whole journey and how your use of information will build affinity and cultivate trust.

Companies seeking to empower customers must also think about the technologies they use to seamlessly deliver experiences to customers across channels. In the age of generative AI (gen AI), virtual assistants and smart chat interfaces can connect information across multiple systems in ways that previously required implementing expensive integrations or making the customer click through countless menus and multiple websites. New ways to empower the customer are emerging in every domain—from planning a vacation to planning their financial future—ways as simple as letting them ask for what they want.

Know Me

Empowering the customer—being effective at personalization—requires knowing the customer: not the "typical" customer, or even a customer segment, but each *individual* customer. Fulfilling this second Promise of Personalization entails securely organizing, analyzing, and synthesizing the data you gather on them, and clearly recording how that data can be used. When the customer sees that you are using information about them in a positive way, that you are aware of their current situation and what they might need at that moment, your brand becomes dramatically more relevant. Using information to support the actions a customer will want to take makes their experience simple, tailored, and fast. You're essentially creating the foundation to know enough about the customer to help them achieve their goal. Building a detailed, 360-degree view of the customer, with their digital permissions in place, powers all of the intelligence in your personalization technology stack.

Reach Me

If a company is not able to connect with the right customer at the right time and place and deliver the right experience, nothing happens. Therefore, a key Promise of Personalization is the ability to reach out to the right customer, in the right channel, at just the right moment. Fulfilling this promise entails having the insights to know what is relevant to the customer at that moment, based on all you know about them. The customer must first grant you permission to contact them and use their data in certain ways. Proper permissioning involves knowing how to ask customers and respecting their privacy (a topic we explore, along with the associated risks, more in chapter 10). From there, the company might reach out based on the contextual information it has: the customer's physical and virtual location, device in use, time of day, weather, or some trigger (such as the customer's browsing behavior or an app download). Or the customer might directly interact with a digital channel. Both the right timing and access require having enough knowledge about the customer, and the right intelligence layered on top of that data, to know which customers to contact, and when.

From a technology perspective, this means having the right targeting intelligence (models and algorithms derived from the data), experiment design and activation (decisions about which customers get which experiences), and next best action orchestration (decisions on the timing, sequence, and cross-channel coordination of the experiences).

Show Me

Giving the customer relevant content is an essential element of personalization. This might be an informational email with tailored text and video, a web or app image, personalized guidance or problem-solving in real time from a call center rep, or a chatbot interaction. Content should be tailored to the information customers expect the company to have on them. Too often personalized messages, even those from leading digital brands, are generic and uninspiring. Companies need creative content design and operational processes that can generate variations for every type of customer.

Fortunately, new approaches to content delivery and the application of gen AI in content creation are making this much more feasible. Personalization leaders are building content libraries with dynamic templates and modular assets that can be mixed and matched to address different audiences. Instead of duplicating efforts by channel, teams are developing content from the start with omnichannel in mind. Gen AI is increasing the productivity of creative teams by making it easier to create additional content variants (e.g., for different segments, languages, personas) and to manage existing content via better tagging.

Delight Me

Masterly personalization should feel magical to the customer. Getting the experience just right requires deeply knowing the customer and discovering what delights them over time. One interaction won't be enough—companies need to set up the processes and ways of working to continuously and rapidly test new ideas to improve the level and accuracy of their personalization. Learning comes from gaining more information about the customer, as you constantly innovate and try new ways of interacting within each journey, always aiming to delight the customer further. Data that you capture on the outcomes of those interactions then informs the next interaction. And sometimes the lessons involve what *not* to do.

Companies that fulfill this promise, for example, will stop advertising cars to you when you're not in the market for a new vehicle and don't plan to be in the next few years. They will also stop sending offers for items you've shown no interest in, using the data from your lack of engagement to update their models. And they will stop sending you any repeat purchase offers while you're sorting through a major issue with customer service. Their systems collect and connect information systematically, animated by a fundamental shift from "send and forget" campaigns to "next best action" ones. The drive for continuous improvement is what enables companies to build the competitive moat—of richer information, smarter predictive capability, and more receptive customers—by which they can distinguish themselves from competitors.

Therefore, delighting customers requires the organizational commitment to relentless innovating, testing, learning, and optimizing. It also necessitates investing in the tools and data flows to quickly put the right information at the personalization working team's fingertips, so they can learn faster. Fortunately, with gen AI and automation, teams can quickly query multiple systems as long as the underlying systems are set up to ensure the right data is accessible to all who need it.

With every interaction, leading personalization companies capture more feedback about what works, because testing different possibilities is a cornerstone of their approach. When you have the capability to test rapidly, you can constantly try new things. Instead of spending time setting up the tests, you can let the technology manage them, and focus on pushing the limits of new ideas that will truly delight each customer.

Delivering on the Promises in Wine and Spirits

One of our favorite stories of helping a company deliver on the Five Promises of Personalization involves a wine and spirits retailer. For those of us who enjoy a great wine, it's easy to see what makes this consumer category a natural for personalization. Mark loves exploring the nuances of pinot noirs from the Pacific Northwest and occasionally kicks back with an espresso martini; David is obsessed with the wines and ports of Portugal (especially dry white port) since his recent trip to vineyards there. The customer's joy of discovering new varietals represents an endless opportunity for purveyors to tailor the customer journey.

Starting in 2021, a growing wine and spirits retailer set out to become the Spotify of wine by introducing customers to products they would love. Its story brings to life what it takes to deliver on the Five Promises of Personalization.

Empower Me. First, the company needed to figure out which steps in the customer journey to personalize. Customers were often overwhelmed by the vast number of products to choose from, so the company identified a broad array of marketing actions: recommending items that the customer had never bought but might like; highlighting new and trending products; and educating customers who preferred a certain varietal about other wines in that category. This set of actions was in addition to reminding customers to replenish regularly purchased items, suggesting favorites on sale, and offering surprise-and-delight gifts to loyal customers. The company also offered in-store wine classes and tastings. For all these actions, the personalization team created thousands of messages, with different tones of voice, images, videos, and copy to appeal to different types of customers based on where they were in their customer journey. To move quickly, the team started with email, but soon expanded to the app, web, and customer service channels. Content relevant to the customer (e.g., the announcement of a newly launched product) was synchronized across these channels.

Know Me. The company aggregated each customer's information in a single-view, comprehensive profile to create its Customer 360 database. This master repository included all the data needed to maintain a current score for each individual, based on more than a thousand data points. These data points reflected such things as the likelihood of someone being a merlot lover versus a cabernet sauvignon fan; their price sensitivity and propensity to respond to offers; their likelihood of not returning in the next ninety days; their typical spend and visit frequency; and their channel preferences. The cloud-based analytics system automatically recalculated the scores every day and fed them back into the Customer 360 database, thus determining which audience the customer would be classified in for any given marketing action.

Reach Me. Next, the company focused on its intelligence capabilities. The team in charge of personalization—a group of marketers, merchants, graphic designers, copywriters, product managers, data scientists, engineers, and marketing technology (martech) experts—built a personalization tech stack they nicknamed "Sensei" (for the uninitiated, a reference to a wise instructor of Japanese martial arts). Sensei's set of cloud-based AI models scored the relevance of each piece of content in the content library for every customer, based on the Customer 360 data, and determined the appropriate piece to send at that time. For example, merlot lovers who were at high risk of leaving might get the merlot discount offer that week. Each new customer interaction generated another three hundred data points to add to Sensei to further improve targeting—such as whether the customer clicked on a particular email and how long they spent viewing it, whether they purchased the item being offered, and whether they provided feedback via reviews. Realizing that any marketing action actually consisted of some twenty different decisions, the team embedded twenty different modules in Sensei, designed to optimize a different aspect of each interaction. Take email messages, for example: one module contained different types of themes for the email (say, a recommendation, a reminder, or an offer); another, the different types of products to showcase in the message body (based on individual predicted preferences); the next module contained which types of customers would receive the message (e.g., based on hobbies and interests, location, or level of loyalty); another guided when the message should be sent (e.g., times of day and week when that individual is most likely to engage); one showed what tone the copy should take for that particular customer (e.g., educational, inspirational, or fun); and still another stated whether a reminder should be sent a few days later, and so on.

Show Me. The company set up a "factory" to develop its library of content so that it would be able to escalate both the volume and variety of interactions with customers. Working in two-week sprints, the content incubator team—a dozen-plus marketers, copywriters, graphic designers, and technologists—filled the library, and within a few months had accumulated three thousand unique ways to talk about each SKU in the company's product catalog. Given the number of products and the number of possible content permutations, the team ended up with more ways to talk about its products than it had customers. In this way, it was able to "hyper-personalize" by selecting from its rich content library exactly what would resonate with each customer, based on their unique situation.

Delight Me. The company developed a rapid test-and-learn capability to continuously optimize the experience, based on each interaction. The team ran thousands of experiments to fine-tune the data and algorithms and to determine which types of content worked best in each channel. It created dashboards to track and measure new actions in real time. All of this feedback was used to tailor the next best action. To further delight customers, the team programmed Sensei to continuously learn and improve: 10 percent of the time, the algorithms would prioritize a message about something the customer might like but hadn't seen yet, over sending the optimal revenue-maximizing communication. The cross-functional team, which expanded beyond its original thirty members as the program was scaled, eventually transformed the approach to become the standard way in which the marketing, analytics, and digital teams would collaborate.

The company credits its personalization program as a major reason it grew faster than competitors, gaining significant share. It is no wonder that other traditional, brick-and-mortar wine and spirits retailers around the world are adopting similar approaches.

This retailer's experience demonstrates that you needn't be a digitally native business to build a world-class personalization capability. Established businesses, even smaller or midsize ones, can as well. Digital natives certainly have an advantage: their entire business model is built on digital customer relationships, so they are capturing data from all of their customers from day one. They also can design their technology stack smartly from the start, avoiding the tech debt that plagues many of their established peers. Most traditional companies today lack the foundational data and technology stack that personalization depends on, which means they must rearchitect their legacy systems. Nonetheless, as we show next, those that are able to do so are among the most successful in their categories, substantially accelerating growth and successfully fending off new competitors.

Measuring Personalization Performance

Over the past decade, our team has worked with hundreds of companies across dozens of categories and countries to build personalization capabilities. Early on, we noticed a pattern among those that were succeeding as a result of their personalization efforts. Since 2016, we have quantified these findings into the **BCG Personalization Index**. It provides a numeric score from 0 to 100 that reflects a company's performance in delivering each of the Promises of Personalization. Analysis shows that a company's Personalization Index correlates with its financial performance.

For this book, we updated our annual survey of more than one hundred leading companies around the world. The companies, which range from $250 million to more than $100 billion in revenues, represent twelve key sectors (spanning both B2C and B2B), including retail, fashion, telecommunications, financial services, health care, and more. We scored each company on more than one hundred dimensions representing every aspect of what it takes to become a personalization leader (see table 1-1 for a simplified view of the criteria we used). The assessment consisted of a systematic review of how effectively personalization is deployed in each step of

TABLE 1-1

Assessment criteria for the Personalization Index

Empower Me	Know Me	Reach Me	Show Me	Delight Me
• Level of personalization by channel and step in the customer journey	• Number and depth of digital customer relationships	• Data is used to target each customer based on their needs	• Ability to create content that speaks to each customer at scale	• Ability to run rapid test-and-learn process at scale, with iteration cycles measured in days
• Personalization efforts focused on the most important channels/ journey steps	• Retention and growth in digital customer relationships	• Experiments designed at scale using automation	• Ability to rapidly launch personalized experiences	• Clear, rapid measurement with actionable KPIs
• Overall impact of personalization on customer experience	• Integrated 360-degree view of each customer and quality of data	• Next best action orchestration across channels, sequence of messages, timing	• Sophistication of content management capabilities	• Personalization has clear ownership and committed funding
				• Cross-functional teams work in agile ways

the customer journey (from awareness and consideration to purchase, post-purchase, and loyalty), and in each channel. Importantly, this assessment is tailored by industry, as the objectives and practices of personalization vary markedly from sector to sector. (The latest results are regularly refreshed and are available on www.personalizedthebook.com.)

Several clear insights emerge from the Personalization Index results.

Companies still have far to go to achieve the full potential of personalization

Across all twelve of the industry segments, the average company today scores only 49 on the Personalization Index. The top decile of companies score, on average, only 72. Not surprisingly, the Index leaders are digital natives such as Netflix, Uber, Alibaba, and Amazon and early movers such as Starbucks and Sephora.

It is possible to be a personalization leader in any industry

As figure 1-4 demonstrates, the differences *within* sectors are more pronounced than those *across* sectors. Besides the digital natives, the food,

FIGURE 1-4

The Personalization Index by sector

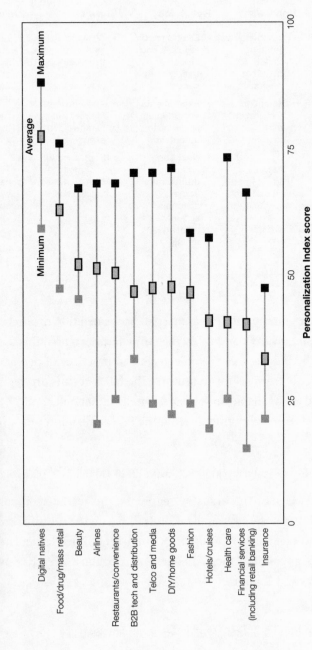

Note: Excludes companies outside of listed sectors.

Source: BCG Personalization Index research, 2023 (n = 98).

drug, and mass-retail sectors also rate highly as a group—not surprising, given that the high purchase frequency, volume of touchpoints, and number of products in these sectors enable companies to collect more data in less time. Although more-highly-regulated industries, such as insurance, financial services, and health care, tend to score lower, there are nonetheless companies that have handily leapfrogged their competitors.

The Personalization Index findings prove it is possible to build personalization-at-scale capabilities in practically any industry. One example of this is Allianz, the global insurer and asset manager. Although regulations limit insurers' ability to personalize, companies like Allianz are nevertheless personalizing claim detection and management to make the customer experience more seamless at the moment it most matters, thereby reducing the time it takes for anxious customers to get their claims resolved.

Personalization drives growth and customer satisfaction

The survey data reveals an unambiguous pattern: on average, companies that score higher on the Personalization Index enjoy faster growth than their lower-scoring peers (see figure 1-5). This same correlation was observed across sectors and regions, and even held during the pandemic years. Thus,

FIGURE 1-5

Companies that score high on personalization grow revenue faster

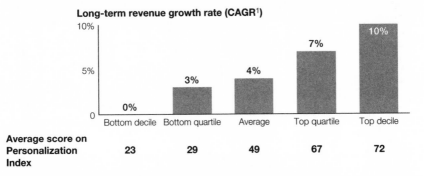

| Average score on Personalization Index | 23 | 29 | 49 | 67 | 72 |

1. Compound annual growth rate, representing 2018–2023 growth for publicly listed companies where data was available and excluding companies with major acquisitions.

Source: BCG Personalization Index research, 2023 (n = 87).

personalization leaders are consistently growing faster, even during times of disruption.

The top decile's 10-point annual growth-rate differential compared to the bottom decile—the size of the competitive advantage from personalization—is consistent with our findings from prior years, and clearly demonstrates that personalization leaders are capturing market share in their respective sectors. The longer-term effect is even more striking given the compound nature of growth. It is no coincidence that every one of the personalization leaders we benchmarked is also a market-share leader in its category—and maintained its dominance through recent downturns (including during the pandemic).

We believe this is a consistent trend that will only accelerate over time. Over the next five years, the net effect will be an almost $2 trillion shift in revenue share, as personalization leaders capture the bulk of growth in their respective sectors, at laggards' expense. Figure 1-6 projects the monetary value of this shift by industry, assuming the current differences in personalization capability remain and the leaders continue to outgrow their competitors.

FIGURE 1-6

$2 trillion in revenue is expected to shift to personalization leaders

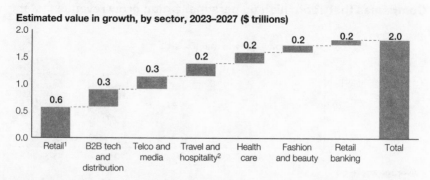

Estimated value in growth, by sector, 2023–2027 ($ trillions)

1. Retail includes food/drug/mass retailers, restaurants/convenience stores, and DIY/home-goods retailers.
2. Includes airlines, hotels, cruise lines, and online travel agents.

Note: Growth in value was determined by comparing the calculated growth rates of personalization leaders with those of laggards and multiplying by industry market size. Growth reflects a five-year period.

Source: BCG Personalization Index research, 2023 (n=87).

Personalization leaders consistently achieve some of the highest customer satisfaction scores across brands

We also looked at the link between customer satisfaction and the Personalization Index. There are certainly some companies with exceptional service and value that don't personalize, such as some of the low-cost airlines known for their on-time performance. However, the highest customer satisfaction companies in our dataset were the personalization leaders. They were the same companies that saw the fastest growth. By building personalization-at-scale capability, companies can stand out among the world's top companies.

Personalization leaders deliver superior value creation

Finally, we assessed the value-creation track record of personalization leaders over time. Companies in the top quartile outperformed both the market index and personalization laggards over all three time frames we examined (three, five, and ten years). As figure 1-7 shows, leaders' and laggards' performance was already diverging prepandemic, but the pandemic further accentuated their differences as digital customer relationships

FIGURE 1-7

Personalization leaders enjoy greater total shareholder return

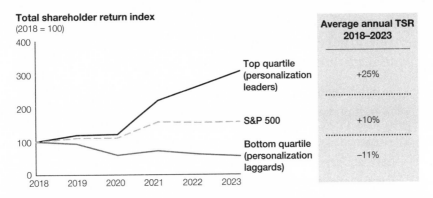

Note: Market data as of April 2023. TSRs run April 30 through April 30 and are calculated in each company's reporting currency.

Source: S&P Capital IQ; BCG ValueScience Center; BCG Personalization Index research, 2023 (n = 100).

became even more important. The gap has widened further most recently. One dollar invested in a personalization leader would have yielded three dollars by the end of the five-year period, while the same investment in a personalization laggard would be worth only about fifty cents.

Taken together, these results show that companies that successfully execute personalization at scale are growing faster, delighting their customers, and creating superior value, as they capture share from competitors.

Accelerating Your Personalization Journey

Now that you have a foundational understanding of what personalization is and why it is so critical to growth and competitive advantage, the rest of this book will focus on helping you turbocharge your own personalization efforts.

In part 1, we delve into the playbook for fulfilling each of the Promises of Personalization, providing a blueprint for how to achieve the needed capabilities. We share questions to ask and pragmatic steps to take to advance your personalization capabilities. We explore the components of the personalization technology stack and how to smartly integrate them. Throughout the book, you'll find industry spotlights that illustrate the path personalization leaders have taken in retail, fashion and beauty, travel, financial services, health care, and B2B distribution and technology, as well as detailed examples of successful companies.

In part 2, we offer broader strategic and business guidance to help you lead the transformation, including:

- How to unite the C-suite to drive the change and lead the charge, through current and new organizational roles

- Insights about the value of personalization and how to measure its impact on your financial performance

- The various risks companies face—in particular, the tension between personalization and data privacy and security—and the steps companies should take to manage these risks. Given AI's rapidly growing role in personalization, we suggest actions companies must take to combat potential bias and inaccuracy in AI output

- Practical ways to accelerate your company's personalization journey and further weave personalization into your corporate strategy, no matter your starting point

- Trends that will shape the future of personalization

Throughout the book, we discuss how AI unlocks the analytics, insights, automation, and optimization that enable personalization at scale. AI gives companies the ability to create exponentially more variations of content, faster, thus fueling the "personal" in personalization to an extent previously unimaginable. As we will discuss throughout this book, gen AI is complementing more "traditional" AI approaches by simplifying the customer experience through its ability to write code, pull together information across systems, and interact using natural language. Fortunately, the technological capabilities, advances in analytics, and explosion of available data that make personalization a reality are available to companies big and small. New companies are being built natively based on these tools, while more-established brands are innovating and transforming their operations, with the expected bumps along the way.

The segment-of-one marketing introduced more than thirty years ago to help companies unlock the potential of customer information seems almost quaint when compared with the personalization practices of today. Personalization at scale is much broader and more powerful than anything we can simply place within the marketing function. It takes a full-on corporate effort to assemble the insight, creativity, technology, automation, and processes necessary to execute and optimize it.

And importantly, it also takes speed. Time-based competition, essentially the value of a superior ability to respond to changing markets, was an important breakthrough in our understanding of the elements of strategic advantage. Personalization leaders are designing and using every interaction to innovate, rapidly test, learn, and empower their customers, making customers' lives easier with each step.

Time is ticking, and the race is on.

PART ONE

THE PROMISES OF PERSONALIZATION

Chapter 2

Empower Me

Empower Me

Empower Me is the first and most important Promise of Personalization. It involves using information about the customer to help them achieve a goal, by providing them a great experience in the channel they choose, at the moment they need it. That great experience could consist of any number of actions on your part: educating the customer, or helping them find something they need, get something done, fix a problem, or treat themselves to a reward. All entail delivering value that the customer expects. Success stems from fostering a closer bond with the customer—keeping them engaged, from awareness to interest, and ultimately to an enduring relationship.

Personalization flips the traditional product-centric approach to marketing on its ear. When empowering the customer is the goal, the individual transaction or interaction is not an isolated event but, rather, part of the continuum of engagement. No matter what the business or product category—even those with long sales cycles—every day is an opportunity for engaging the customer. Consumers may buy a new car on average every eight years, but they drive almost daily, and every trip they take (especially in a connected vehicle) generates engagement opportunities.

Interaction throughout the customer journey enables a deeper understanding of the individual and their context, and provides the fuel for personalization to help the customer. It is also a source of competitive advantage for the company—the speed with which companies understand customers is ultimately dependent on the number of touchpoints they have with each customer and how quickly they integrate those learnings into their personalization efforts.

Traditionally, companies have had to rely on transactional and third-party data to derive insights about customers' desires. But today, companies can create interaction points throughout the customer journey and capture the signals from each of these (whether the customer responds or not) to keep tailoring the next action with increasing precision.

Customer Priorities, Not Technology, Should Drive Your Personalization Game Plan

Thanks to groundbreaking new technologies—notably gen AI—companies can now create personalized content and messaging at volumes, levels of granularity, and speed they could only have dreamed of a mere decade ago.

Because gen AI systems can interpret, assemble, and produce text, speech, images, music, and video—and especially code—they enable customers to accomplish their own tasks simply by asking the system. These systems are designed to contain the customer's complete history and information, their current context, and any goals already indicated (e.g., "remodel my kitchen," or "create meal plans for my family with special dietary needs"). They also know the user's format preferences (e.g., text, audio, video).

However, in pursuing these dazzling possibilities, many companies proceed in the wrong order. All too often, they put the data and technology in place before articulating *how* they want to empower the customer. In all of the personalization implementations we have guided, we have always first pressed leaders to define the crucial applications that personalization can

FIGURE 2-1

Key needs along the customer journey

Awareness	Consideration	Purchase	Post-purchase	Loyalty
• Inspire me • Educate me • Connect me with a community	• Help me find what I want • Make it easier to navigate the process • Give me better value	• Make my purchase experience simple • Give me a great deal • Remind me to repurchase	• Help me use what I bought • Make it easy to resolve issues • Complement my purchase	• Recognize me • Surprise and delight me • Make my future experiences seamless

TABLE 2-1

Questions to identify personalization use cases

Which customers?	Where in their journeys?	Which channel?	How personalized?
New	Awareness	Site	Macro-segment
Active	Consideration	App	Micro-segment
High-value	Purchase	Email	Household
Price-sensitive	Post-purchase	SMS/push	1:1
Declining	Loyalty	Paid media	
Lapsed		Physical	
		Call center	

uniquely enable. Naturally the use cases vary, based on the brand, customer base, customer journey stage, company starting point, and the economics of a company's business. But there are nonetheless use cases that commonly rise to the fore. From our experience, we've identified a list of fifteen core needs covering the five steps of a customer journey, taken from the customer's point of view. (See figure 2-1.)

Mapping use cases

First, to map the full set of opportunities, ask a few key questions. Table 2-1 provides a starting point for your thinking.

There are many ways to select use cases to launch or accelerate your personalization effort. At the highest level, though, the guiding approach is simple. Ask:

- What outcome is most valuable for the customer?

- What value does it create for your business?

- What can you test and scale quickly, especially in a way that will help you build more intelligence to support more use cases?

Your answers will tell you how to prioritize your actions across those potential customer needs, which then become your top use cases. In some cases, building a common fact base can help rally the various functions around the use cases to prioritize. Start by using data to identify where in the journey customers seem to be getting frustrated, wasting time, or giving up. Analyze call center data to understand the problems common to certain types of customers, and try to preempt those problems with targeted educational messages. Or find customers who spend a lot of time searching on your site, and think of questions you could proactively ask or information you could use from their previous purchases to help them find what they are looking for more quickly. But don't let all this analysis stall your efforts.

Some organizations waste a lot of time on use case mapping. However, a cross-functional team working side by side can quickly identify the most important ones based on value and feasibility. Table 2-2 shows high-priority

TABLE 2-2

Fashion and beauty personalization use cases

Product recommendations	Offers and promotions	Experiences	Journeys
• Personalized product pages	• Private promotions	• Personalized clienteling	• Personalized onboarding
• In-cart recommendations	• Personalized gifts with purchase	• Personalized beauty and style adviser	• Lifestyle triggers (to prevent churn)
• Triggered replenishment	• Gamified offers	• Targeted fashion inspiration	• Conquesting (to target switchers)
• "Complete the look"		• Personalized customer service	

use cases developed by a cross-functional team at a fashion retailer during a single workshop.

Making rapid progress on the priority use cases

The real difficulty usually arises after compiling the list. Teams might flounder because there is no single companywide leader who owns personalization and can marshal the resources needed. Business-line and functional teams might go off on their own and develop disconnected customer experiences—emailing an existing customer to introduce a product the customer is already using, texting a customer with an irrelevant offer as they enter a store. Such misfires result in disjointed experiences that only confuse, if not irritate, customers.

To get started with a priority use case, bring your cross-functional teams together to create an integrated road map, one that considers opportunities as well as dependencies. Suppose you want new customers to register for your site and download your app. Don't just send a simple email. Instead, test different kinds of incentives, different versions of the copy, different prompts in the call center (for customers needing help), different ways to create the call to action right after the order is placed. Such tactics involve different functional areas—for instance, marketing, customer service, operations, technology, product management—all of which must be aligned in order to execute any high-value use case.

It's easy to see why organizations get bewildered by the countless permutations of use cases and the internal alignment that is needed to execute them. The inherent complexity of these decisions and their enterprise-wide implementation is why we believe so strongly that personalization is central to the C-suite agenda. Time and time again, we've witnessed the power that a CEO or other senior executive can have in rallying leaders around personalization as a business strategy. Arti Zeighami, the former chief data and analytics officer at H&M Group, recommends starting with "a couple of simple use cases, based on actual business problems, that would deliver the most value to the organization."[1] These should be projects that would be highly visible and could be scaled up quickly to win advocates for the new ways of working that personalization requires. "Training the organization to be more data-driven will create pull for personalization rather than it being pushed on the enterprise," he adds. What variables can we influence (such as reducing abandonment rate or increasing order size), and what holds customers back? Pioneering executives like Zeighami distill the opportunities personalization represents into a single customer-centric objective that the organization can rally around, such as simplifying a customer's ability to put together an outfit for an occasion. "They just get going!" he says.

This is precisely what Starbucks did at the outset of its personalization effort.

Starbucks and the Coffee Connection

In 2016, Howard Schultz, Starbucks's legendary leader, rightly predicted that the company's new "one-to-one personalized marketing capability . . . [would] prove to be a retail industry game changer."[2] Shortly thereafter, spend per loyalty member grew 8 percent, a company record and no small feat at a time when same-store sales growth in the quick-serve restaurant sector was below 2 percent.[3] Analysts and company leaders alike repeatedly cited personalization for its contribution to the company's revenue growth in the ensuing years: a total of 44 percent from 2017 through 2022, a period encompassing the Covid-19 pandemic. How did Starbucks achieve these impressive outcomes?

Personalization wasn't part of the company's strategy in 2015. But Aimee Johnson, then head of CRM, loyalty, and analytics (and later SVP of digital customer experience), saw personalization's potential to transform the customer experience. The Starbucks brand had always been about the human connection that happens over coffee: the company's mission, in fact, was "to inspire and nurture the human spirit—one person, one cup, and one neighborhood at a time."[4] The best baristas brightened their customers' day with a smile and a great cup of coffee. Johnson wondered: What if this same, personalized coffee connection could be extended to the company's digital channels—and scaled?

The vision started with a white paper. She and her colleagues kept coming back to the idea until it came to life.

Forging a strategy. From there, Johnson and her team worked hard to articulate a personalization strategy and the business case to support it. They identified the necessary tech and people investments and tallied the sources of upside: the reduced churn and increased frequency and spend per visit. Developing a strategic and economic case for personalization required collaborating with other senior executives across many functions (many of whom had similar but slightly different priorities) and getting their buy-in to support the plan.

In parallel, the team pondered the ways that Starbucks could empower its customers. They explored the use cases and channels where they could quickly bring personalization to life in a way that showcased its power and laid the foundation for more innovation. They mapped out customer journeys, organized and sized use cases, and assessed their feasibility and priority.[5] Importantly, even before gaining consensus on the strategic road map, a small tiger team got to work on the first set of journeys: personalized offers. They aimed to solve one of the most common customer pain points: making it easier to discover just the right beverage for you in the moment, while having fun and being engaged in the process. The best baristas were already solving this issue for their best customers, but now Starbucks sought to do it for every loyalty member, through digital channels. In addition, personalized offers could be a way to reward members with loyalty points (Starbucks "stars"), which would save them money on their next purchase and allow them to enjoy Starbucks more often.

Scaling up. Given the number of manual steps involved in launching a personalized offer, the team was limited to no more than thirty customer segments. Still, it took a dozen people more than eight weeks to produce a typical campaign. Every customer in the "never bought, but might like food" segment got the same recommendation: the slow-roasted ham, Swiss, and egg breakfast sandwich.

To scale up, the teams worked to automate 1:1 offers through email. Every customer could thus potentially receive a different offer. (In fact, this hyper-personalization approach meant that Starbucks now had the ability to develop more variants than it had customers.) In a Menu Quest challenge, for example, customers would have to buy a certain number of items over a certain number of days. With hundreds of items to choose from and the ability to vary the number and sequence of items, the number of days, and the time of send, the permutations became almost endless. Starbucks was not just able to segment customers by food preference (vegan, low-calorie, or meat-loving) and by beverage preference—each customer got the *individualized* recommendations that were right for them. This required rebuilding the martech stack and hiring a new team of data scientists and engineers, as well as redeploying the marketers who had been doing tedious manual work to more-strategic offer-design and -optimization efforts. Customers once annoyed by an endless barrage of Frappuccino offers they never redeemed could now get beverage recommendations suited to their tastes. Morning regulars who had never considered visiting in the afternoon for a pick-me-up beverage discovered a new way to recharge during the day.

The first six months' results were dramatic enough to persuade the CEO and the board to ramp up investments. Personalization doubled customer response rates and tripled the net incremental sales results of individual campaigns.[6] What began as a tiger-team effort to prove one use case quickly turned into one of the company's top strategic initiatives.

Going mobile. The next step was to extend personalization to the mobile channel to reach customers wherever they were on the go—during their commute, while shopping or running errands, and so on. Doing so required obtaining real-time data and integrating new tools into the martech stack so that the Starbucks app could become the focus of the effort to escalate engagement. Starbucks "gamified" its personalized offers, and customers could track their progress in real time and immediately see their star balance grow as they completed a challenge. The new capabilities, which tracked the customer's purchase history, the preferences of similar customers, real-time inventory levels at a given store, even the local weather, also enabled the next use case: adding specific item recommendations to the order-and-pay function of the app, pre-checkout.

The number of app users, many of them Gen Zers, doubled. At a time when the customer base of many large companies was aging, Starbucks's actually grew younger.[7] Starbucks's mobile personalization push helped the brand's new beverage and food platforms take off swiftly.[8]

Empowering Customers across the Journey

At its core, Starbucks's personalization approach was about growing loyalty: rewarding customers as they made repeat purchases, tried new products, and explored new occasions. But personalization can be applied at any point across the customer journey, not just to engender loyalty. This is as true for the B2C companies mentioned below as it is for B2B companies (see the sidebar "Empowering Customers in B2B Industries").

Awareness. Personalization may seem challenging at this stage, because the company knows little about its prospective customers. But new tools are available to help companies understand whom they are reaching, how often a prospect sees content, where they encounter it, and whether they linger or click to learn more.

For example, a leading houseplant retailer has used a journey advertising platform, illumin, to find consumers who have recently moved. Depending on a person's location and type of housing, the company shows them an initial set of ads that explain the benefits of decorating a house with plants. The tool tracks the number of ad impressions (each instance the ad is displayed to the prospect) and the specific ads the prospect saw. After seven impressions, the ads are changed to new ones that explain the varieties of plant best suited for the customer's likely dwelling type, based on predictive modeling drawn from the prospect's location. After a few exposures, the ads are once again changed to targeted offers to click through and buy a plant online. If the prospect clicks on any of the ads along the way without buying, the next ads they see will depend on what they were exploring on the site. The goal is to design the flow of ads through a journey, running constant tests, with targeting based on what is known about the prospect, and using sophisticated identity-matching to maintain contact with the prospect as they move around online. Personalized advertising doesn't always make sense, as precision targeting typically carries a higher cost per impression, but in this case, the associated conversion lift more than compensated for the higher costs.

Consideration. Here, a company knows the customer, but may not yet understand their needs and how best to help them. Having a rich set of metadata about your products and services is critical at this stage to help customers navigate to what they need.

Fashion and luxury brands face this challenge constantly, given their broad product lines and the number of new items every season. Many are using personalization to simplify how customers discover and explore new arrivals. A large fast-fashion retailer we work with started by building out its product database with descriptors for each item that included not just the name, size, and color but also its style (e.g., modern or traditional), what occasion it was for, what patterns it had, and other variables. It then built a style engine based on preference indicators modeled from its interactions with millions of customers, combined with data gathered by surveying customers directly ("zero-party data"). To spur excitement ahead of a new season, the style engine generated inspirational style ideas, personalized for each customer, on the company's website and on Pinterest, as well as in emails. The more detailed the product database got and the more recommendations that were made, the more accurate the style engine became, with the models ultimately predicting what customers would like over 90 percent of the time.

Purchase. Clearly, most personalization today focuses on the moment of truth: the actual purchase. Personalized on-site search and individualized add-to-cart recommendations are hardly new. But leading companies are going well beyond the "customers who bought X might also buy Y" logic, and instead powering recommendations with their knowledge of the individual customer's context. More recently, companies with much longer purchase cycles (like those selling cars and major appliances) are hyperpersonalizing the purchase journey. Such companies leverage every bit of data the customer has shared to help customers narrow their options, understand financing, and place an order.

Consider what leading auto insurance companies are doing. Once a customer enters a Vehicle Identification Number and zip code into their application, the company pulls up the car's entire history, along with the ownership information, and then immediately provides the customer with accurate pricing for a policy, even autofilling much of the form. Many insurers have begun continuously testing experience improvements in different stages of the customer journey, such as purchase and claims.

Post-purchase. As we will see later in this book, financial services and health-care companies are leading the way in personalizing for the post-purchase stage, thereby making customers' lives easier. This isn't so surprising, given the traditionally longer-term nature of their customer relationships. Their ongoing, direct interactions with customers provide more opportunities to gather rich information. Most of these companies are shifting their marketing focus from the initial sale and service needs to a more proactive, longer-term orientation, to make it easier for the customer to adhere to a journey to achieve a goal. For example, fintech companies, which by definition are digital natives, are going well beyond personalizing transactions to help their customers improve their financial health. Many are offering automatic-savings features, such as depositing a portion of every paycheck to savings. Some, like Chime (in the United States) and Monzo (the United Kingdom) are also dynamically personalizing these triggers: adapting them not only to the customer's stated preferences but also to the customer's behavior, spending and savings patterns, income, and demographics.

Companies in other industries are keying in to the post-purchase stage. Nike, for instance, has extended the customer relationship beyond selling shoes and athletic wear to creating a community of members. Through Nike Run Club and Nike Training Club, which boast well over 100 million users combined, athletes can track their fitness activities, set personal goals and challenges, and engage with leading athletes to get tailored recommendations.[9]

Forward-looking personalizers will prioritize use cases all along the customer journey and across channels. As our Personalization Index shows, personalization today is most commonly deployed at the moment of purchase and when companies seek to retain customers (see figure 2-2). In

FIGURE 2-2

Prevalence of personalization in the customer journey, by channel

Customer journey step	Email	Web	App	In-store
Awareness				
Consideration				
Purchase				
Post-purchase				
Loyalty				

Legend | The dark gray shading in each Harvey ball represents a score out of 100 (how often personalization is observed in each step of the customer journey, by channel across companies).

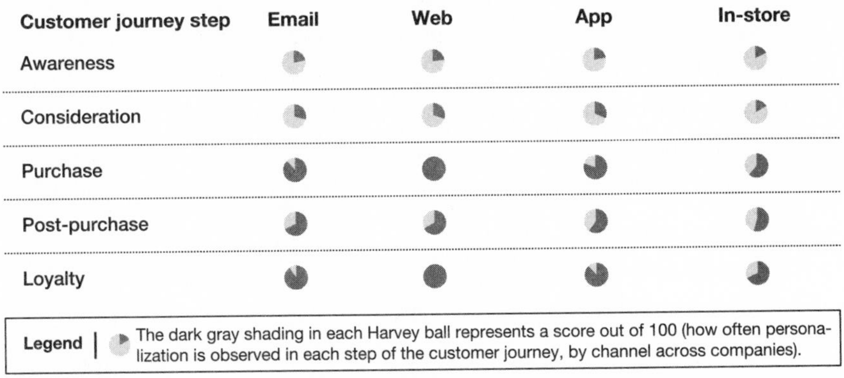

Source: BCG Personalization Index research, 2023 (n = 100).

Empowering Customers in B2B Industries

On the one hand, empowering B2B customers with personalization should be more straightforward: their utility function is generally simpler to understand than that of B2C customers. Personalization in B2B is about delivering business outcomes. B2B customers want to grow, become more cost-efficient, serve their customers better, manage their cash flow, and so on—and these business goals drive their buying behavior and decisions. It has become increasingly easier to model and predict these goals. The B2B seller is thus in a better position to make more-personalized recommendations, establish their brand image as a partner helping clients achieve their goals and manage their own supply chains more deftly.

On the other hand, business accounts are generally more complicated than individual accounts. The same master account might have not only multiple users and logins but also multiple buyers. B2B companies must therefore take extra steps to manage their client account data to keep it organized, including using one of a growing number of identity-matching AI tools to enable them to tie together the many different parties within each client company in an organized way. Companies must manage multiple layers of personalization: the account itself, any number of individual users and decision-makers, and, in many cases, a salesperson or channel partner.

As digital channels have grown, a new type of B2B buyer has emerged: one who does not expect, and in many cases does not *want*, to deal with a salesperson until it's time to close the deal. A majority of all B2B purchasers today, small businesses and enterprise customers alike, have only limited interaction with salespeople. These buyers rely on digital resources—such as suppliers' and third-party websites, videos, buyer reviews, blogs, and social media. And they increasingly use mobile phones to get that information, mostly through search and social media. Half of all B2B customers today expect a supplier's website to be a helpful channel, and more than one-third expect the site to be their *most* helpful channel.[10] In this digital environment, merely pushing products or services on customers is not an effective sales strategy. Both marketing *and* sales must become more "pull" oriented, helping each customer as they go about learning which B2B services can help them, how those services work, their economics, who the best suppliers are, and so on through the full journey of buying, using, renewing, and expanding.

What's more, B2B buyers today look for the same online and mobile experiences and features that they encounter as consumers. Personalizing digital experiences has become essential. B2B customers, on average, now complete 57 percent of their buying process online, before they ever make contact with a sales representative, according to a study from Google. More than half of all B2B buyers view at least eight pieces of content during the purchase process, and an additional 30 percent view five to seven pieces.[11] They want concise and coherent interaction however it occurs, and when they don't get it, they often eliminate a vendor from consideration before any direct sales contact takes place.

Many B2B products have long sales cycles that entail many steps, through initial contact with decision-makers, proposal creation, price negotiation, and so forth. So B2B personalizers are adept at thinking through the leading indicators that reveal where the customer is in their journey. They build intelligence on the steps different types of companies tend to take, and use that to manage a continuous dialogue with the customer as the customer moves along. Every website visit, email opening, content request, and discussion with a salesperson is critical to capture, and the best companies build next best action models based on taking customers to the next step, rather than on the expectation of an instant sale.

In the post-purchase part of the journey, B2B companies are also pushing fastest in using personalized content for customer support. As more B2B interactions require customers to use some form of software, issues constantly arise when new users or features are added. The complexity of some B2B pricing models also can lead to questions about how bills are calculated. Often, this generates emails and calls to a support center. To address this, many companies are

(continued)

building "knowledge bases" of content that can be surfaced during an interaction with a service rep or a chat bot. AI-based solutions, such as SearchUnify and others, are jumping into this space and making it easier for companies to provide automated, personalized support while also using those interactions to get feedback on issues customers are raising, so they can improve the product or other aspects of the offering.

In the race to decommoditize their products and alleviate the endless pressure from clients' procurement organizations, B2B personalizers are finding ways to add value from the experience of using their core products. Personalization done right ties the seller's success to the customer's success, helping clients achieve better performance, and building stronger relationships as a result.

other words, personalization is still widely considered a transactional tool. But personalization leaders are already applying it at other key stages of the journey, especially in the awareness and early consideration stages, and going beyond email and web as the channels of activation.

Technology and AI as the Power in "Empower"

In summary, empowering customers to reach their goals is the core objective of personalization, not exploiting high-powered technologies to bombard customers in a push for more sales. Companies that are leaders put technology to use in service of the primary goal of empowerment. They build an engine for personalization (see figure 2-3), essentially the data and technology stack to deliver on each of the Five Promises of Personalization:

Empower Me stems from having the technology connected in the right way to deliver the experiences in the right channel in a timely manner, whether it be an owned channel, such as email, an app, a call center, or the website, or a paid channel, such as social media, search, or display.

Know Me happens by integrating and enriching data sets, built through direct customer relationships. This data is augmented as needed (e.g., with third-party data) to produce a detailed, real-

FIGURE 2-3

The personalization data and tech stack

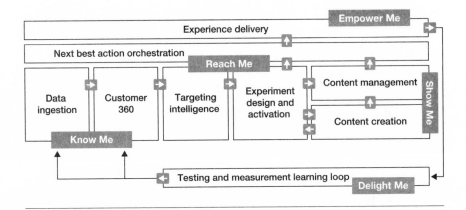

time, 360-degree view of the customer (what they want, who they are, where they are in their journey, and how they have engaged with personalized content). This is the fodder that enables more-relevant interactions.

Reach Me takes advantage of the targeting intelligence (models and algorithms derived from the data), the experiment design and activation (decisions about which customers get which experiences), and the next best action orchestration (decisions on the timing, sequence, and cross-channel coordination of the experiences). Through these elements, we reach the customer in the right channel at the right time, with the right experience.

Show Me is enabled by the content creation and management capabilities (the design, storage, and tagging of text, images, video, and new emerging forms of interaction) that facilitate assembling a resonant, relevant experience dynamically, increasingly assisted by gen AI.

Delight Me is powered by the measurement feedback loop and dashboards that give agile teams the data and learnings they need to make rapid improvements.

Which companies in your category are already building the operating approaches, backed with data and tech, to add value throughout customers' journeys? Are there powerful tech companies encroaching on your space? Companies whose large base of customers gives them a data advantage? New, focused disruptors? Or has no one seized the personalization advantage yet?

The game is still evolving, but the needed capabilities and business philosophies are already taking shape.

Personalized Customer Experience Self-Check

Ask yourself: How would you and your teams rate the current state of your personalized customer experience?

- What are the overarching goals for our personalization efforts? How will this empower customers? How will this benefit the business?

- Where can customer data be used to make the experience better, faster, easier? Where would customers expect it to?

- How much of each step of the customer journey do we personalize today? How much should we?

- How much is each channel used for personalization today? How much should it be?

- What common pathways do our most loyal customers take over time? What actions most contributed to their customer lifetime value? How do we enable these pathways for more of our customers?

- What is the potential value at stake from personalizing the most important parts of the customer experience across channels?

- What use cases should we personalize next, based on feasibility and value to the customer and business?

- What could we do tomorrow to accelerate our existing efforts to personalize the customer experience?

Travel

Travel is, at its core, a fundamentally human endeavor. It taps into our desire to explore new places, experience new things, and connect with others across time and space. It can also be a profoundly emotional experience; for many of us, our most vivid memories come from the journeys we have taken and the people we have met along the way. Personalization in travel is thus about meeting the needs of the individual throughout their entire journey in a way that makes the trip feel effortless and easy, removing anxiety about all the things that can go wrong and allowing us to enjoy the experience.

The mantra of our book—that personalization is, above all, about empowering customers—applies to travel even more than it does to other industries. Planning travel involves making hundreds of intensely personal choices about where you sleep, what you eat, how you get there, and how you do so safely and enjoyably. Today, because of the fragmentation of the travel industry, customers have many choices to navigate, which can be overwhelming. Moreover, personalization in travel is expanding well beyond sales and booking, going deep into each customer's experience.

Marriott: Personalizing Moments of Truth

"With personalization, we're talking about how we make people feel," says Peggy Roe, Marriott International's chief customer officer. The emotional aspect of travel, she claims, is what keeps people coming back to Marriott. And what creates loyalty? Most often guests credit "an interaction they had with an associate while staying at a property, a memory created at our hotel when celebrating a special occasion, or how they were treated on a particular trip"—sometimes recalling the details of a single gesture shown by a hotel associate.[1]

Marriott International is the largest hotel company in the world, with more than thirty brands in more than ten thousand destinations. Marriott Bonvoy, the company's loyalty platform, is also the largest in the global travel industry, with roughly 186 million members as of mid-2023. The platform was born from a combination of Marriott's original loyalty programs, Marriott Rewards, The Ritz-Carlton Rewards, and the Starwood Preferred Guest loyalty program, which came with the company's 2016 acquisition of Starwood Hotels & Resorts. These direct customer relationships, together with Marriott's global reach, give the company unmatched insights about global travelers and position Marriott Bonvoy as a gateway for the end-to-end travel experience.

"We believe that the future of service should always be human-centered, but [also] data-driven and tech-enabled," says Roe. "Great service delivery starts with having the right people building trust and confidence with their customers." She adds: "Many companies don't get to know customers the way we do, but we also recognize how important it is to use what we know carefully, to provide exceptional service." To preserve this trust, Marriott gives customers the opportunity to share and update their own preferences so that hotels can use that information to deliver personalized experiences. The level of personalization varies by brand, tier, and member level and can often be driven by the creativity of an associate on property. "We don't want personalization to be systematic. Ideally it should feel more like a surprise and delight."

The decision to create a unified Customer Experience Design and Innovation (CEDI) team proved to be pivotal for Marriott's personalization effort. The team's leader had worked extensively in operations, and also had a deep passion for customers and a collaborative personality. The team's mission was not to "own" the customer experience directly—an impossible task in an enterprise where virtually every function has direct (and consequential) impact on the customer. Rather, it was to teach the organization how to identify "pain points" and inefficiencies, and then design future-state customer experiences. The team often serves as program leader or coach, working across the enterprise to orchestrate the execution of the envisioned customer experience.

Traditionally, hotel companies are organized around departments—food and beverage, front desk, housekeeping, marketing, and digital and tech— each operating separately. Personnel thus tend not to see the customer's experience holistically. The CEDI team rallies these functional areas around a unified vision, using customer journey and experience blueprints as the starting point. Then it aligns those teams' work around key *moments of truth*: those instances where customers may feel highs and lows. This framework accounts for both the customer's *functional* journey and their overall *emotional* journey with Marriott. The team can then focus on fixing the most critical pain points in the functional areas (such as when a room is not ready upon check-in) while also looking for opportunities to create emotional high points (such as doing something special for guests on their birthday).

The CEDI team also redesigned the company's customer data strategy. To start, it spent many years centralizing multiple sources and types of data into a modern data platform. With a major technology transformation underway to replace much of Marriott's global technology infrastructure, the team championed the importance of marrying the data and business transformation with tech modernization efforts. As Roe and her team debated, it made sense to conceive of the user experience and the back-end infrastructure migration in an integrated way. Roe worked early on with her peers to ensure that the organization started with defining the target customer experience. This informed what tools the cross-functional teams would need to deliver great experiences, and determined the data and technology requirements. Behind the scenes, Marriott also established an internal governance structure to bring decisions about customer data collection and use to the organization's senior leaders, and to bring together numerous stakeholders to carefully contemplate regulatory changes, consumer protection, and the resources needed to enable delivery of great experiences.

Starting in 2020, Marriott launched a dedicated personalization team— the Marketing and Personalization Acceleration (MAPA) team—that included experts from multiple functions. From the start, the MAPA team focused on building data and martech capabilities to serve specific use cases. They secured investment by crafting a business case that articulated the necessary technologies and competencies. New personalization capabilities were embedded in the cloud analytics environment, across the marketing technology stack (for example, in the content management system), and in associate-facing systems (such as the management and reservation systems used at check-in).

It was important, Roe notes, to delineate the roles of everyone on the MAPA team: that is, who would be responsible, accountable, consulted, and informed. Senior team leaders jointly defined distinctive yet complementary roles (e.g., digital, data and analytics, and marketing played unique roles), aligning process and technology platforms across business and IT functions. This delineation of roles and responsibilities allowed the team to focus on cutting their learning-cycle times and moving the needle on the key metrics of their test cases.

Next, they further centralized customer data, creating a robust data architecture, accelerating content automation and personalization, and developing the decisioning intelligence engine and algorithms that determine the next best action to provide the customer. Finally, Marriott needed to upgrade its martech systems and various supporting platforms.

To secure alignment on their broader goals, the team proposed a string of use cases that could produce quick wins in four key areas:

- Giving Ambassador program members the opportunity to share more of their travel preferences so that dedicated Ambassadors and hotel associates could better personalize their experiences

- Personalizing offers and marketing messages to drive specific behavior that deepened loyalty—for example, making reservations for a second stay or getting a Marriott Bonvoy credit card

- Curating offerings and experiences for luxury travelers

- Using data to tailor localized food and beverage recommendations for customers (particularly in Europe, the Middle East, and Asia)

Roe teamed up with leaders of Marriott's luxury brands to accelerate certain early projects. These included launching a customer data platform (to enable marketers to create use cases leveraging real-time customer signals) along with a set of early pilots. The results convinced key stakeholders of the value of personalization. While in the past, email marketing did not distinguish between Marriott's brands, now luxury customers were consistently tagged across channels to receive targeted luxury communications. Click-through and engagement rates doubled. In addition, Marriott reintroduced its personal Ambassador service in 2023. Providing such individualized service after the pandemic rebuilt customer engagement with valued members. Customer satisfaction scores for the Ambassador program rose significantly.

These use cases did more than produce tangible results and prove the importance of personalization to the rest of the organization. They also clarified the business requirements for the tech transformation and additional process improvements that would be needed, and underscored the urgency of the high-priority investments. But there is a lot more to do, Roe says. She is particularly excited about the potential of partnerships and the opportunity for Marriott Bonvoy to cement its role as a gateway to all things travel. She cites the role of partners like Rakuten, Rappi, and Alibaba in jointly signing up new loyalty program members. (One-third of new members in China came from the company's joint venture with Alibaba.) Partnerships with MGM Resorts (e.g., sponsoring concerts and culinary experiences) and Allianz (offering travel insurance) represent opportunities—when powered by personalization—to meet even more of the customer's needs and deepen loyalty.

Reflecting on the program and her work, Roe says,

> I have a simple construct for talking about creating loyalty through personalization: "love and money." "Love and money" has been our mantra for the last three years. We use personalization to make "big" feel "small," and to make our customers feel understood and special. As we deepen their loyalty and engagement . . . we also drive business results. Our most valuable members stay deeply engaged with us for more than fourteen years, [but] we aspire to have them stay with us for a lifetime.

Looking Ahead: The Rise of Travel Ecosystems

In the future, as Marriott indicates, we expect more collaboration among destination travel brands, hotels and airlines, and travel agencies to enable a more seamless and rewarding travel experience. For example, airlines and hotels will be able to work together directly to ensure that when a customer's flight is delayed, their hotel reservation is adjusted automatically.[2] Companies are racing to become the gateways for end-to-end, personalized travel experiences that make customers feel special and that satisfy their desire for exploration and discovery.

Gen AI is already enabling customers to access many different systems and sources with a single query, simplifying the research and booking phase. Expedia Group was one of the first to embed gen AI in its app, making it easier for customers to find what they want among the platform's 1.26 quadrillion travel options. The gen AI chatbot even presents users with exclusive rewards and discounts as they narrow down their options.[3] And gen AI's adoption will only grow.

The next applications of gen AI will be within the travel journey itself. These tools will become smart companions to travelers—for example, helping them discover off-the-beaten track options in a new city. As gen AI is increasingly applied to facilitate travel planning across providers, this capability may end up further shifting the balance of power from travel companies to online travel agents like Expedia and Travelocity and technology platforms like Google and OpenTable. At the same time, as travelers increasingly search for unique and customized experiences, travel agents, hosts and ambassadors, and tour operators will continue to play a role in delivering personalization throughout the travel journey, especially at the high end of the market and for more-complex bookings, such as cruising and destination travel.

With so much still evolving in personalized offer management and ecosystems built around the end-to-end experience, the travel industry is an exciting laboratory for how to use customer information to empower customers. It offers lessons and insights for the many sectors that are in the earlier stages of personalization. Given that travel decisions are among the most emotionally driven ones we make, it is only fitting that this industry continues to show the way toward personalization's next frontier, much as it did in the early days of loyalty programs.

Chapter 3

Know Me

Know Me is foundational to enabling the other Promises of Personalization. Believing that they will get value in return, individual customers share their data with you and grant you permission to use it for their benefit. As each customer realizes the value of this data exchange and engages more, your insights about them grow significantly. The more engaged they are, the more data you obtain. You can augment your knowledge about a customer with data from outside parties, and can ask the customer specific questions, but the richest source of insight will still be the frequency and way in which they engage with you, and the granularity of the data you capture from those interactions. Success at Know Me is thus measured not only by the breadth of your direct customer relationships (the number) but also by their depth (the level of knowledge you have).

Customer data is the very essence of Know Me. So naturally, personalization starts with collecting, integrating, enriching (adding attributes or new information), and managing it. The data that companies already gather from customers and would-be customers is strewn across many systems—marketing, sales, billing, customer service, and product usage, among others. Beyond integrating what's in hand, companies should augment it with new types of data, directly from customers and prospective customers, as well as from external sources.

Historically, many companies have relied heavily on third-party cookies to target specific prospects on digital channels. Companies have also bought and sold such third-party data. And while the data has usually lacked identifying characteristics (such as the customer's name or email address), in many cases, the specifics of that data made it fairly easy to identify an individual customer, or at least find them online.

As privacy concerns have grown, new laws (notably the EU's General Data Protection Regulation and the California Consumer Privacy Act) have placed limits on the use and sale of customer data.[1] Apple, Mozilla, Google, and others have steadily introduced more privacy features and permission requirements. Consequently, marketers have had to rethink their approach. In a 2022 BCG survey, a majority of the participating marketing executives said that the transition away from third-party cookies was putting at least one-fifth of their current data used for targeted marketing at risk.[2]

As we will see, new ways of using third-party data to know customers are constantly emerging. However, these changes are also prompting companies to rely less on external data sources and to redouble their efforts to acquire their own data through more direct customer relationships. Companies are also starting to pursue data partnerships.

Let's start with a brief layout of the levels of identifiable customer data a company could have, defined by how it is sourced.

Zero-Party Data: What Your Customers Tell You Directly

Any information the customer willingly shares when explicitly asked is known as zero-party data. Though zero-party data includes all the information a customer provides when creating their account, it can be collected at any point. For instance, recording a customer's call to customer service or virtual chat generates information about the customer that the company might use to personalize, including whether to send a follow-up communication, what tone to adopt in that message, and how to route a future call from that customer. On e-commerce sites, the ratings and reviews that a customer posts represents data that's useful in many ways, such as what it reveals about them. When a company is providing clear value to customers, they are more willing to directly share their personal information—answering such questions as "What are your investment goals?" (if you're a financial advisory service) or "What type of camping do you and your family enjoy?" (if you're a sporting goods retailer).

As the capacity of AI tools to turn unstructured text into codable data keeps improving, companies are finding it easier than ever to gather and use zero-party data from open-ended questions and the content of their dialogues with customers.

First-Party Data: What You Know from Customers' Engagement

The core information every company should be using comes from the transactional and behavioral data created by recording actions the customer takes—browsing different pages on the site, hovering over specific items, making purchases, and so on. This data, known as first-party data, comes directly from the customer and is owned by the company. Often, its power lies not so much in the specific actions it records but, rather, in what companies can infer about customers from their behavior. With first-party data, a company can predict what the customer is likely to do when it sends them a certain type of message, shows them a new product or service, or connects them with a customer service rep. For many years now, companies have been using their first-party data to identify look-alike audiences in social media platforms and find new high-value customers.[3] They are also building propensity models that predict each customer's likelihood of purchasing a specific product or service. And, more recently, they're constructing headroom models that estimate how much more a particular customer could spend in a category, based on what similar customers already spend in that category.

Collecting zero-party information through direct customer interactions and integrating it with transactional first-party data is critically important for creating a customer profile. But to gain enduring competitive advantage from personalization, companies must steadily accumulate and extract insights from data that reflects a customer's engagement—whether a customer opens an email they send, how long the customer spends in different areas of the company's website or app, and what channels they engage with, and when. Engagement data can be the gold in a company's first-party-data mine if it is continuously collected and accurately stitched with customer data. It enables a company to go beyond merely inferring what customers might do and allows it to gather massive volumes of data to learn about what customers actually do in each interaction. Companies can also discern what customers *don't* respond to, which is equally valuable. Marketers can use these insights to stop sending irrelevant messages and to glean which products or services customers dislike. They then feed those learnings back into their systems and processes in a perpetual loop, further deepening their understanding of how best to serve, and retain, the customer. The more engagement data you can gather, and the greater the specifics of that interaction (e.g., when it happened, exactly what the customer saw and clicked on, how much time they spent), the richer the intelligence you can build to power predictive models.

Loyalty programs are another critical source of first-party data. Indeed, loyalty data is a uniquely valuable source of such data because it provides information about a subset of customers who are often two to three times more engaged with the company than the average customer.[4] Deeply engaged customers are substantially bigger spenders. Loyalty programs also generate engagement data by their very design, as customers regularly check their loyalty points and status. This gives organizations opportunities to build on those moments of connection.

In the rush to capture more first-party data, most businesses have overhauled their loyalty programs or are introducing new ones. And over the past decade, loyalty programs have become more personalized: many are free and easier for customers to join; they offer rewards; and with a broader reach, they capture data about a wider range of customers. Some loyalty programs also gamify the experience of participation to drive even more engagement. As we saw in chapter 2, Starbucks's Menu Quests, for example, challenge customers to try specific items over a specific period of time, enabling them to earn more points. Some loyalty programs, like Amazon Prime, Walmart+, Rakuten Super Points, and Aldi Plus, are designed for deeper engagement with high-value customers and require a subscription. In return, they provide customers with access to unique content, such as bundling Amazon Video streaming with Amazon Prime, or offer perks like free shipping. These programs tend to generate higher engagement and loyalty, although they can also be costly to run; many companies do not take in enough subscription fees to offset the costs.

Regardless of where first-party data comes from—whether loyalty programs, direct digital interactions, or website or app registrations—personalization leaders are constantly hunting for ways to increase the number of digital customer relationships so they can feed their first-party data pools and secure digital routes for sending messages to customers. These companies are building digital customer relationships that number in the hundreds of millions, with brands like Alibaba, Tencent, and Spotify exceeding 500 million monthly active users in 2023. They understand the importance of maximizing breadth (the sheer number of relationships) and depth (the array of channels and ways to interact with each customer). That's why so many focus avidly on getting new customers to register or existing ones to download their app.

Second-Party Data: What Trusted Partners Share

Second-party data comes from a company's trusted partners—other businesses that collect first-party data from customers who give their explicit permission to use that data more broadly. A classic example is a co-branded credit card. Merchants might send offers to their cardholders, generating data in the process, and then share that data with the credit card company, under the terms of the permission granted by the customer when they signed up for the card.

Second-party data is now being utilized by a rapidly expanding pool of partnerships. After obtaining permission from their customers (via opt-ins), companies link their loyalty programs to partner programs or promotions. They create joint experiences that make transactions more convenient for customers or use the joint data to offer rewards. Such partnerships will become more commonplace as companies maneuver to become the main gateway for customers' particular needs. Application programming interfaces (APIs) supporting the information exchange essential for such partnering are becoming more standardized, even as AI is facilitating synchronized ways to classify, clean, and organize customer data. Increasingly, companies will tap a variety of complementary partner brands to deliver an end-to-end personalized experience. Imagine Angi (formerly Angie's List, the marketplace for home improvement services) coordinating the complete remodeling of a kitchen with a large home improvement retailer, or Best Buy and Roku teaming up to create a media center in a customer's home.

Third-Party Data: Sort the Good from the Bad

To further enhance data already in hand, companies can obtain third-party data through several different means. Most companies tap into what is available from paid media platforms. Meta and Google allow companies to target customer segments in-platform via their data, based on topics of interest to customers. Data-poor companies, which lack the ability to create their own look-alike audiences using first-party data, depend on media platforms' data to target specific audiences. But these "walled gardens" have limitations. For example, a company can't distinguish different individuals using the same device unless they sign in to their own account each time. Moreover, advertisers might lose track of users as they move across multiple devices.

One class of software-as-a-service providers addresses the limitations of using third-party data in walled gardens or of relying on third-party agencies. LiveRamp and Neustar, alongside startups like Bridg from the United States and Sqreem from Southeast Asia, provide identity-resolution services that help companies grow the number of customers they can market to in targeted ways and follow along their journey.

Take Japan's Rakuten, one of the world's largest e-commerce platforms. Rakuten created a joint venture with Sqreem to use Rakuten's AI-driven behavior-analysis data.[5] This partnership drew on Sqreem's ability to target leading indicators of potential conversion, plus Rakuten's extensive member network and device fingerprint mapping to drive customer acquisition for Rakuten Ichiba, Japan's largest e-commerce platform. (Fingerprint mapping relies on tracking the user based on the characteristics of their device as they engage with servers across the internet.) Winning new customers in a saturated market like Japan is challenging, but this approach enabled much-more-precise targeting of prospects most likely to convert. It also cut out the intermediaries in the ad-serving value chain. The payoff was impressive: a 50 percent reduction in cost-per-acquisition and a tenfold boost in return-on-advertisement spend. Rakuten also applied this approach in its retail media business, where it sells ad space on its site. (For more on retail media, see Industry Spotlight: Retail after chapter 4.) For instance, it helped cosmetics companies acquire customers at a cost 85 percent lower than before.

To further expand marketers' options, new data "marketplaces," tools, and mechanisms for acquiring third-party data are emerging. Some of these supplement or supplant third-party cookies. The largest data software providers, like Snowflake and Databricks; cloud service providers, including AWS and Azure; and specialized firms, such as Narrative.io and Bloomberg, have all set up such data marketplaces. Many of these services enable companies to rapidly standardize their database schemata and integrate information from across the business. Data scientists use such services to refine identity-matching, and to spot more triggers that can drive a recommended action. These services also enable data scientists to build new predictive and attribution models based on the expanding range of variables they can now access, such as weather, geolocation of customer devices, traffic conditions, and an endless array of indicators that reveal individual customers' online behavior. While this application is a common trend in certain markets, such as the United States, we expect practices to keep evolving as data privacy concerns grow.

Some third-party data marketplaces use AI to sense the structure of the importing database and to reformat the data to easily mesh with a company's own tech environment. This eliminates the need for extra data engineering work and even provides "streaming" services to fill data gaps and remove duplicate data from multiple sources, all in real time.

Despite its advantages, third-party data has its drawbacks. For one thing, it can be highly variable. In testing data sources for a major fashion brand, for example, we found that gender data obtained from a well-known third-party data provider was less than 50 percent accurate (i.e., worse than a random guess) when compared with data that a subset of the brand's own customers had provided about themselves. Worse still, in large third-party databases, new data can coexist alongside old data, and high- and low-quality data can be intermingled.

More worrisome is the fact that third-party data can be misused or abused. For example, a 2023 report by Duke University found that information from mental health apps about diagnoses that users had received of conditions such as depression, post-traumatic stress disorder, and bipolar disorder, was making its way to data marketplaces.[6] Imagine the outcry and regulatory backlash if information like that were to be incorporated into credit scoring systems, recruiting algorithms, or targeted marketing programs. Every brand must build trust with its customers and be mindful of its fragility, given the many situations where data abuse could wreck it. To avoid such disasters, companies must be aware of what data is coming to them via the walled gardens, data platforms, and marketplaces; carefully screen it for appropriate use; and understand the permissions it comes with. In chapter 10, we delve into privacy issues and risk, as well as responsible AI practices, but we can't stress enough the importance of managing one's data supply chain and data use from the perspectives of ensuring it is correctly permissioned and its use actually adds value for the customer.

Because no one source of data gives full insight into customers, personalization leaders build their understanding of the customer from a wide range of sources. As our Personalization Index research shows (see figure 3-1), fewer companies focus on engagement data, zero-party data, and data derived from customer preferences and goals, but these are the areas of data collection where leaders stand out.

How One Company Reconciled Data throughout the Customer Journey

So how do companies make sense of all the data generated from the various possible sources? Consider this example of a telecom provider that decided to expand into an adjacent line of business and compete based on offering a far better service experience. From the start, the company focused on how best to use customer data.

The company organized the most important customer data such that relevant team members could easily access it. The company started by identifying which data it considered most critical. Call center interactions fit the bill because they would provide early warning signs of customer dissatisfaction. The company set up processes for digitally recording every call center interaction and running call routing data through natural language processing to convert customer conversations into insights. This data would tell the company why the customer called; when and from where; the length

FIGURE 3-1

Types of customer data collected and derived

Percentage of surveyed companies

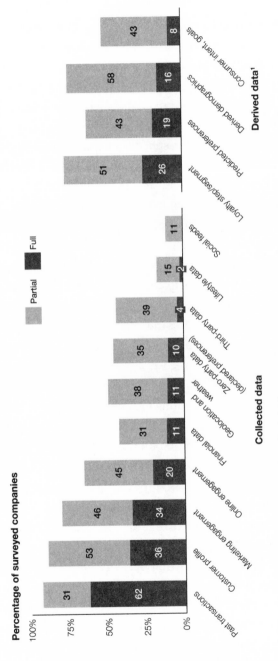

1. Derived data is calculated with models using collected data.

Source: BCG Personalization Index research, 2023 (n = 100).

of the call; and the customer's attitude, language, and implied education level. It also revealed the outcome, and what, if any, direct next steps were needed. In addition, the digital team used Pointillist, a tool that pairs an identity-resolution solution with customer journey analytics, to be able to tag customers' actions through their journey, across channels (the web pages, mobile apps, call centers, billing systems, marketing systems, and retail payment platforms). By time-stamping customers' actions, the technology created new kinds of data sets, now oriented around a journey framework.

Next, the team used AI to spot deviations in journey patterns and to look for correlations in data characterizing customers who were grappling with problems. For example, if calls to a company helpline were spiking, the AI would trace all of the actual journeys in which customers were calling, to see whether there was simultaneously an unusual increase in a particular prior customer action, such as using a new feature of the app or paying a bill. The team could then alert the reps to what customers were calling about, so the reps could help customers while the headquarters tech team worked on a solution. The data also enabled the team to understand developments as they were unfolding, such as where visitors were on the website when they ended up purchasing services. This feedback positioned the team to quickly enhance the website's content and flow.

A cross-functional team comprising people from service operations, marketing, field ops, and billing took charge of keeping customer data clean and consistent, integrating needed technologies, setting up and refining dashboards, and taking action on the resulting insights.

The journey teams met daily to review customer KPIs (satisfaction scores, call center volumes, app downloads, monthly active users) and respond to problems. They also tracked the impact of design changes they were making to the onboarding journey. Such changes included newly designed web pages, videos explaining new services, simplified scheduling tools for field representatives, and better data feeds to call center representatives.

Their new offering quickly became recognized in social media for its enhanced experience. Call center volumes ended up well below forecasts. And the company outperformed its rivals, in both the percentage of customers who used the website and app as well as the percentage who gave permission for data usage.

Three Principles for Managing Customer Data

The immense volumes of and variations in the types of data a company must manage in order to know its customers are, in a word, overwhelming. The data is often messy (e.g., shows different spellings of a person's name), sits in disparate systems across the organization, and contains different definitions. To extract maximum value from the data, personalization leaders need to formulate their data strategy; build the right customer data platform; and put in place the right people, processes, and governance to manage it all.

Data strategy: Decide what data you need and how you'll use it

Too many companies get so bogged down in building a 360-degree view of their customers that years pass before they can actually *use* the data. One large airline spent three years and tens of millions of dollars building a comprehensive data lake. The technology team led the effort, with little involvement from the business teams. Consequently, before they could launch personalized campaigns, marketers still had to create many new data attributes (such as customer segment descriptors, customer propensities, whether the customer uses the app) and bring in additional data.

Savvier companies build their data systems and infrastructure with the end use cases in mind from the outset. They start by defining a data strategy that prioritizes the ways in which they want to empower the customer, and in which channel. This way, companies know what data is most vital and what tools that data should fuel. For instance, to power personalization for a leading retailer, we set up a data platform with three thousand data assets tied to each individual customer ID. Data about category-purchase intent informed which item recommendations would show up in customer emails or on the website's carousel. Media-usage data influenced which social media platform customers would be targeted on, and how often. Email-response data determined message frequency. Data about the customer segment (such as category shopper, price-sensitive shopper, or recent mover) shaped decisions about which types of ads, deals, or inspirational messages they received.

A sound data strategy prioritizes the data types that are most critical for targeting customers, and, when external data is the only option, rigorously tests the business value of purchasing data versus just using mass advertising. It establishes which data assets should be built first and how they will support the most worthwhile use cases. Teams need to evaluate data sources across zero-, first-, second-, and third-party data, as well as consider data types. Any business with a digital platform like a website or an app can generate mountains of clickstream data. But to make sense of it, leaders must think through which events are most critical to track within this data: for instance, how much time a user spends on specific website pages or when a user abandons a shopping cart. Companies can use some data elements to measure which personalized experiences are most effective—but only if they capture and store such data properly. Finally, companies can't tag and store all of this data forever, so their strategy should also clarify what data is most important to keep and how long it will be relevant.

The customer data platform: Stitch data together across your systems

Once a company has crafted its data strategy, it needs to bring disparate sources and types of data together into a single view of the customer. It is the data that initiates the flow through the personalization tech stack.

As we've noted, first-party data comes from many disparate systems, such as billing, customer support, and website visitors' actions. Historically, few companies anticipated the need to link all of these systems when they were first set up. Every database has its own customer identifiers—anything from a customer ID number, Social Security number, or date of birth to an email address, physical address, or mobile phone number. Under these conditions, compiling a single, complete view of each customer from all the company's functional and business areas is no small feat. But *not* doing so can sabotage a company's personalization efforts.

Customer data platforms (CDPs), such as Amperity, Treasure Data, Salesforce CDP, and ActionIQ, are software-as-a-service providers that help companies surmount this challenge by enabling them to stitch together all their data about individual customers and make it readily available to analyze or to power interactions. For example, the bookings data an airline might receive from its website and from third-party online travel agents is separate from the rest of its customer data. With a CDP, the airline can immediately identify when a customer made a booking and contact the person during the "golden" hours (those first few hours after booking) to ensure they've noted everything they'll need (such as wheelchair assistance) or to suggest additional services (e.g., a rental car, hotel, or vacation package).

The power of CDPs comes from how they use AI to match an individual customer's identity across data sources and then aggregate the data, either in a new integrated database or on an as-needed basis. The AI looks for any combination of the various customer identifiers used in the company's different systems, and couples it with other insights (such as matching a repeated location of interaction) to assemble all the data on a customer. Some CDPs even use probabilistic matching, meaning they can identify when a customer is likely (although not certainly) the same person showing up in another digital venue (say, on social media posts). The company can then take into account how it is using this data, treating probabilistic data with more prudence than data it knows to be certain.

This stitching together of customers' data to create their customer record activates a personalization "flywheel": the more signals that get pulled together, the more insights a company can gain, generating a 360-degree view of the customer—all leading to more-effective personalization.

People and processes: Get data governance right

No matter how strong AI's data engineering capabilities become, executives will still need to agree on their basic data definitions, how precise predictions from AI must be in order to formally match data, and what guardrails to put in place to preserve the privacy of permissioned data. This is where data governance comes in. Many companies are putting in place chief data officers (CDOs) and establishing data stewards across the organization. CDOs define the data governance process. The data stewards—the actual data users, such as a marketing executive or the head of call center operations—help agree on common definitions for different types of data, such as a "lapsed customer." Otherwise, having conflicting rules for what counts as "lapsed" results in an uncoordinated reengagement strategy that can prevent the company from taking immediate, effective action to win back a customer. A strong data governance process can align these definitions so that the instant a customer is lost, everyone tasked with retaining customers knows it, understands what to do, and can roll into action.

But governance work doesn't stop there. Cleaning the data, setting standard definitions, and putting the data into structures that can be combined—these tasks call for the skills of data engineers. So it's no surprise that in many markets data engineers are the fastest-growing job category, even more so than data scientists. Data engineering practices that ensure consistency, accuracy, and metadata about one's data, such as permission rights, source, and timeliness, enable the transparency needed to understand data and ensure its appropriateness. That, combined with policies on the "red lines" that a company won't cross (i.e., types or uses of data that are off-limits) as well as with periodic audits of data, is the critical foundation of good governance.

In addition to having the right talent and strong data governance practices, companies must set up their data architecture to capture, connect, and make accessible the rich potential of customer information they have across their systems. Data architecture is the lifeblood of the enterprise, with data from a variety of sources flowing along critical arteries and response data flowing back, in a feedback loop. As we've explained, the company's data architecture requires careful management. After all, it determines how quickly incoming customer data can be accessed and used. As such, management of the data architecture must be a priority for the C-suite and the board of directors. These leaders need to meet regularly with the CDO or similar executive to address vital issues, such as how customer data is being enriched and improved, how well the company is protecting customers' privacy, and how the company is activating its personalization agenda.

Data Diagnostic Self-Check

Ask yourself: What is the current state of your data strategy, platform, and governance?

Data Strategy

- What are the most critical types of zero-, first-, second-, and third-party customer data needed to power our top personalization moves?

- How effective is our approach to growing the volume of our digital customer relationships over time?

- What do we directly ask customers about versus draw inferences from? How useful are their responses?

Data Platform

- How well are we aggregating and using insights from customers' responses to power our personalized experiences over time?

- To what degree do we stitch together customer data to create a single, unified view of each customer that enables decision-making?

- What roles do data lakes and/or customer data platforms play in our data architecture? How well are these systems integrated to ensure smooth data flows in our personalization stack?

- For customer actions that require an immediate triggered action, do we have real-time access to data about those actions?

Data Governance

- How well do our data governance processes ensure consistent and clear management of our data? What do we know about the provenance and quality of the third-party data we use for customer interactions? Are there better, safer alternatives?

- Do we have the right talent in place to set up, maintain, and monitor our data pipeline, engineer our data for data science applications, and analyze the data? Where are our greatest talent gaps?

- How will we implement and adhere to ethical AI principles in our data and analytics approach?

Financial Services

Financial service companies have historically competed on the personal service they provide. The bank knew your name, the loan officer knew your business, and the investment adviser knew your goals. But then the consumer finance industry underwent massive consolidation. Banks implemented more technology to digitize operations (especially for routine transactions) and cut customer-facing staff. In the process, much of the human touch and the personal connection people felt with providers were lost. It was hard for consumers to see how those companies could truly be thinking about them when their operations seemed so remote.

Given all their digital channels and AI-enabled capabilities, financial services companies should be able to mobilize mountains of customer data, not only to drive the sale of their products but also to expand access to services and offer end-to-end support to customers throughout their life stages as their financial needs change.

In a 2022 BCG survey of financial services CMOs, 46 percent reported that revenue growth was a number-one priority and 70 percent said personalization was also a top priority. But spending cuts had turned the pursuit of these priorities into a major balancing act.[1] The search for opportunities to expand the customer relationship via personalization has been challenging for the larger players. Despite the breadth of first-party data acquired through transactions and services, companies often still lack insight into customers' personal circumstances, goals, and attitudes toward investing, or their broader financial picture. Companies need strategies for gathering customer insights at every point in the journey—from the customer's initial interaction with marketing to enrollment, from getting feedback on recommendations to testing the ways customers prefer to consume content.

The transformation of two financial services players, Fidelity and Voya, illustrates the changes required to provide customers more-personalized support.

Fidelity: Tailoring Investment Advice at Scale

Boston-based Fidelity Investments is one of the top-three money managers in the United States. It serves millions of customers at every point in the wealth, income, and investment-attitude spectrum. Traditionally, investment management services came through a broker or wealth manager, a human adviser with whom an investor would discuss plans and trading activity. Today, Fidelity continues to offer that option to its customers but has also created an enormously scaled digital operation. Across its multiple physical and digital channels, Fidelity aims to use personalization, with clear permission for it granted by the customer, to distinguish itself from other investment houses and drive more engagement.

Given the company's scale, growth from new-customer acquisition is particularly challenging. People tend not to open new investment accounts as frequently as they establish other financial accounts, such as credit cards, CDs, or even checking accounts. Fidelity's growth thus depends partly on expanding each customer relationship, to serve customers with the broadest array of products and services that fit the individual's circumstances—their age, family status, income, wealth, and goals. But growth also, and perhaps more importantly, depends on encouraging customers to let Fidelity serve more of their financial needs. With its focus on building customer lifetime value rather than on stimulating brokerage transactions, engagement has become a top priority.

However, as David Dintenfass, former chief marketing officer, observes:

> Many customers don't engage with us except to periodically check on their balances or make a trade. If we can encourage customers to read an article, watch a video from one of our analysts, or check whether their investments are progressing according to their plan, we can use the opportunity to educate them on smart moves that make sense specifically for their situation.[2]

Doing so, he says, requires building trust, being relevant, and being sensitive to the customer's level of financial savvy—none of which are easy to do in a personalized way at scale. Fidelity has had to build up its ability to track the customer across all of its lines of business and from every angle, so it can understand each customer's context. Increasingly, the company is going straight to customers to ask them questions firsthand, especially about their attitudes toward investing.

One of the most valuable bases for a personalized relationship is working with the company to develop an investment plan. Customers with a wealth manager relationship tend to develop a plan at the start, which then guides their interactions with their account manager and the company more broadly. Fidelity encourages those customers with only a basic digital relationship to take a longer-term view and also develop a plan. It emphasizes the importance of a plan for improving outcomes and for providing a way to receive timely, tailored advice. Fidelity can then notify customers when they are falling behind or need to rebalance their investments, and suggest new strategies to address inflation.

In addition, Fidelity monitors which articles on its site customers have read, which funds they look at, and what they check on regarding their account. Based on that information, it provides links to new articles and videos. If a customer adjusts their account in a way that signals a life change—say, a marriage, new baby, job change, or divorce—Fidelity might follow up to suggest actions to take, such as changing one's beneficiaries, opening a 529 plan, or changing their investment allocations. Through its workplace business, the company can even detect a job loss and, depending on the context, gently reach out to provide advice. All of this incoming data from the customer's activity becomes a trigger for actions that would benefit the customer.

But being relevant also means eliminating actions that make no sense. A few years ago, Fidelity was sending some customers daily emails. Every product area saw email as a low-cost opportunity to reach the same customers based on a trigger. The result was customer overload. The pile-up of messages led to higher opt-out rates and declining engagement. Realizing it needed to pull back, Fidelity began to build better next best action models for each trigger, whittling down the number of messages to a handful each month. Initially, product managers were worried that their businesses would suffer as some of their messages were deprioritized. But, notes Dintenfass, just the opposite happened: opt-out rates fell, and engagement rose so much that the "pie" actually grew for each one of Fidelity's businesses.

Personalization, Dintenfass observes, is not just about rational analytics. "Relevance can come from how we gather and use information. Empathy, however, is a whole other story. We must communicate with you in a way that is approachable and matches your level of expertise with investing."

Determining that right way takes considerable experimentation. Fidelity organized its personalization team members into fast-moving, agile pods. These pods constantly test new ways of connecting to see what resonates. The company also classified the profiles of people's attitudes into segments, and these segments continue to evolve as the company learns.

Fidelity also took a hard look at the nature of the content it was producing, realizing how important it was to talk to its customers in a way that recognized their personal context. Customer feedback revealed that Fidelity was better at reaching more-sophisticated investors, but didn't always connect with younger or more-inexperienced investors as well as it could. That led the company to simplify the editorial style of its content. In the past few years, Fidelity has begun posting content on TikTok and Instagram—content that is more fun—along with putting follow-through experiences on its landing pages that feature the kinds of graphics, text, videos, and ways of interacting that appeal to younger customers. The company has even overhauled its product line to make it easier for younger people to engage with its services. For example, Fidelity now offers investing solutions for teenagers through its own app (the product features parental supervision).

Looking ahead, Dintenfass sees even more focus on the emotional side of personalization and on taking advantage of Fidelity's operating velocity to expand the innovations the company can deliver. By way of helping people set longer-term goals, the firm has experimented with a "gratitude questionnaire." The questionnaire, says Dintenfass, "asks people . . . what they are thankful for and encourages them to think through what had to happen to lead up to that. It gets them in the right mindset to plan for the future and stick with it."

Voya: Supporting Complete Financial Management

New York City–based Voya, one of the top-ten US providers of employee benefits, takes a somewhat different approach. Spun off from Dutch financial services conglomerate ING in the early 2010s, Voya used the launch of its new brand name to reposition itself in a highly competitive market. Voya aims to help its clients' employees be best prepared for their retirement and future health situation by making the most of their employer benefits and of Voya's supplemental offerings.

Voya wanted to move away from a chiefly transactional, intermittent way of dealing with customers (for instance, when filing a claim or during open enrollment) and instead build relationships characterized by an ongoing exchange, continuously creating value for its customers. But to be that kind of adviser to millions of employees requires having an extensive set of capabilities. This took some time to build: the company had to know each person's context, generate advice, reach them with it, make transactions easier, and build the kind of trust that fuels steady engagement.

In 2019, Voya undertook an ambitious research initiative to understand how consumers thought about the advice they were receiving; the challenges they faced; how they defined their retirement, investing, and health-financing needs; and what it would take to gain their trust. Voya not only discovered endless variations in people's contexts, financial savvy, and tastes, but it also found that people's very definition of retirement varied. Retirement could mean anything from moving to a warmer climate to starting a small business, traveling more, or something else, all of which would have different implications for the advice they would be requesting.

As Santosh Keshavan, Voya's chief information officer, explains, executives discovered that no other company was helping people plan for both their financial and health needs. Few other financial planning brands, moreover, looked at the customer's context beyond the products the company sold. He says:

> We then sketched our vision for "myVoyage"—a tool into which you can provide links to as much of your financial and health information as you want. As you provide us with more information,

we can track the dynamics of your situation and provide recommendations such as paying down your student debt when we notice
extra savings building up. [Such guidance] . . . helps to build trust
for when we do make an appropriate product or added investment
recommendation. We want to be seen as the company that helps
people make smarter choices.[3]

Once the research was complete, Keshavan's team built the architecture
for myVoyage in under a year, integrating a stack of third-party, cloud-
based software services using a flexible, open architecture. They started
testing their model with Voya's own employees and, seeing a positive response, then began scaling the model to clients, personalizing the whole
pathway. As Voya continues its IT development, its marketing teams are in-
tensively testing messages, designs, sequencing, and even whether messages
should come from Voya or from the customer's employer.

The customer journey begins with Voya asking customers about their
goals, attitudes, and starting points. The company then gathers more data
about customers externally to get a richer picture. Depending on their interests and needs, Voya provides brief content to educate them; for example, when to use a bank savings account versus investing money in mutual
funds, stocks, or bonds; how to think about different ways of accessing
credit; how to understand college savings accounts, 401(k)s, health savings
accounts, and other tax-advantaged investment vehicles; and especially how
to think about prioritizing investments generally. As Keshavan observes,
"We may even tell someone that they just do not need more life insurance—
even though we sell it." Taking the customer's position, he says, "is key to
[winning] the trust we need." Through links it has established to other financial services companies, Voya enables customers to execute transactions
it doesn't manage. Then, "we share aggregate data on how employees are
doing with the benefits managers, so plan sponsors can see the impact we
are making on their behalf."

This transformation toward being truly customer-centric, personalized, and integrated is also driving a fundamental transformation at the
heart of Voya's operations. One major change: the narrowing of the organizational divide between Voya's health and wealth businesses. Voya
now has one product team and one salesforce serving what were once

two separate businesses. Marketing and tech development operate as an integrated agile team, constantly putting out new ideas and testing them. Along with pulling data from customer interactions, Voya has set up a "listening post" team to capture feedback from surveys and call center interactions. Using natural language processing, that feedback is converted into usable data about issues to address, especially where customers are confused or are having problems. Mobilizing to constantly act on all of that rapid input, Voya has shifted its corporate planning away from annual strategy to setting eight-week update cycles. A strong emphasis on improving the velocity of its operations propels its adaptability and ability to test new ideas.

———

Fidelity and Voya—both, enterprise-scale financial services players—have pivoted from an institutional feel to one of partnership with their customers, bringing back that sense of personal support that had been lost in the age of consolidation and automation. And in doing so, they maintain their focus on building customer trust. Customers have noticed: Fidelity was named one of the Most Trusted Wealth Management Companies in 2023 by *Investor's Business Daily*, and Voya was recognized as one of America's Most Trustworthy Companies by *Newsweek* in 2023.[4]

Our Financial Future Will Be Completely Personalized

As these examples show, financial service companies recognize that today's consumers, especially younger ones, expect their interactions to be digitized and more personalized. And consumers' expectations will further evolve as consumers learn about and use new capabilities offered by companies that push the envelope. In a 2021 speech, BlackRock CEO Larry Fink opined that personalization will extend in the future to "creating completely tailored baskets of securities driven by one's values and sense of the market."[5] New customer data and metrics will be used to create portfolios based on customers' goals and interests, not just their age and wealth. Already, there are simple versions of "self-personalizing" investment portfolios—such as Vanguard's Just Invest (acquired in 2021), which allows customers to invest in index funds and then strip out companies they don't want to include.[6] The bar will keep rising. Staying on top of it, as Fidelity and Voya show, will require a shift in mindset from selling products to providing goal-based services, whether that's access to credit, saving for retirement, or managing finances through changing life situations.

Chapter 4

Reach Me

Reach Me is the promise that personalization will be relevant and timely. It starts with having the customer's permission to contact them in relevant channels. It relies on having the always-on intelligence to identify the right experience to deliver and the right moment and channel to deliver it in. Critically, a company must also know when not to reach out, sparing the customer from irrelevant or unseemly interactions, like pushing a new product amid a major service issue. Success is measured by how well contactability (the number of customers and channels a company has permission to reach) and knowledge of the customer is used to drive engagement.

Once you know your customers, personalization is all about reaching the right customer, in the right place, at the right time. Doing this well relies on three "intelligence" components of the personalization tech stack: *targeting intelligence, experiment design and activation,* and *next best action orchestration.* These components are more than just collections of data science models. They fuel scale and speed, enabling rapid optimization based on data gathered from each interaction with customers.

Targeting intelligence. This component sorts through a wide variety of data that is used to decide when to deliver an experience, including:

- **Trigger events,** such as an abandoned cart, customer complaint, new user sign-up

- **Scores,** such as churn likelihood, customer lifetime value

- **Propensity models,** which gauge the likelihood a particular customer would buy a given product or take a certain action, based on purchase history and similar customers' behavior

- **Affinity models,** which predict which companies, channels, or categories customers prefer

- **Headroom models,** which calculate the incremental sales-growth potential from customers based on comparing them with similar customers

- **Channel preferences,** such as mobile app, website, email

It is not enough to develop this intelligence once. Companies must set up, monitor, and maintain data pipelines and automated analytics to continuously update this information, making it available for activation and also to flag trigger events that require a response.

Experiment design and activation. This component decides which customers are eligible for which experiences based on the targeting intelligence, the available content, and the key rules (as described below). It automates the match-up of actions to take with customers. A new customer is prioritized for a welcome message, a customer who just made a booking gets a cross-sell trigger, and customers at risk of lapsing get prioritized for churn-prevention interventions.

For many companies, this step is done manually, so it generally takes weeks to set up scheduled personalized campaigns (i.e., proactive customer outreach). This pace therefore limits the degree of "activation," or response to the customer's action. Personalization leaders, however, automate much of the work in this step.

For one thing, they create a rules "layer" that guides their actions:

- **Exclusion rules,** such as "Consumers under eighteen cannot be targeted with certain actions"

- **Antirepetition and frequency-cap rules,** such as "Customers should not be shown the same content more than x times"

- **Activation rules,** such as "Bias toward showing new products for customers seeking variety"

- **Business rules,** such as "Favor higher-margin products," and "Don't show certain items together"

Critically, leading companies also think about experimentation from the start. Unlike most companies, they set up multivariate tests, which go well beyond simple, sequential A/B testing. (See figure 4-1, which summarizes our Personalization Index research.) They run dozens or even hundreds of experiments in parallel, often testing multiple variables in each. They withhold personalized interactions from a control group of customers in order

FIGURE 4-1

Experimentation types used for personalization

Companies surveyed using various types of experimentation (%)

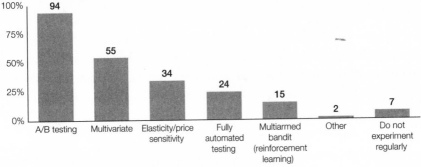

Source: BCG Personalization Index research, 2023 (n = 100).

to measure the impact on the business as well as on the customer experience, allowing teams to identify ways to optimize them. Building experiment design into the activation step and automating it is what enables the rapid measurement and learning that is essential for personalization at scale.

Next best action orchestration. The most sophisticated personalization leaders have this component in place to guide how experiences are delivered. This layer prioritizes actions across channels; for example, it might skip sending a paid ad when a customer has already clicked on an email. The orchestration also acts as "air traffic control" to avoid detrimental interactions; for example, it ensures that the company suspends scheduled messages to customers when a conflicting trigger event, like a customer service incident, has occurred. It can also be set up to harmonize content across channels; for example, coordinating what gets shown across the website and in emails to reinforce a message, or taking into account channel preferences in prioritizing how and when to issue an outreach.

One emerging tool for next best action orchestration is the so-called *state machine*, which tracks the progress (or "state") of each customer in a sequence of predefined actions. This is particularly important when a company wants to engage customers in multistep actions, such as a loyalty onboarding journey or purchasing multiple items over time; the machine keeps track of steps the customer has already taken and the steps that come next. The sequence could be as simple as visiting a store three times or as complex as navigating the steps in a financial-wellness journey toward a concrete savings goal. Implementing a state machine requires moving from a product- to a customer-centric orientation. Financial services companies, for instance, traditionally set up dozens or even hundreds of trigger-based campaigns to push actions related to each line of business, with complex (and sometimes conflicting) rules governing which ones take priority. Instead of such an undiscriminating barrage, a state machine provides a more modern way of setting up journeys centered around the customer, and then managing each customer's progress.

Most sophisticated companies incorporate reinforcement learning—training AI algorithms by constantly updating customers' responses—to optimize the sequence of actions created, say, to onboard new customers for a subscription service. Unfortunately, this orchestration layer is often

When Less Is More:
Orchestrating Message Suppression

Orchestration is as much about what *not* to say as it is about what to tell customers. Personalization leaders are setting up rules engines that govern which types of triggered messages should force others to be suppressed: for example, if the customer files a complaint, "stop all product messages for the next month"; or if the customer just made a booking, "stop all other booking recommendations and prioritize cross-sell messages." Digital and marketing leaders are also auditing all of their communications across the enterprise. In the typical large company, they often find that three to five teams might be using a given channel (like email or the app) to push communications, with no central coordination.

Personalization leaders are implementing frequency caps, tailored to each individual customer's appetite for content. This practice, when paired with an effective next best action engine, can reduce "unsubscribeds" and opt-outs by 30 to 50 percent and can *increase* open rates and click-throughs by even greater percentages. Product teams, eager to meet their financial targets by sending more push messages, are often reluctant to implement it. But customer-focused leaders are proving that it works, by testing the new approach on a portion of the audience, and forcing change based on this value proof. A regular audit of what customers are experiencing is critical for preserving existing digital customer relationships; no company wants to spend to acquire new customers only to see them quickly exit when they get inundated with irrelevant content.

implemented in only a few channels, or is missing entirely. As a result, companies' most valuable customers, who are rated "high propensity" for a broad range of actions, end up getting inundated with content.

Even before the advent of AI, overload was common. "Flooding" can happen when product P&L owners narrowly pursue metrics such as cost per acquisition (CPA) and conclude that they should bombard customers with content until they hit their target CPA.

The trick is to determine the optimum number of messages—just enough to help customers as well as the organization meet their goals without overdoing it (see the sidebar "When Less Is More"). Data analysis can help. At one employee benefits provider, marketers closely examined the correlation between the number of emails they were sending to a customer each week and the customer's click-through rate, which showed a massive falloff beyond two messages per week. To optimize the number of messages, marketers consolidated all contact management into a single platform, assigned prioritization weights to different types of messages (based on their importance for the customer and value to the business), killed messages whose value could not be proven, and then tested the effectiveness of various mixes of message content. The outcome? Click-through rates doubled, even as the volume of emails dropped by an astonishing 75 percent.

While initially, companies might use off-the-shelf tools to power the intelligence components of their personalization tech stack, personalization leaders often choose to selectively customize key parts (while still leveraging and integrating off-the-shelf elements). Let us dive into two examples from different industries.

Starting a Company with the Next Best Conversation in Mind

Companies of all sizes can achieve personalization at scale. From the start, many consumer brands launched in the last two decades have been built with personalization in mind. Take Warby Parker, which integrated personalized recommendations and augmented-reality try-on features into its app early on.

Another example is a company we worked with that makes a popular brand of outdoor equipment. From the get-go, the company built strong direct-to-consumer engagement by connecting with its fans, who raved about its products to friends and family at local events and festivals and through social media and email. By the time it launched its IPO, the company had several hundred million dollars in sales, with the ambition to become a multibillion-dollar company and expand into more product categories that its passionate fan base would crave.

To accelerate growth, the company decided to personalize its product communications to customers: recommendations, educational messaging for new customers, deals to lure back lapsed customers, messages from brand ambassadors, and personalized offers for existing customers. The company built out its martech stack; for example, choosing Braze and Segment as core engines for delivering messages across channels. To automate the targeting, experiment-design, and activation processes, the team deployed the relevant modules of Fabriq, BCG's prebuilt personalization codebase. They tailored and customized Fabriq into what became their Conversation Management System, an integrated platform for managing campaign creation, business rules, and rigorous experimentation and measurement.

The first step was to build a customer 360 database. The team started with thirty critical data features, which were eventually expanded to more than two hundred (and growing), including purchase behavior, product preferences, customization choices, web activity (such as views and clicks), campaign engagement, posted product ratings, and social media activity. Using this feedback, the data science team developed machine learning models to power the targeting intelligence. For example, propensity models predicted the likelihood a given customer would purchase a given product within the coming two weeks, and response models predicted such outcomes as how well certain subject lines would perform in an email or how well certain themes (such as camping, or hiking) or specific images would work in cross-channel campaigns.

The codebase managed the remaining steps, turning the raw ingredients into automated, themed journeys. These personalized communication sequences are far more complex and dynamic than segmented campaigns: they comprise a series of outreaches that continuously deepen the dialogue on a specific theme (for example, items for an avid mountain climber) or pivot to other themes (e.g., new products, different vacation topics) when interests wane or change.

By integrating best-of-breed marketing-activation tools and augmenting them with the codebase, the company was able to launch pilots in market, and then turn them into dynamic campaigns in days, not weeks. These tests combined the machine learning output with business rules (e.g., limiting emails to no more than three per week), experimentation cells (groups of test-versus-control customers for any given action), and automated measurement (e.g., real-time engagement data feeding dashboards). All marketing-response data was fed back into the Conversation Management System, further enhancing the targeting capabilities.

Marketers remained in control by crafting new ideas and variations of campaigns, but technology assisted them along two dimensions: first, by automating the experimentation process; and then, by developing dashboards that allowed marketers to track click-throughs and incremental revenue generated by the campaigns, both of which (click-throughs and revenue) grew by double digits.

After the initial success of these personalization efforts, senior executives quickly realized the power of scaling this new capability. The company doubled down on this approach by further investing in its in-house data and analytics team.

While great products and a focus on building a satisfied customer base drove the company's first decade of growth until its IPO, personalization played a pivotal role in the next era, as the company onboarded new customers and offered new product categories to its most loyal customers. Over a five-year period (2018–2023), sales doubled and market capitalization grew three times faster than the S&P 500. Senior executives and industry publications alike have credited personalization with materially contributing to the company's impressive growth.

Icario: Delivering Health Outcomes with Intelligent Personalization

All health insurers and their clients (plan sponsors) have a deep interest in encouraging plan members to be proactive about their health. For example, the US Medicare program adjusts its reimbursement to insurers based on its Stars Rating system, which rewards them with more stars (a valuable marketing tool) and extra compensation for better health outcomes and greater customer satisfaction. But managing such an approach for millions of plan members is challenging. Which members should an insurer spend money on to reach? When should it reach out, and through which channel? And with what kind of message, creative design, or incentive?

Executives at Minneapolis-based Icario, which develops consumer engagement content and strategies for 80 percent of the nation's leading health insurers, recognized AI's potential for orchestrating outreach to plan members.[1]

Drawing on a huge volume of data (its own and that of customer data suppliers), Icario's analytics team initially clustered people into "message theme" segments (e.g., lifestyle, diet, health, fitness). Icario amassed more than 15,000 data points that could be applied to every person. It surveyed plan members about their health attitudes and correlated their responses with their individual data. From this enriched data, Icario created more than a hundred types of message programs, grouping each of its clients' members into one of those programs. Based on how customers responded, the team continued to refine the segments and further tailor its approaches.

The volume of the data and the number of variables quickly exploded, so Icario began to automate orchestration. It personalized the choice of message (phone call, text message, app notification) and the timing and sequence. The company aimed for the most engagement using the cheapest channels, but when it realized a customer wasn't responding to digital messages, it switched them to direct mail or phone.

As Icario's personalization effort grew more complex, and the variations in member responses to the same message grew exponentially, the company added AI capabilities to automatically assign and manage members on the front end as well as analyze the back-end response data. Through randomized testing, the data science team developed a better sense of which contact strategies were most effective for each subsegment and how to orchestrate those strategies.

Over the course of a year, Icario began seeing dramatic jumps in program performance—with up to four times the response rate of Icario's prior average member outreach. The combined membership of two top health insurers—more than three million people—gave Icario the initial data set for building its advanced machine learning algorithms. On this foundation, it built the intelligence components of its personalization tech stack.

In the targeting-intelligence step, the company scored its clients' plan members according to the right next best action that would improve their health, lower the plan member's cost, and help boost the client's star rating.

Moreover, members were prioritized according to their predicted level of responsiveness (e.g., "easy," "need a nudge," or "unresponsive").

Icario's approach considered activation and next best action orchestration simultaneously. For any assigned action goal, Icario determined the best channel, sequence, and timing for each member. Next, Icario chose the best message (and possible incentive) for that channel, using both its findings on the psychology of different messages and guidance from behavioral economics experts. For example, some people are more motivated by the value they themselves would derive from a given action, while others are motivated by its value to their family. Still others follow what those around them are doing.

Because most clients have a limited budget for outreach and incentives, "Icario modeled how to optimize that spend," says Peter Eliason, former analytics leader at Icario. "We measured the value of each action to the client, the probability of customers taking that action, and the cost of outreach in each channel."[2]

Based on customer response to outreaches, Icario's machine learning models update the prediction accuracy of the models that determine the outreach plan in real time as feedback comes in. Having a continuously updated view of the prediction accuracy has enabled the models to decide where additional learning would be more useful—information used to guide the next wave of activation and experiment design.

Practical Considerations for Leaders

Based on our insights from dozens of personalization-at-scale implementations, we would emphasize five key lessons for leaders seeking to build and optimize the intelligence underpinning their personalization efforts.

- **Keep investing in contactability with your customer base.** This provides the foundation for reaching customers. Run periodic app-download offers, give customers reasons to log into the website, and provide easy sign-up options across digital channels. Clearly explain how signing up provides value through, for example, loyalty rewards, offers, easier returns with e-receipts, and educational newsletters. Spur customer sign-up in physical channels by properly incentivizing both customers and sales associates. Monitor unsubscribe rates and address issues promptly. Ultimately, the higher the share of customers who can be contacted, the higher the rate of learning for personalization.

- **Tailor your targeting approach based on your data and technology starting point.** While there are many software-as-a-service solutions for key portions of the tech stack (such as Braze, Segment, and Fabriq by BCG in our first example), this does not obviate the need for cleaning up the data architecture. Understanding which use cases can be quickly activated with the available data is an important jumping-off point for making the necessary build-or-buy decisions.

- **Regardless of your data and technology approach, prioritize scaling your customers' personalization response data.** This data provides critical insights into what works and what doesn't with your customers, and it's a key source of competitive advantage. As you add more personalized experiences and channels, such data will help you further improve targeting and activation in these instances, and you do not want it to sit exclusively in outside tools that are difficult to access and integrate. The Conversation Management System cited earlier is a great example of how companies can build personalization as an advantage by pulling together all the learnings on which interactions customers find relevant.

- **Automate the activation step.** This can massively reduce the time traditional marketers would otherwise spend on pulling customer lists and manually assigning customers to content; such handoffs between teams can add weeks to the process and decelerate learning. Add experimentation into the activation process, ensuring multiple variants are tested to enable continued optimization (as Icario did), and also that you are holding out an appropriate number of customers in a control cell to measure the impact of personalized variants on the rest.

- **Consider where orchestration across channels is important to the customer experience.** We find that most companies don't make obvious connections across owned and paid channels (e.g., email and social media), online and offline channels (e.g., web and call centers/stores), or even email and web, because of the way internal teams are organized. The examples cited in this chapter illustrate the power of this cross-channel orchestration to maintain contactability and avoid "burning the channels" (running the risk of large numbers of customers unsubscribing). Product teams will want to push their messages to customers without regard to customers' overall appetite for outreach, so it is important to move from a product-centric approach that allocates customers to messages to a next best action approach that prioritizes the best possible message and channel for each customer across scheduled and triggered actions.

These considerations enable personalization teams to build the right intelligence to power their efforts. But this intelligence would be soulless without the personalized content to feed it. As we will explore in the next chapter, with the emergence of gen AI and new atomic and dynamic approaches, the possibilities for creating, managing, and delivering 1:1 content at scale are more exciting than ever.

Intelligence Diagnostic Self-Check

Below are practical, specific questions you should ask yourself and your teams to assess the maturity of your personalization intelligence.

Targeting

- What can we do to increase contactability across our customer base by channel? How do we compare on this metric against competitors?

- Have we developed the data science models we need in order to target customers in a personalized way at the most important steps of the journey?

- Are we updating these models often enough, and are these models based on high-quality, accurate data with minimal time lag—keeping in mind the use cases they are driving?

- Do our models conduct machine learning based on customer response data to fine-tune the initial targeting of actions?

Activation

- What portion of our activation is triggered versus scheduled? How does engagement vary for the key types of activation, and what can we learn from this to further hone our strategy?

- How long does it take to activate major types of campaigns and personalized actions? What level of automation are we applying to the key steps of the activation process, and where should we increase this?

- Are we building experimentation into how we activate by testing many potential variants? Are we comparing test variants with control groups to enable statistical measurement of the impact? How manual is our current process for setting up an experiment?

Orchestration

- Are we taking a next best action approach to prioritizing actions by customer?

- Which channels are we orchestrating across? What marketing technology and process changes would be needed to enable closer coordination across paid and owned channels or key online and offline owned channels (e.g., email, web, apps, and call centers/ physical channels)?

- How well do we select the channel to use for each customer, and how well do we control the frequency of communications? Are our unsubscribe rates above the industry average?

- How well do we suppress irrelevant content?

Retail

So far, no sector has been more transformed by personalization than retail. That's hardly surprising, given its success harnessing the power of AI to reach customers with the right experience at the right time. Whether shopping for groceries, stopping by the local pharmacy, or buying electronics, office supplies, or materials for a home improvement project, consumers transact with retailers regularly and often engage with them in between purchases. Retailers are using first-party data from these interactions to fuel more-personalized experiences that make the next visit—whether in person or online—faster, easier, and more convenient. Consumers are more likely to return to retailers that do this best, generating yet more data in the process.

Now, hundreds of retailers worldwide have added another arc to this "digital flywheel": an advertising business fueled by first-party data. This new activity, known as retail media, is altering retail's traditional economic model; some retailers are now earning as much, if not more, from data-driven advertising as they are from their merchandise. This enables them to plow even more investment into improving the customer experience. That's why we predict that personalization leaders will see the largest gains: by our estimates, some $570 billion in growth before the decade's end. That's more than a quarter of the total personalization value at stake across *all* industries.

Woolworths: Rewarding Grocery Shopping

Woolworths Group is Australia's largest food retailer, with more than a thousand stores in the country and a significant presence in New Zealand. During the past decade, the company (known as Woolies to locals) has evolved its AI, digital, and personalization capabilities to become one of the world's leading grocers. Woolworths' success in becoming a data-driven retailer was underpinned by three key pillars: its leading loyalty program, Everyday Rewards; its data and digital division, known as WooliesX; and its partnership with Quantium, a global leader in data science and AI.

Everyday Rewards has more than nine million active members, which translates to an active loyalty membership in over half of Australian households. Thanks to the program, 70 percent of Woolworths Group sales are tied to known Everyday Rewards members. As with many grocery loyalty programs in Europe and Asia, every dollar spent at Woolworths earns a point. Through its loyalty partnerships, including with Qantas, Australia's leading airline, Woolies further expands the wealth of insights available for personalization and the value of its loyalty currency. Considering the vast number of its digital customer interactions, the frequency with which customers go grocery shopping, and the breadth of nonfood categories its banners also sell, Woolworths Group clearly has an unparalleled view of the Australian consumer.

One of the primary use cases for personalization in grocery is providing individualized value. Most grocery businesses operate on razor-thin margins. But their customers are highly price-sensitive, and will readily shop elsewhere if they aren't getting value in their weekly purchases. And yet the lion's share of marketing activation in grocery is built around mass promotions funded by the grocers themselves as well as by the consumer packaged-goods companies (CPGs) whose products they sell. Woolworths has undertaken two substantial streams of work to optimize promotional investments. For mass offers, its AI-driven NextGen Promotions capability drives spend efficiency and ROI. In parallel, Woolworths found a clever win-win solution to amplify customer value: it established a "currency" in its loyalty program—points customers can earn and apply to a wide range of rewards. This currency offers more ways to personalize value beyond the simple discount promotions available to any customer.

Despite the advances in AI and personalization, BCG estimates that more than 95 percent of promotional spend in global retail today is allocated to mass offers in the form of storewide deals, circulars, and product coupons. In our view, this share should be no more than 75 percent overall (and at most 50 percent in many categories), with the rest of the value investment shifting to personalized offers that yield a much higher ROI to retailers and their vendors. Thus, the more the customer shops and engages, the greater the value they perceive, which reinforces their relationship with the retailer. Leading retailers understand this payoff and are now more proactively managing their overall value investments.

Like Woolworths, grocery leaders throughout the world—Kroger (the United States), Tesco (the United Kingdom), Carrefour (France), Shoprite (South Africa), and Dairy Farm (Southeast Asia)—are building advanced personalization capabilities. Woolworths started early, in partnership with Quantium, before doubling down and creating an organizational structure that accelerated innovation and P&L ownership of digital: Woolworths Supermarkets operates the company's grocery stores (under a number of banners), WooliesX is its digital business unit, and wiq has been the group's AI arm since 2021.

WooliesX has P&L responsibility over the company's e-commerce, its grocery and loyalty apps, Everyday Rewards, its digital marketplace (Everyday Market), and Cartology, its retail media business. As such, it directly controls key teams, including digital and technology talent, and has a strong connection with supporting functions like HR, finance, and strategy via its agile operating model. WooliesX has been pivotal in making Woolworths a leader in personalization, creating a platform where the essential ingredients of data science, technology, customer strategy, and contact channels could be developed under a customer- and digital-focused leadership team. WooliesX has enabled the company to move faster than most other large retailers in expanding its digital capabilities. Speed proved crucial during the pandemic, when consumer demand in e-commerce and delivery skyrocketed. New data-driven businesses (like retail media) took off, and the WooliesX teams had to build and scale new capabilities at breakneck pace.

In 2013, Woolworths took a minority stake in Quantium and licensed the capability to create data-enabled services out of its own data, such as providing shopper insights on customer segment behavior and trends to CPGs. Over the following years Woolworths partnered closely with Quantium to drive data science innovation throughout its business. In 2021, Woolworths became a majority owner and integrated Quantium's team of cutting-edge retail data scientists and engineers with its in-house advanced-analytics talent to create wiq, whose purpose is to unlock the power of data to reimagine retail. Wiq's more than 800-member team is further accelerating the use of AI throughout the group, including personalization efforts, as well as making solutions developed at Woolworths available to noncompeting retailers globally.

Woolworths has put considerable effort into making it easy and compelling for customers to engage with personalized offers. Sophisticated personalization engines can gear promotional investment, such as loyalty rewards offers, toward price-sensitive customers who often base their purchasing decision on promotions, as opposed to customers who may not even realize they are getting a deal. But for personalized offers to be most effective, customers must opt in. Many companies force customers to leaf through hundreds of deals to clip coupons one by one (either from flyers or the app) for their preferred items. Woolworths' Everyday Rewards app shows customers offers that are suited for them. Customers can click once and "boost" their loyalty card with the selected offers, thereby loading them onto their card, ready to be applied to their next purchase in-store or online. Requiring a customer to indicate their interest in an offer through "boosting" means that companies don't waste their promotional spend on customers who are unaware of the offer. This enables companies to fund more offers from a set budget, as well as to invest more in each offer, thus making each offer more compelling.

As Woolworths' machine learning techniques became increasingly sophisticated, the company's ability to provide customers with the most tailored, relevant offers began to hit constraints. Many grocers are limited in the sheer number and variation of personalized offers they can execute at once, because their point-of-sale technology requires that each discount coupon be set up manually, and only so many coupon codes can be "live" at any one time due to system limitations. Thus, of the tens of thousands of SKUs and numerous categories that a typical grocery chain sells, and the hundreds of promotional combinations that may exist (which would theoretically yield tens of millions of permutations), only a few thousand can be active at any given moment. Woolworths has managed to overcome this obstacle by automating the underlying technology, including direct integration into point-of-sale systems with the help of Eagle Eye, its technology partner. Now, whether it's a loyalty-based points offer, a loyalty member-only discount, or a free sample, Woolworths can individualize offers to every customer. Most personalized offers incentivize customers with loyalty points (which tend to be higher in ROI), thereby enabling them to accumulate points that they can convert to Everyday Rewards Dollars to apply as they wish to future purchases.

Beyond personalized offers, consumer satisfaction in grocery comes from making weekly shopping easy. Here, too, personalization is playing a role, providing consumers such conveniences as prebuilt shopping lists, autoreplenishment, scheduled delivery for frequently purchased items, and even recipe suggestions. At Woolworths, personalization powers chatbots to help resolve customer queries. Olive, the company's virtual assistant, provides personalized suggestions to customers based on their order history. In addition, if a customer logs in to report "my eggs were broken on delivery," Olive will look up the order, confirm purchase, inquire whether the customer had any other complaints, and process the refund (noting the reason), without any human intervention.

Woolworths' progress illustrates the value that personalization can bring to a business with historically thin margins and cutthroat price competition. Indeed, when we compare the growth of loyalty programs, personalized offers, personalized service and experiences, and data monetization with the economics and competitive pressures of the core grocery business, it's no wonder that, as an executive at a leading European grocer told us, very soon, grocers will be making more money from data than from food.

Home Depot: Getting the Job Done for Every Customer

Beyond grocery, big-box retailers are also demonstrating the power of personalization and the value of data. Home Depot has long been one of the world's biggest brick-and-mortar retailers, and over the past decade, has also become one of the biggest e-commerce sites.

Several years ago, Home Depot's marketing team realized that it needed to personalize communications. "Customers come to the Home Depot to solve a problem," says Melanie Babcock, VP of retail media+ and monetization.[1] So, she explains, the company needed to communicate with customers in ways that corresponded to the level of help they required. The company launched a new marketing strategy, initially in paid-media channels, to target different audiences based on their individual needs. Under the new strategy, movers, project-based customers, contractors, and single-item, infrequent shoppers receive different communications. For example, the website will suggest a brand of appliance that is tailored to the search history of a customer who is remodeling their kitchen. A single-item, infrequent buyer who recently purchased a grill might get an ad promoting pellets, while a contractor might receive an invitation to the company's Pro Xtra loyalty program, which features offers specific to their trade.

As its online business rapidly grew, Home Depot saw a huge opportunity to help its vendors as well as its customers. Using its ample first-party data, it could help kitchen and bath suppliers like Kohler and Delta, and toolmakers like Milwaukee, reach customers with a high propensity for their products—both on homedepot.com as well as on social media and other ad platforms. Through the same audience-based media-targeting capabilities it applied to its own sales, Home Depot developed a robust retail media ad business. As Babcock says, "We leverage the power of Home Depot audiences and personalization to differentiate our Retail Media+ offering in the marketplace. The work we do to really know our customers, including their projects, items they are buying, and whether they are pro contractors, is what makes our retail media network stand out."[2]

Say, for example, the customer remodeling their kitchen is looking for a new faucet. Home Depot can sell a vendor the right to display particular faucet models (e.g., by price point or style) to the shopper at that moment. Not only does the vendor get its particular wares in front of just the right customers, but customers are spared time looking for the products they need to complete their project.[3]

What's powering this capability is data science. Home Depot's analytics team developed a suite of cutting-edge data science models that enable it to select the appropriate item from tens of thousands of SKUs in stores and millions of SKUs online. And in presenting just the right item, Home Depot goes beyond basic specs: the company takes into account other important details it has on hand regarding the customer's project.

Just as important as data science (that is, the algorithms) is the data engineering foundation on which it is built: Home Depot's ability to stitch together a full picture of each household from data captured in its different channels. During Covid-19, customers increasingly elected to order products online and pick up the order in store; and since the pandemic, more customers are shopping online as well as in the store. In response, the company has invested heavily in building a single view of each customer across channels, whether professional contractor or DIY household. Its award-winning app helps customers find items in the store, which can be particularly challenging, given the typical size and scale of its stores. Home Depot even offers virtual reality views, so customers can see what an item would look like in their house. All of these efforts have given the company new ways to build digital relationships with customers, in order to engage with them more frequently and understand their unique circumstances over time.

As Woolworths and Home Depot illustrate, the digital flywheel—the synthesis of the digital customer relationships, personalization, and new business models fueled by digital channels and retail media—will power the future of the retail industry.

Leaders will dream and aim big. They will explore bold partnerships and acquisitions to build scale in digital customer relationships. They will innovate with connected and experiential loyalty programs. They will launch new personalized experiences that vastly increase convenience and grow digital sales and contactability. They will compete for more than their fair share of what we estimate to be a $100 billion–plus retail media opportunity globally. They will hire the best AI and human-centered design talent, break down silos across channels and functions, and reshape their organizations to be customer- and not product-driven.

The prize: $570 billion in incremental revenue will accrue to the few retailers that can turn their personalization ambitions into reality first.

Chapter 5

Show Me

Show Me is about how a customer experiences the various forms of content that bring a company's Promises of Personalization to life—informational emails; images and videos on a website or app; text messages; exchanges with call center reps, store associates, or chatbots. Companies that excel at Show Me have the right content at their fingertips, tailoring each piece of content precisely to be most relevant to the individual customer, while also affirming the brand's voice. Success at Show Me stems from effectively creating, managing, and delivering huge volumes of personalized content to strengthen customer engagement and thus drive sales growth.

One CMO we worked with early on in her company's transformation effort put it well:

> Once you automate the data science, a new bottleneck crops up: content. In the past, we were routinely frustrated over the data and analytics teams' inability to execute campaigns fast enough. But

once the intelligence was up and running, it was our creative teams that couldn't keep up. Now our limiting factor was how quickly we could create great content to test.[1]

As crucial as analytics and AI are to the intelligence components of a personalization tech stack, personalization at scale comes down to content: whether a company has enough of the right content, can deliver it rapidly, and knows how to manage it strategically. In the age of AI, cranking out one asset at a time won't cut it. Companies that make this mistake vastly limit the variation in content that they can produce, test, deliver, and learn from.

The crucial job of the personalization tech stack is not just targeting the right customer; it's delivering the best interaction for each customer at the right step in their journey. Alongside rapid advances in AI and data-related technologies, new approaches to content strategy and creation are evolving rapidly. These changes have big implications for creative design and marketing operations, and they're happening across all three stages of content operations: content creation, management, and delivery. Consider:

Content creation is now modular and increasingly automated. We've come a long way from yesterday's one-size-fits-all approach to content development. Personalization leaders are creating reusable components that can be arranged in configurations tailored for each customer. What's more, gen AI is helping companies accelerate the creation of variants from existing marketing campaigns customized for unique audiences. For example, a call to action can be written ten ways (within approved parameters) and tested to see which versions most often strike the right chord with customers.

Content management systems can read, store, and describe every granular bit of content as data. As the content components of an experience become more modular, each piece can be tagged with metadata, such as the nature of an image, font type and size, word choice, and channel fit. Then, as a company deploys content, more information can be layered onto it from the resulting interactions. For instance, did an insurance customer respond better when a message contained an image of an outdoor activity or location that has special meaning for the customer? What about when the message was upbeat and inspirational versus cautionary? What impact did a larger font size or certain color or background image have? All of these layers of data inform AI systems' predictions about which content component to use as new customer interactions take place. Instead of tedious manual tagging, AI systems can now scan each piece of content to tag its main attributes, and today's content management systems (CMSs) can pull in data about the outcomes of interactions from the interfaces where experiences happen—channels such as the company's app, website, or call center.

Content delivery brings together the components for each customer, increasingly in real time. In response to an opportunity to interact with a current or prospective customer, decisioning engines choose what content to deliver, when, and through which channel, linking to the systems that manage the interactions in each channel.

Let's probe how personalization leaders take advantage of these trends to build differentiated content.

Craft the Content Strategy

Not all content needs to be personalized. Nor is it practical for companies to do so. Take news media. Digital news sites typically present general-interest articles to all readers, but personalize sections of their sites based on their readers' individual preferences. They also ensure that content is optimized for each device it is being viewed on, whether phone, tablet, or computer.

Some actions that a company wants a customer to take may not need much content personalization beyond the right timing and delivery channel. For instance, if a bank wants someone to download and enroll in its mobile app, it would create different calls to action for different types of customers. But the basics—conveying the app's value, emphasizing its ease of use and the fast enrollment process—are fairly consistent.

Now consider a restaurant chain that wants to encourage customers to order breakfast in advance, through its app, and pick it up at one of the company's drive-through stores during customers' morning commute. Accomplishing this will probably call for personalized content related to the nature of the breakfast choices, the drive-through location, and even the timing of the interaction.

So, to craft a sound content strategy, start by asking: What do we want to personalize? For which customers? At what stages in their journey? How will doing so enhance the customer's experience? and What business goals will it enable us to achieve?

Many companies that offer subscription-based services are realizing that the complexity they've brought into the design of their products—tiered pricing, different levels of service, random discounts for various add-ons, changing restrictions, and so forth—are leading to customer confusion, calls into their service centers, dissatisfaction, and higher overall costs. As many analyze the biggest problems that their customers encounter, they are realizing that they must either radically simplify their products or better educate customers from the outset about what they have bought. Since it is exceptionally difficult, and often economically undesirable, to radically change one's product line, many are turning to new tools to educate customers during the onboarding process.

One such tool is personalized video. Video's attractiveness is obvious. According to a 2022 report by Wyzowl, 73 percent of the consumers surveyed said they preferred learning about a product or service through a short video, compared with just 11 percent who'd rather read a text-based article, website, or post.[2] Think about it: Would you rather learn about your new car from a 300-page manual or from two-minute videos you can watch at your own pace? Videos that don't just explain your particular model but that also describe your dealer's services, the options you bought, and the process for setting up your car's dashboard-based features?

Personalized video is changing content strategy, as it shifts the content development process toward making video components and leads to exploring the use of techniques such as animation to convey important information every new customer needs. You can set different priority goals for different customers, such as encouraging people to download and register the company's app, or making others aware that they are eligible to join special programs.

These moves are paying big dividends. At several telecom companies, for example, more than half of new customers are watching an entire onboarding video, a very high percentage for video viewing. Thanks to enhanced customer education, call center volumes are decreasing by double-digit percentages, an improvement that translates into millions in annual savings.

The Shift to Atomic, AI-Generated Content Creation

At one time, the biggest impediment to personalizing content was producing the sheer volume of components needed. Even creating simple content for mass distribution was traditionally a tedious and time-consuming process. Today, personalization leaders are using many strategies to create content at scale. Gen AI is turbocharging these efforts.

With a content strategy in place—what to personalize, for whom, when, in which channel, and how to measure the results—the next step is to create the modular pieces of content that will come together to personalize each customer's experience. Instead of developing fully designed content pieces for each interaction, personalization leaders start by creating templates for each channel: an email template with blocks for header copy, the call to action, images, offer descriptions, and incentives, or a mobile app recommendation card with space to drop in an image and a call to action. These templates become the "containers" that receive the personalized content the organization designs.

The companies then create *dynamic content*: multiple variations of each type of creative asset (text, images, video, other graphical elements) as possible components that can then be preassembled into appropriate, targeted communications. Companies populate their templates with these personalized content elements, mixing and matching them as needed for each recipient, and then deploying them across channels. By creating, approving, and quality-controlling a library of templates and content pieces, marketers thus avoid the once painful process of constructing each campaign manually from scratch.

For example, we helped a large global airline increase the volume of its personalized content fortyfold without the need for any additional resources. We used gen AI, plugged into the company's CMS. This way, the creative team wouldn't have to make any necessary changes manually or risk copyright issues (because only the company's own content was used). The content was then generated with the brand's voice, and it adhered to guardrails (e.g., rules about the appropriate message tone or blacklists of inappropriate words) and covered different formats, backgrounds, and imagery for different customer segments. A quality-assurance step ensured that marketers still had final say over what content was used. Gen AI enabled us to create countless content variations from these elements for each

FIGURE 5-1

Traditional versus personalized content

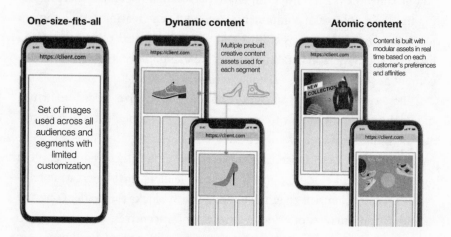

One-size-fits-all

Set of images used across all audiences and segments with limited customization

Dynamic content

Multiple prebuilt creative content assets used for each segment

Atomic content

Content is built with modular assets in real time based on each customer's preferences and affinities

Source: Taking an Atomic Approach to Content Personalization, BCG.

key travel destination and to target customers based on their background and interests. Text and images corresponded to each customer segment and their position in their customer journey. For example, for a Disney-loving family of four, the airline could suggest one set of activities in Orlando, while a weekend-warrior couple would get an entirely different set of recommendations.

Atomic content creation goes one step further, drawing on real-time data (e.g., location, weather) to update content in the moment, even after the original message has been sent. Suppose the customer has just purchased the dress advertised in the original email; the AI changes the product recommendation from a dress to shoes that would match by the time the customer opens the message. (See figure 5-1.)

Manage Your Proliferating Content

To enable personalization at scale, you must carefully structure and manage content to allow different components to be combined for each contact. The systems tasked with these activities must be able to handle volumes of content that are growing exponentially.

Digital asset management (DAM) systems house databases of photos, videos, and logos. These, together with CMSs, were the key to enabling personalization, and are now crucial to managing the growing volumes of all types of content, their components, and their metadata. CMSs, initially designed to manage blocks of content on websites, expanded to handle content across digital channels. Today, most of the major systems also include an integrated DAM. However, these tools are only as good as the data, tagging taxonomy, and processes that feed them. Another common pitfall: companies often find that their creative assets are housed in multiple systems.

Increasingly companies are using AI to overcome the challenges of content management. As content assets that are created with one set of tools (possibly a gen AI program) get loaded into a CMS, they need to be tagged with descriptive metadata about all of their attributes, so that they are searchable. Then, the system must track every aspect of each piece of content when it is used. That way, the CMS can learn which attributes of which content components work for which customers, while also managing timeliness of delivery, copyright permissions, and compliance. In personalization, the possible combinations of attributes of content relevant for an individual customer interaction are so vast that companies are increasingly using AI to scan the content and create the tags automatically at the most granular level possible. A whole class of software solutions is emerging that enables and automates AI-driven tagging.

Some content creation solutions, such as Adobe Firefly, Jasper, and Stanley.ai, are integrating gen AI capabilities to combine variation and tagging. One such offering can take an initial creative concept and build a wide range of incremental variations as well as multiple language versions, tuned with images appropriate to different cultures. What's more, the solution can vary the concept for use in different channels that each have their own formatting requirements, such as a digital web ad, a mobile phone ad, an email, or a web image.

Specialized solutions are also emerging, such as ones enabling retailers to generate all the variations of a product image they could need.[3] Software not only tags the variants but also looks at the image itself and creates a broad array of tags that can help shoppers search—product design, color, fabric, size—and that renders the versions they seek. With such a tool, a company can test hundreds of permutations of images and text to determine which works best for which kinds of customers.

Consider how a mobile telco used gen AI to encourage customers to upgrade their phones. It designed a campaign with special offers on devices and service plans, including the option of receiving a new phone free for a trial period. The telco's ad agency fashioned the associated words and phrases into copy that formed the basis of the campaign.

In a traditional campaign, this copy would be developed by a copywriter relying on insights from research, data analysis, experience, and intuition, and would be used uniformly across the entire campaign. Success would rest largely on a process driven by guesswork. In contrast, the AI creative-content generation tools that the telco now uses are vastly more precise, scientifically selecting the optimal words and phrasing for every message, even varying them for the time of day and channel of interaction.

The algorithm breaks down the basic copy into its component parts (format, emotional appeal, call to action) to gauge the impact of each part on different consumer segments. Using an existing, and continuously expanding, database of words and phrases, the algorithm then generates all possible permutations of the copy, which can run into the hundreds of thousands or even millions. Based on past campaign experience and brand guardrails set, it selects a manageable universe of, say, one or two dozen alternatives for marketers to approve for testing. In-market experimentation reveals the specific copy that is most effective in each channel—email, website ads, in-app offers, and the like—for each main consumer segment, at different times of day, in different types of locations.

These efforts have produced impressive results for the telco, including a 36 percent increase in engagement and 83 percent more conversions than the control group. Further, because the company could break down how different parts of the content drove performance, it was able to pinpoint and quantify the sources of effectiveness. It found that the engagement lift stemmed from three key elements: language with an emotional appeal (69 percent), specific words on the company's positioning (14 percent), and how the company highlighted its call to action (17 percent).

Next, let's delve deeper into how another company—not a digital native—upgraded its content development strategy.

Brinks Home: Personalizing to Deepen the Service Relationship

Texas-based Brinks Home recognized that the home security market was being reshaped as a result of the data explosion generated from digital interactions with customers and from the modern security systems themselves. It also realized that its standard renewal offers were giving away more of a discount than was necessary for many customers, while skimping on the premium needed to persuade others to stay. The company was sitting on a data goldmine. Every day, Brinks's core products—motion sensors, security cameras, smart-home apps, and other devices—generated mountains of information, and the company had accumulated a wealth of historical customer-level transaction data from its call centers. Field reps, moreover, had been gathering competitive data. On top of all this, new biometric identification methods were becoming commercially available, sources for a whole new array of security data.

For Brinks, the choice of who to target and who to prioritize was fairly straightforward: everyone who was facing a renewal, everyone with an outdated system, and everyone who had moved to a larger home presented an opportunity to expand the relationship. You don't need AI to spot those opportunities. But different aspects of the service appealed to different customers. Therefore, to start out, the company focused on personalizing the content to communicate its offerings to each potential customer, and on establishing the feedback loops to continue refining the process.

To keep the flow of the customer experience as personalized as possible, Brinks connected the marketing-activation engine to its call center systems, so that reps would know exactly what content had been sent to any customer who called in. It also added the capability to collect more information from call center interactions, like what offers the reps made and what key messages they delivered. This revealed such things as which customers tended to call, which offer and message combinations were most likely to lead to a conversion post-call, and which combinations led to costlier calls. Such feedback informed decisions about optimizing the content and layout of the marketing messages for the highest conversion rate at the lowest cost. Building on its initial approach, Brinks is now using information from its call center calls (teased out by natural language processing) to learn what kinds of questions customers ask, their attitude, and the words that reps should use to nudge customers over the threshold to convert.

Instead of developing a proprietary intelligence engine, Brinks chose to adopt OfferFit, an off-the-shelf orchestration and optimization solution, for its customer retention and renewal journeys. By connecting it with Brinks's CMS, and modularizing all of its email, SMS, and website templates, the company tested and then optimized thousands of different combinations of messages and offers (including variations in creative content), as well as of channel and delivery timing.[4]

Brinks started out with an advantage: abundant data that, once harmonized and cleaned with AI, was sufficient to feed into the marketing-activation engine. Over time, Brinks has developed not only new types of deal offers but also new and smarter ways of reaching out. Beyond learning the time, messaging combinations, and frequency preferred by each customer, the company has focused on continuously testing new copy in its marketing messages to help it understand the motivations of individual customers. The company can now know which calls to action work best: those that emphasize savings or those highlighting security (or other factors). Brinks's efforts have helped yield a 400 percent improvement in net present value from its renewal expenditure.

Gen AI: Put the Right Processes and People in Place

Personalization leaders don't merely push out campaigns to broad groups of customers or let every product team send messages to customers they would like to target. Instead, they prioritize interactions with each customer at the right moment in their journey, and at a time when and through a channel where they are most likely to engage. Such companies cut the volume of outreach, while sending more-varied and more-relevant touches to each customer at any given time. This is a major shift in philosophy and operating model: more strategically managed, and less "Wild West." To make this shift while also managing the risks of gen AI, we recommend an agile, iterative approach that calls for new processes and new mixes of skills.

Let process, not just tools, drive performance. Moving to a modular approach requires several intermediate steps. You need to design the templates into which the content elements will go. You need to establish guardrails for brand voice, compliance, or other factors that limit risk. And your creative teams (increasingly, those managing AI tools) will need to think in modular terms instead of whole blocks. Beyond varying the backdrop image based on the individual's location, do you want to vary the action in the image based on the recipient's age or family structure? Does your data indicate that someone has responded better to more-prominent financial incentives? Gen AI can produce endless variations to test, but strategically, you need to think about the segments and angles to address.

Establish governance processes. Companies need to establish the right governance processes to ensure that the many content components they develop are appropriate, free of bias, and meet compliance requirements. Bias can especially creep in when content has been created only for specific types of customers, not new ones whom you may be aiming to serve. It can also come from algorithms trained on data that was simply not diverse enough. AI tools can help, but humans must review random samples and any outliers the AI identifies to ensure that these edge cases are not veering far from established guidelines. Many companies put their own employees in their customer database as "frontline" recipients of marketing messages, with the variants those employees may have in household structure, or their status as an actual customer. That way, marketers can get rapid feedback if problems occur. (See chapter 10 for a deeper discussion of bias and other risks.)

Bring in the right skills. Content development may be evolving from a primarily creative capability to one that draws extensively on digital and data skills, but that doesn't lessen the importance of human creativity. On the contrary, creativity will become even more essential, as the power of human innovation is unleashed by tools that make idea generation and testing vastly easier and faster. The human ability to understand customers' emotions and reactions to the company's communications can be a springboard for developing content variants using AI, or for adapting gen AI's outputs to ensure they're appropriate.

To do all this, creative directors and their teams will need to excel at a range of skills vital for rapidly testing content and learning from the testing process. Such skills include knowing how to measure success using digital metrics and understanding how to apply the resulting data to optimize the impact of the company's creative assets. Beyond traditional writing and design skills, teams will have to be cross-functional, and include data and analytics experts, data scientists, martech experts, and software engineers.

As the scale and breadth of content that companies generate dramatically expands, teams will also need people who know how to manage the prompts for gen AI by which the business generates variations, set guardrails for content design and development, and check content samples for appropriateness and bias. For example, a quick-service restaurant company set a rule that its marketing emails should not feature items that, when combined, exceed a certain calorie limit. A fashion company defined a guideline stipulating that webpage pop-up ads for apparel items must show items—such as a dress, handbag, shoes, and jewelry—that would work together to "complete the look." And an industrial-parts company put a screen on all emails that any product recommendations had to be compatible with a client's installed base.

In the early days of segment-of-one marketing, and even as digital marketing began to take off, companies focused on customer data and targeting, not on content creation, management, and delivery. The unlocking of content management as an engine for personalization—mainly due to advances in natural language processing, gen AI, and database design—is driving an explosion of content, along with the ability to tailor it on a massive scale. Personalization leaders, using new tools—and also new ways of working, as we will explore in the next chapter—are pushing the frontiers of how to modularize and innovate content and test innumerable configurations to learn what works best.

Content Diagnostic Self-Check

How mature is your content personalization process?

Content Strategy and Creation

- What types of personalized content (in which channels) are most critical for delivering a great experience for our key customer segments across their journey?

- How finely targeted is our content in our most important channels (e.g., completely personalized, just segmented, tied to real-time data)?

- How should we apply gen AI to increase the volume of content generation, increase content quality, and/or lower our content creation costs?

- How well can our content creation process accelerate the legal and regulatory review of modular creative assets?

Content Management

- How much of our content is dynamic and templatized?

- How much of our content is tagged and managed in a content library to allow reuse and automated delivery to customers?

- How well have we implemented and standardized the use of content management and digital asset management systems across our business?

Fashion and Beauty

As an expression of our individuality, style is among the most personal choices we make. Each day, we make fashion choices about what to wear, how to accessorize, or what makeup to put on. Leading brands don't just sell products, they inspire us with new looks, traditionally captured through expensive photo shoots in glamorous locations. But brands like Pandora and Lululemon are showing a new way to engage with and delight legions of customers across digital and physical channels.

Pandora: Reigniting Growth in a Mature Category

Denmark-based Pandora is the world's largest jewelry brand (and not to be confused with the music streaming service). It grew explosively in the early 2000s with the introduction of its charm bracelets. These customizable yet affordable items—crafted mostly of sterling silver at the company's facilities in Thailand—appealed to a mass market.

By 2018, however, growth in Pandora's core business had begun to slip.[1] Loyal customers had already bought all the charm bracelets and charms they would buy, and new customers weren't coming along fast enough. The company worked hard to reignite growth, and in 2021, launched Phoenix, a new strategic initiative based on four pillars: brand, design, personalization, and core market growth.

Personalization took center stage. Says Jesper Damsgaard, senior vice president, global marketing and head of go-to-market and data-driven growth:

> Our purpose as a company is to give a voice to people's love.
> Whether you love your wife and kids, horses, or music, we give a

physical manifestation to that love, and you have thousands of products to choose from. So we decided that personalization needed to be at the core of not just our brand proposition, but also of how we engage the customer.[2]

To jump-start the personalization part of the program, Pandora applied many of the strategies already described in these pages: establishing a direct relationship with millions of customers via its own retail network and online touchpoints, and building a strong foundation of customer data—purchase history, website visits, and email and paid media engagement.

The company created a personalization center of excellence, with cross-functional teams consisting of marketing, tech, and data science experts. Organized around key customer segments (such as repeat buyers or "gifters"), each team was assigned well-defined goals.[3] The gifting team, for example, focused on identifying more potential occasions for which consumers would consider a Pandora gift appropriate.

One challenge Pandora faced was determining how much of its core product its most loyal customers had already purchased. With its traditional brand-campaign approach, the company was able to maintain interest in its core offerings, which represented 70 percent of its sales. But it still struggled to grow new and niche products, an effort critical to its next phase of growth. Such offerings might include limited-time "collab" items (those created jointly with a celebrity or with other brands, like Disney), items made from new materials, or entirely new designs. Personalization seemed like an excellent way to identify the right customers to present these new products to: those who were already big Pandora fans but who were unlikely to buy more of the core items.

To achieve this objective, the personalization team launched initiatives in the following three areas:

- **Product recommendations.** Using first-party customer preference data gathered from Pandora's website, the analytics team built propensity models that scored customers' preferences according to the particular "look" they desired (e.g., "fun," "elegant," "special occasion," "casual," or "themed") and other attributes. By incentivizing customers with loyalty points, the personalization team succeeded in collecting additional preference data directly from them to enrich their profiles; data-capture rates more than doubled when a small amount of points were offered. With this newly enriched data, Pandora could prioritize what each customer saw at the top of the website and in other digital touchpoints. This strategy unlocked growth in sales of the company's long-tail offerings, such as its rose- and yellow-gold items. Pandora ultimately adopted a new marketing approach: pairing tried-and-true, mass brand-marketing campaigns for key occasions (like holidays) with personalized marketing touches tailored to individuals.

- **Gifting.** Because most jewelry is purchased as a gift, the team assessed the different ways that people approach gifting. One successful early win involved tailoring separate messaging to gift-givers (who often seek reassurance about choosing the right item and price, along with convenience) and recipients (who seek inspiration and the latest trends). The team also personalized the outreach based on where each segment was in the buying process.

- **Customer journeys.** Some new products required a multistep process to move customers from interest to purchase and beyond. For example, Pandora was betting big on a new product line: lab-created diamonds, which have only five percent of the environmental footprint of mined diamonds. The team created a new journey for customers who expressed an interest in diamonds: it introduced the new line, educated them on the manufacturing process, and finally, persuaded them to come to the store to try on pieces, buy them, and recommend them to friends.

Once the foundational elements were built, the team could tackle the ultimate challenge: personalizing creative content. In the jewelry business, helping customers visualize themselves wearing a product in their context—for example, showing ads featuring relatable models representing a wide range of lifestyles, body types, and ethnicities wearing the bracelets rather than showing the same model for everyone—drives conversion. Traditionally, developing campaign content required expensive location photo shoots and twelve-month timelines. While this approach was still crucial for maintaining Pandora's brand identity, it was no longer enough.

The team augmented the traditional method with dynamic personalized content creation. Using a new process aided by technology and a content library, this approach took just days. Knowing that success on this front would hinge on getting the imagery right, the teams ran tests to determine which customers would respond best to different product presentations: in a particular context (say, a festive background), on a model, or in a stand-alone product shot with accompanying descriptive text. The team leveraged Bloomreach, the campaign-building tool, to automate workflows and enable marketers to create multichannel campaigns on their own in minutes. To further slash content development times, the team partnered with gen AI vendors, focusing first on simpler techniques (such as using the technology to change the background). They continued with custom photo shoots for the hand-model images that gen AI couldn't yet autogenerate. Damsgaard explains:

> You do one use case, you learn, you do another one, and then another . . . and pretty soon, you get a snowball effect. Soon we had an innovation hub working with many leading tech players around the world. So when something like gen AI comes along, we can immediately take advantage of that innovation—something that would have been very difficult for us in the old Pandora.[4]

Pandora's efforts led to resounding success. Within the first year of its Phoenix program, it returned to growth: the first three personalization initiatives in particular drove substantial incremental sales growth. Even before the latest rounds of improvements, the company achieved record sales overall, with growth in the high single digits, despite the fact that charms, its flagship line, were a mature product.

Lululemon: Extending Grassroots Marketing into Digital Channels

Lululemon's spectacular early rise was as much a testament to well-timed product innovation—creating yoga pants when yoga went mainstream in the West—as it was to grassroots marketing. Founded in 1998, the company built an impressively large community of extremely loyal fans during its first two decades. It did so by making use of "ambassadors," local athletes and trainers who evangelized the brand in their yoga and fitness communities, and "educators," store associates who hosted yoga classes and shared information about the "sweat life" that Lululemon encouraged its customers to lead. Essentially, Lululemon was built on the personalization its ambassadors and educators delivered to each customer.

However, it wasn't until 2015 that the company hired its first head of customer relationship management to scale and extend this personalized approach to digital channels. Lululemon's leadership at the time also set about reshaping the company's operating model across its data, technology, and people processes. The new CRM leader put in place a plan centered around three objectives: knowing, understanding, and engaging customers across all channels.

To know the customer, the company began systematically collecting email addresses from everyone who had signed up in its store for yoga classes and events (such as running events it sponsored). It also launched e-receipts (containing the customer's phone number or email address), which allowed customers to return purchases without a paper receipt. Lululemon enriched its first-party data with second- and third-party data attributes (such as demographic and lifestyle information); cleaned, deduped, and enhanced the data infrastructure; and invested in a customer data platform and a master-data-management capability. Within just a year, these actions had filled the company's database with millions of names and the details of each customer's purchases.

The company also augmented its tech stack with new cloud tools for digital asset management, marketing automation, web and app optimization, and clienteling. Given its scale at the time ($2 billion in revenues in 2016), Lululemon lacked the hefty tech budgets enjoyed by giant retailers. Nevertheless, it was willing to become an early adopter of new software-as-a-service solutions that gave it preferential pricing and additional implementation resources in exchange for becoming a reference customer. All this allowed the company to build its initial personalization engine in months, not years, and at a lower cost.

To truly understand the customer based on all this data, Lululemon assembled a team of data scientists and engineers to serve as a center of excellence. The team developed segmentation and data models to power personalization and became part of a broader agile cross-functional accelerator group that played a crucial role in rapid testing and learning. In parallel, the company implemented web analytics and a robust test-and-learn program in its paid and owned channels to gather marketing-response data on customers (e.g., which emails they opened or which social media ads or website banners they clicked on). The findings revealed customers' purchase intent, browsing behavior, and channel preferences.

One early success involved a holiday campaign. Using personalized app notifications, emails, and paid-media ads, the team beat the marketing plan's revenue target by tens of millions of dollars. Building on its initial wins, the team started personalizing communications across owned and paid channels. It ramped up its frequency of contact with existing customers and began recommending new products and new categories, such as accessories, tops, and shorts. With its personalization technology stack in place, reaching new segments, such as men and yoga enthusiasts in markets where Lululemon had no physical presence, became much less expensive.

Like Pandora, Lululemon soon found that its traditional content development process was creating a bottleneck in its personalization efforts. Aiming to engage the customer wherever they were, Lululemon moved from photographing content for each channel separately to an omnichannel approach. It developed different types of content for different segments and leveraged a mix of in-house and agency talent to reduce production time. The team was already creating millions of pieces of content and spending a large part of its marketing budget on this effort, so the solution lay in working in a more coordinated way across channels. For instance, the team ensured that output from every photo shoot could be used across all channels. The result: more relevant content in each channel, without the need for additional creative resources.

The company's operating model transformation also extended beyond headquarters. In a pivotal move, Lululemon tied bonuses for its "educators" to customers' online as well as in-store sales. The company armed its educators with personalization tools for growing sales in both realms, such as handheld devices for making contextual recommendations and daily CRM reports that let them track engagement with their top customers.

Personalization has played a huge role in Lululemon's meteoric growth. Throughout its transformation, Lululemon focused on pivoting from transactions as the primary metric of customer engagement to dialogue and connection with customers. It fostered a mindset of pursuing limitless growth, with the goal of maintaining double-digit growth to become a $10 billion company over ten years (by the late 2020s). With 2023 revenues exceeding $8 billion, that's a goal the company is now very close to achieving.

What's Next for Fashion and Beauty?

We predict that fashion-and-beauty players will increase their investments in personalization. Creative content will continue to be a competitive battleground: companies will create inspirational personalized content at scale using gen AI tools in tandem with dynamic templates and AI-driven content delivery. As a result, creative teams will boost content tailoring by a factor of fifty or more. Personalized clienteling at scale will spread from high-end luxury brands to call centers across the fashion-and-beauty industry, improving the customer service experience, including facilitating rapid problem resolution. Finally, given ongoing cost pressures and inflation, brands will continue to shift funds from costlier mass promotions to more-cost-effective personalized offers.

Using these levers, established large brands and multibrand fashion houses, with their superior breadth and depth of knowledge about their customers, can reclaim some of the share lost to newer, direct-to-consumer brands that captured most of the category growth in the early 2020s. Amid this change, new business models will emerge as social media networks like Pinterest and as style apps become one-stop marketplaces for customers to get styling advice and buy what they like with one click.

These many advances give brands across the fashion-and-beauty industry new and exciting opportunities to realize the full potential of personalization.

Chapter 6

Delight Me

Delight Me

Delight Me is the promise that makes personalization feel magical. It is fueled by agile ways of working, organizational structures and processes, and technology, which together constantly improve personalized experiences with each customer interaction. It's about embedding a test-and-learn culture and measuring improvement in performance indicators at least weekly. Fundamentally, success hinges on people. The result is sales, value creation, and brand love.

Delighting customers by constantly improving their experiences takes a significant degree of internal coordination and quickly learning what individual customers want. It calls for designing customer journeys with numerous touchpoints that cut across channels. This requires collaboration, along with agile ways of working, to foster constant innovation and rapid testing. Think back to the Sungevity story in the preface of this book: the ever-more-tailored nature of both the purchasing journey and the ownership journey would not have been possible without close-knit coordination across marketing, sales, financing, and customer service. Delighting the customer happens only when you can quickly innovate, test, and scale up great experiences, especially those that use customer information for customers' benefit. Sungevity also made sure its outreach got progressively smarter as the customer engaged, and that learning flowed to its call centers. Delighting the customer is never a one-and-done exercise—and it necessitates an internal operating model that can iterate rapidly.

So far in this book we've talked a lot about data and technology. But our Personalization Index research shows that the top pain points cited by leading companies in their personalization efforts relate to dealing with functional silos and challenges in how people work (see figure 6-1). It's the people issues that constitute the lifeblood of personalization: how you scale agile ways of working, revamp incentive systems, reengineer manual processes, and reimagine organizational structures. Ultimately, these are the catalysts of "delight": they are what differentiate personalization leaders from the rest.

FIGURE 6-1

Most common pain points in personalization efforts

Percentage of companies surveyed citing as a pain point

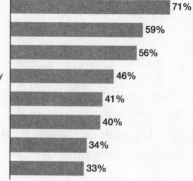

Siloed operating model with numerous handoffs	71%
Manual work due to technology limitations	59%
Creative design speed and flexibility	56%
Lack of shared vision for personalization across the company	46%
Lack of centralized customer data	41%
Lengthy legal, compliance, and risk reviews	40%
Lack of FTE or agency resources	34%
Data quality	33%

Source: BCG Personalization Index research, 2023 (n = 100).

The 70/20/10 Rule

Looking at the most successful AI transformations of the past decade, we have observed a common thread: what we call the 70/20/10 rule. Seventy percent of the effort in AI transformations involves people: processes, ways of working, incentives, and performance targets. Twenty percent entails getting the data right. The remaining 10 percent is about the technology foundation. This empirical finding comes from reviewing the level of resources we and our clients have deployed across hundreds of digital transformations. In fact, it holds equally true for transformations dedicated to personalization. This distribution doesn't mean that data and technology are easy, but it underscores the complex change management that personalization requires. That 70 percent piece is the focus of this chapter.

Many organizations, however, get this formula backward: they see transformation, including personalization, chiefly as a technological issue. Or else they understand the implications on people and processes but find them too daunting to address. Yet we've seen time and again how this approach causes so many transformations to falter. Why?

A lack of agile ways of working across functional teams. Although *agile* has become a corporate mantra, in our experience very few big companies do it well, especially outside of their IT teams. Without the proper tools and methods to facilitate rapid experimentation and learning, companies end up giving customers inconsistent and static experiences across channels. Implementing agile approaches is the biggest change necessary for successful personalization, and the hardest one to get right. Many companies thus shy away from taking this major step first.

Processes that are slow and not scalable. When processes are not tightly coordinated across silos, collaboration among teams involves long lead times and dozens of handoffs. Cycle times for personalized campaigns often run between six and twelve weeks, and learning slows down. Nimble teams can cut down the number of handoffs and automate key parts of the work to reduce the cycle time to three days or less.

Lack of automated measurement and embedded analytics. In many organizations, the impact of personalization is not measured consistently, and measurement is delayed. When it takes anywhere from two to four weeks to analyze an email campaign's performance, your target customers may end up receiving the same email you've just tested, because you've had no chance to process the findings. The same applies to monthly coupons sent to price-sensitive customers. Sending out July coupons without knowing how May's performed can have considerable revenue impact. Furthermore, data is often not accessible to decision-makers—meaning even longer delays in deriving insights.

Solving for the 70/20/10 Rule at a Major Retailer

So what can companies do to overcome these challenges and achieve that 70/20/10 balance? One client, a large global retailer, took a phased approach, starting with the "70" part of the formula.

First, the company piloted new agile ways of working

The company started by setting up a personalization "lab." This is an approach to accelerating personalization, where an agile, cross-functional team ("pod") reengineers core personalization-related processes for speed and scalability, and also tests the value of quick-win use cases by taking a group of customers (a control group) offline. Initially, the team piloted three targeted use cases across two channels. For each use case, the team was tasked with working toward a specific, measurable six-month goal, such as testing and scaling personalized product recommendations on the website or designing new, multistep personalized offers in the app. Within a year, the same working model was applied across the five core customer strategies: increasing new-customer acquisition, expanding digital engagement, growing loyalty members, increasing the share of Gen Z customers, and growing multicategory cross-selling.

Figure 6-2 shows what a typical agile pod looks like. Representatives span a wide range of cross-functional areas, including marketing, analytics, IT, creative, data scientists, and engineers. All are "doers" who could quickly execute their ideas on their own, or in some cases (like technology) could readily tap broader organizational resources.

What a typical agile pod looks like

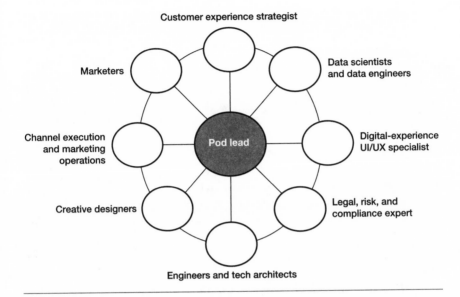

Next, the personalization team identified ways to streamline the process

Personalization-lab team members mapped how personalized experiences were traditionally launched. (See figure 6-3.) They identified thirteen hand-offs that could be eliminated, and nineteen steps that could be whittled down to eight, with automation reducing the resources needed by two-thirds. The traditional twelve-week campaign development process was cut to five days. (See figure 6-4.)

Importantly, the personalization lab allowed the agile pods to put the streamlined process into action, demonstrate that it worked, and refine it. When the time came to scale this process across the organization, there was a proven blueprint to work from, making it much easier to achieve alignment for the many changes needed across the functional teams. Senior leaders, seeing the substantial time and resource savings, quickly rallied behind the changes.

FIGURE 6-3

Before: The traditional 12-week campaign process

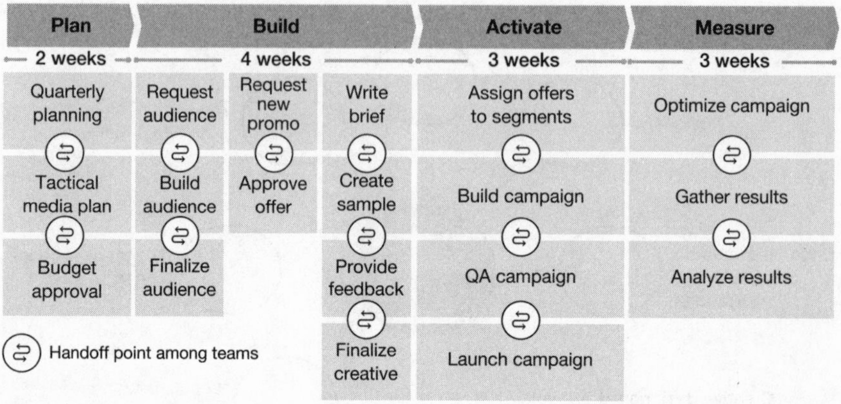

Plan		Build		Activate	Measure
2 weeks		4 weeks		3 weeks	3 weeks
Quarterly planning	Request audience	Request new promo	Write brief	Assign offers to segments	Optimize campaign
Tactical media plan	Build audience	Approve offer	Create sample	Build campaign	Gather results
Budget approval	Finalize audience		Provide feedback	QA campaign	Analyze results
			Finalize creative	Launch campaign	

Handoff point among teams

FIGURE 6-4

After: The new, improved 5-day campaign process

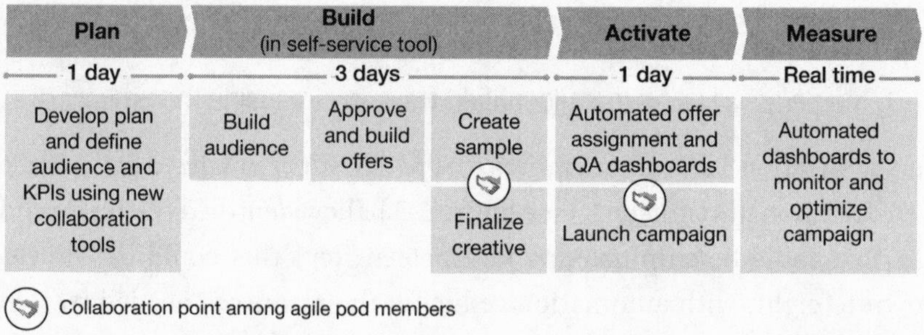

Plan	Build (in self-service tool)			Activate	Measure
1 day	3 days			1 day	Real time
Develop plan and define audience and KPIs using new collaboration tools	Build audience	Approve and build offers	Create sample	Automated offer assignment and QA dashboards	Automated dashboards to monitor and optimize campaign
			Finalize creative	Launch campaign	

Collaboration point among agile pod members

Finally, the personalization team set specific, measurable goals

The team decided on several specific goals, and then set up automated measurement dashboards that provided real-time customer engagement metrics for all experiences launched. Each personalized experience was designed for experimentation, so that, using a test-versus-control methodology, the team could measure the resulting net incremental sales. Importantly, these results were automatically loaded into the dashboards as soon as a test was concluded.

The team adopted a "1 percent per week" improvement mantra for all the KPIs. Its strategy of pursuing rapid, incremental improvements yielded dramatic results, with 100 percent gains in customer engagement and 40 percent increases in incremental sales lift in six months. Among the things the team tested were:

- What are the most important triggers to act on?

- Which channel is most effective to use?

- When do we reach out to a customer?

- What's the right message to send?

- What incentive should we offer?

Over time, as more experiments were run and more data was gathered, AI played an ever-increasing role. Machine learning helped in designing and optimizing multivariate tests and in scaling the results to the broader customer population. The net result was a "bank" of value that was used to fund the next steps in the personalization effort, including investments in technology and automation. After a year, the personalization lab had served its purpose, and its ways of working were adopted as the new approach by the full organization.

———————

To drive change—including changing ways of working—you've got to start small. Like the above-mentioned retailer, companies should launch self-governing pods whom they invest with clear goals, budgets, and decision rights. These groups should develop "epics" (to borrow agile lingo) that lay out performance targets for a limited number of experiences that they redesign, such as changing the customer onboarding process to cut call center volumes by at least 20 percent. Within the epics, they should generate "stories" detailing the dimensions they will test to drive improvement, such as trying personalized video. Then, they should create a "backlog" of actions needed to get the tests out in two-week sprints. Underlying the pods, there should be support from an extended team that makes sure the pods have the right tools, access to legal/compliance review, and connections to any key operational teams if needed. While the full potential of personalization can be realized only from scaling these ways of working across the organization (often requiring shifts in org design), an agile pod approach is a practical way to get started.

Faster Measurement = Faster Learning = Faster Impact

Many companies fall into the trap of dealing with the organizational structure first, hoping that a new customer-centric design will be the solution to achieving personalization. But a reorganization is no way to start: apart from being a complex and lengthy transformation unto itself, it makes no sense without understanding what personalization entails (the operational and system requirements, the processes, skills, resources, and dependencies). As our global retailer example demonstrates, it is far more effective to start by transcending silos and adopting agile ways of working in service of launching a focused set of use cases. With their cross-functional connections, teams have the resources and decision rights to act swiftly. But to make this work, measurement is key.

Contrary to what many companies believe, measurement is not simply a tech and data problem. It is also, fundamentally, a people and process problem. In 90 percent of the organizations we've worked with over the past decade, measurement was generally treated as an afterthought. But real-time measurement is the heart of successful personalization. For organizations pursuing this goal, it's critical to know what and how to measure.

What should we measure?

Advancing personalization requires progress on three core measures: engagement (i.e., each customer interaction), the related sales lift, and the impact on the lifetime value of the customer.

Customer interactions. Each personalized interaction must be measured so that learning can happen. Metrics such as open rates, conversion rates, online browse rates, in-store foot traffic, and call center volume provide real-time opportunities to adjust targeting and content. Most organizations already track these metrics, but generally on an average basis. They tend not to capture the different responses across customer types, nor do they track the engagement with different personalized experiences in real time. In addition, they don't probe the underlying causes of lack of engagement. They therefore miss the chance to readily understand why customers thought an outreach was not relevant—and fix it. Starbucks, for instance, set up real-time dashboards to monitor personalized campaign performance even while the campaigns were in market.

Net incremental sales lift. To justify the investments personalization at scale can require, it is critical to measure incremental sales lift. But this is often harder than measuring engagement metrics (such as click-through rates). That's because it involves manual steps, such as pulling data from multiple systems, especially at first. Many marketing teams measure the net incremental revenue gain of an individual campaign (based on test-versus-control populations, net of any promotional costs) but are unable to calculate the total net incremental value across campaigns. Invariably, overlap and extraneous factors fuel the lift, so simply adding up the incremental revenue from multiple concurrent personalization campaigns grossly overstates their collective impact. As a result, teams can quickly lose credibility with finance leaders, jeopardizing their chances of securing funding to expand the program.

Best-in-class companies solve this problem by establishing a universal control group: a set of customers who, for a specific period, receive only mass communications. This may not always be advisable or practical; for example, if the personalized element or experience is considered table stakes (e.g., an abandoned-cart trigger) or if withholding it would materially harm the customer experience. But it is crucial when companies are trying to make important decisions about the investments needed to enable the next level of precision targeting, such as shifting from mass promotions to personalized offers, or investing in guided selling, individualized services, or personalized omnichannel recommendations. Starbucks, for example, used the universal-control-group approach to support quantum-leap investments in personalization that put it five years ahead of the competition.

Longer-term impact on customer lifetime value. Enhancing lifetime value is, after all, the whole point of the deep engagement that personalization engenders. So companies need to understand the drivers of lifetime value—the frequency, timing and value of transactions, customer satisfaction, digital channel engagement, and so on—and continuously track leading indicators over time. For instance, Starbucks not only measured net incremental revenue on a weekly basis; it also increased the volume and recency of its customer satisfaction data exponentially by collecting it via its app (instead of the traditional method, collecting it only at the point of sale via survey invites printed on receipts). This gave the company a much richer understanding of customer satisfaction, a key driver of customer lifetime value.

How often should we track impact?

When you operate under a mantra of driving improvements every week, measurement has to happen immediately. Engagement metrics must be available in real time, but more important, net incremental revenue and the predictors of customer lifetime value (such as customer satisfaction scores) need to be measured daily or weekly. When personalization teams wait for weeks to get data, the learning cycle breaks down. Measurement must therefore be automated.

The learning cycle is integral to personalization at scale, and velocity is essential to a compressed learning cycle. We cannot emphasize this enough. **Learning is a function of the number of experiments, multiplied by the time to measure, plus the time to act on the feedback.** Competitive advantage in personalization stems from the dynamics of these interrelationships. Leading companies have increased the number of experiments by a factor of hundreds, if not thousands, and slashed the cycle time for each by 50 to 75 percent. (See figure 6-5 for a concrete example from a leading bank. For a more detailed case study about the same company, see chapter 7.)

Who does the measuring?

Often, companies outsource measurement to low-cost analytics vendors who put together ad hoc reports weeks after actions are taken. That doesn't work. As we've shown, successful personalization depends on receiving results in real time. Once companies automate content creation and delivery, teams can review results constantly and adjust their strategies to delight

FIGURE 6-5

Personalized-campaign cycle-time reduction at a leading bank

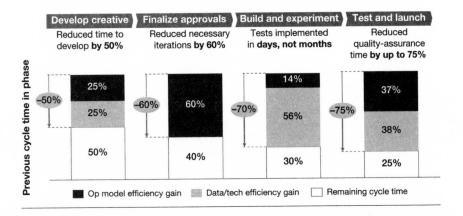

customers. They are freed up to focus on the highest value-added work in personalization: rapid iteration and learning. And not only do customer satisfaction rates surge; team members' job-satisfaction rates do, too. At one global beverage company, thirty people who once handled manual list pulls and quality control for personalized communications were almost all retrained and redeployed to propel the learning cycle. A team once known for high churn and high burnout suddenly became a model of employee retention. The company was able to avoid hiring additional personnel (with all the associated delays) to support its ambitious personalization goals.

Designing Customer-Centric Organizations in the Age of AI

While agile ways of working are critical to launching successful personalization efforts, a company's organizational structure will need to evolve as it scales up. Every functional team will need to consider its level of resources and its talent requirements. Many activities will still need to happen at the functional level, but other activities (such as marketing operations or cross-channel orchestration) will eventually be better managed under one roof, rather than in several different areas of the organization. New roles and organization designs will be emerging that are more conducive to personalization at scale.

Most companies are organized by product or channel. Take the typical bank. Every spoke in the marketing hub—the call center, the in-branch offices, the email and direct-mail operations, the website, the app—is typically run by a different team reporting to a different part of the organization. And for all the talk of customer centricity, most banks are still organized around products—credit cards, mortgages, loans, and so forth. While the marketing organization may generate broad consumer insights, those insights do not directly feed the efforts of the various teams that touch the customer journey. It is no wonder that many banks struggle to put in place cross-functional teams and agile ways of working. All of this explains their low ranking on the Personalization Index. But even retailers, who rank higher, are often organized around product-merchant teams, with limited resources to define and prioritize which customer strategies to pursue and how to activate them with cross-functional teams.

By starting quickly with agile pods, companies can notch up early wins, while sorting out which changes are most critical to the operating model as they scale their efforts. As organizations become more customer centric, they can shift P&L responsibilities, create new roles and functions, and integrate existing functions.

Let's look at four specific ways personalization leaders are doing this.

Reimagining marketing as an integrated function

For personalization at scale to succeed, marketing needs to be an integrated function that brings together all channels to coordinate customer outreach. One senior leader, with analytics support, oversees execution across paid and owned channels, and across upper-funnel (i.e., brand-awareness-driving) and lower-funnel (i.e., conversion) marketing activities. This configuration enables smarter budget allocation and better orchestration of the push and pull conversations with customers across channels. It also ensures that the pods are not stepping over each other. Furthermore, organizations are adding dedicated teams in charge of marketing operations to improve and automate the processes around channel orchestration and channel delivery. Without a strong marketing-operations function, teams across channel silos won't be aware of what the customer is seeing in totality. Execution quality-control issues are also much more likely to arise, such as customers getting the wrong messages or tests being incorrectly measured, because the targeting or the control hold-outs were not executed properly.

Creating new, customer-centric roles

Almost all organizations have consumer insights functions, but the best of these groups are being more explicitly charged with developing customer strategies that help the cross-functional teams advance from insights to action. Many companies are also appointing a senior owner of customer experience design—creating roles such as SVP or VP of customer experience, or charging an existing chief digital officer with these responsibilities. If experiences are essentially a "product" that the company offers, this leader is the "product manager" who oversees the development of the interfaces that customers will engage with online and in the physical world, and then is also accountable for the financial performance of those experiences. Some companies have also created chief customer officers or chief growth officers with explicit P&L responsibilities for driving revenue from digital channels and digital customer relationships.

Elevating data and analytics (D&A)

Companies are centralizing teams and expanding them with additional resources and new senior leadership positions, like the chief data and analytics officer. Teams that previously sat in distinct parts of the organization are increasingly being merged (sometimes even with digital roles)—in particular, at banks, health providers, insurers, and retailers. These data and analytics reorganizations are strengthening the linkage among data science (i.e., model and algorithm development), applied analytics (i.e., business intelligence), and the business functions that apply the analytics, from marketing to digital to supply chain to operations to finance. D&A leaders establish analytics teams focused on improving customer use cases, not just functional productivity. In doing so, they are not only bolstering the ability to deliver value; they are also creating a magnet for world-class talent that seeks out jobs that entail learning, working with like-minded people, and driving impact.

D&A leaders are also creating new tools for data democratization: arming marketing and operations teams with tools that allow them to pull and analyze data themselves instead of being dependent on data scientist gate-keepers. These companies are investing more resources in data engineering to create robust platforms and powerful dashboards and tools that can be widely used across the organization. They are bringing more useful data to the fingertips of managers across the organization, helping the managers make better decisions and create better customer experiences. New, empowered senior D&A leaders are pushing to raise the quality of data and integrate it across functions. They are instituting strong data governance mechanisms (i.e., defining common standards and definitions across the enterprise). And they are also establishing data stewardship processes—identifying the key data needed and how it will be used.

Tapping leaders to spearhead personalization across the enterprise

Many organizations have had a loyalty function for years. Now, we often see these leaders taking on the explicit responsibility for setting the personalization ambition. Given the substantial investments personalization calls for, these leaders are prioritizing initiatives and tracking progress against key P&L targets. Depending on the industry and company specifics, we also sometimes see this responsibility residing within the integrated-marketing, digital-experience, customer strategy, or D&A function. While personalization will impact many teams, regardless of organizational design, it is critical to have a single leader with the mandate to move the enterprise toward its overall ambition. Charging a senior executive with P&L responsibility can increase the accountability for progress. In leading companies, the personalization owner has a standing sixty- to ninety-minute slot every other month on the executive-leadership-team agenda to discuss progress and issues needing coordinated support from other leaders.

How do all these roles fit together? It is essential that they be set up with role clarity vis-à-vis the rest of the enterprise. While the specifics across organizations vary greatly, figure 6-6 illustrates how one company evolved existing roles and added new ones as it scaled up personalization as one of its core strategic pillars and adopted a customer-centric mindset in the process.

FIGURE 6-6

Example of org structure illustrating evolving roles at one company

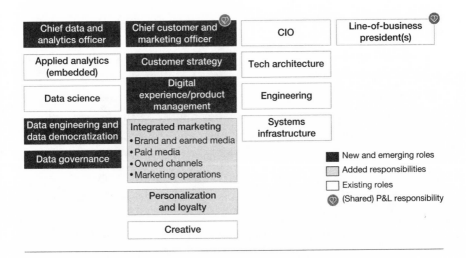

Avoiding the Org-Design Quagmire

When considering these changing roles and responsibilities, it is easy to overdo the expansion of senior leadership roles. Certainly, new areas—especially data, analytics, and digital—are becoming critical corporate assets that require top-level ownership, and the right new leaders with broad mandates can accelerate change. But companies can offset this expansion by streamlining some of the traditional functional leadership roles, thanks to the growing role of more-autonomous, agile teams. And companies should also be thoughtful about which redesigns are truly needed: substantial changes can slow down a company as everyone sorts out their new responsibilities and establishes new ways of working. This is also why we don't recommend starting a personalization transformation with a full org redesign; that is best left for the second or third year of the effort.

Most companies we work with opt to establish integrated teams but retain their functional organization structure. Each function is essentially a center of excellence, responsible for its own recruiting, coaching, performance-standard setting, and talent retention. Most recruits arrive with functional expertise that they want to further among colleagues who will help them develop. So people have their feet in two worlds: one in their functional team, where they learn new skills and seek growth opportunities; the other in their pod team, where they pursue an agenda of constant improvement, working with people of diverse talents. At Spotify, the cross-functional agile teams are famously known as "squads," with members still affiliated with their respective functional teams (e.g., marketing strategy, creative, operations, analytics). By using workflow tools such as Trello to bring transparency to each squad's projects, functional leaders can more effectively allocate resources and manage projects. They can reallocate resources and show their members how they might contribute their skills to the squad's operations. With instant messaging and collaboration tools, they foster communications across the company, so squad members can call on their functional teams for operational support, functional advice, help with resourcing, or support in mobilizing broader teams when initiatives begin to cut across squads.

Leaders such as H&M Group and Starbucks have recognized that the very differentiation they deliver rests on these newer, agile work models, which allow learning to accelerate and insights to snowball. Arti Zeighami, the former chief data and analytics officer at H&M, summarizes how to put this into practice with a "tight-loose-tight" leadership model:

> You need to set a clear vision of the North Star outcome you are targeting, along with tight guardrails for the cross-functional team to follow. But you need to keep it loose between these two bookends: leave it up to the team to decide how to get there. Focus on establishing KPIs that can provide feedback weekly or daily that the teams can respond to, quickly working out what works and what doesn't. Stop guessing what you can calculate. . . . This leadership style fosters a culture of trust in the individuals and teams to solve the technical problems, and in that way, helps attract the right talent.[1]

By creating new roles and evolving responsibilities, companies can cement the new ways of working trialed and adopted by agile teams that pioneer personalization. Ultimately, the goal is to build muscle for the organization, enabling it to constantly try new ideas that can delight the customer and new ways of making an experience more personalized and effortless, while moving the needle on financial performance. With robust measurement, rapid feedback, clear decision-making authority, and increasingly automated execution, companies can scale up what works and halt failure quickly. Ultimately, Delight Me is about learning from the customer. It brings personalization full circle—back to our original goal of seamlessly empowering customers on their journeys—by embedding the organizational capabilities, ways of working, and operating model to constantly improve the experience.

People and Process Self-Check

Below are practical, specific questions that can help you and your teams assess the maturity of your talent bench and ways of working to enable personalization.

- Do we have a well-articulated and aligned vision for personalization?

- Is there a single leader who has overall accountability for personalization?

- Have we set clear targets for customer engagement, net incremental sales, and customer lifetime value? Do we have practical ways to measure them across channels and use cases?

- How long does it take us to launch a typical personalized marketing campaign, from ideation to launch? How many teams and handoffs are involved? What does the process look like when launching a new personalized experience?

- Do we have small cross-functional teams dedicated to our key personalization use cases, working in agile ways to make continuous progress? Or are our experiences dependent on siloed functions that are not tightly coordinated and moving the experience forward?

- How promptly and effectively do we measure our personalization efforts? How quickly do teams learn from and act on the results?

- How well integrated are teams across channels, including paid and owned and online/offline channels?

- How effective is our marketing-operations capability?

- How well resourced are our data and analytics teams? Is their work aligned with the work of the business teams they are partnering with? Are there duplicative teams building similar data assets across the organization?

Health Care

What could be more personal than health care? Your physical and mental state, your age, your genes, your health history, vaccinations, socio- and geodemographics, current location, family structure, caregivers, insurance: addressing any given health issue involves an almost endless list of factors. Managing one's health care is complex and often overwhelming. However, for many health needs, personalization can facilitate the effort, educating, motivating, and empowering an individual to be more in control. According to a recent study in *The Lancet*, more than a quarter of all health-care spending in the United States each year is due to conditions—notably diabetes, heart disease, and cancer—tied to lifestyle choices, conditions that are thus to some degree preventable.[1] There is an obvious opportunity to use more-personalized support as a way to improve health outcomes.

But changing individuals' behavior is not easy, and the factors that will motivate people vary widely from person to person, depending on their knowledge, personality, attitude, health state, influences, etc. Figuring out what will engage each individual and make them receptive to change is a huge test-and-learn challenge.

Already, insurers (payors) and providers (clinicians) are designing large-scale programs to steer patients toward better health, and thus reduce costly and avoidable treatments. The options are many, including encouraging people to get appropriate preventive tests (mammograms, colonoscopies), guiding them to use local urgent care centers instead of hospital emergency rooms for noncritical issues, reminding them to take their medications as directed, and making sure they monitor themselves for chronic or hereditary conditions.

The challenge most large, established players face is how to get past the wall of diminishing returns they inevitably hit after a good start. Once they have sent basic motivating messages to their relevant patients, how do they shift their customer management approaches to a scaled, agile operation that will encourage each individual to take different actions?

Enabled by emerging AI tools, marketing automation, and broader access to medical research, new health and wellness service providers have equipped themselves from the start for fast-cycle test-and-learn approaches and are now using their personalization prowess to broaden their position in health care. Consider the experiences of Noom and SonderMind, two unconventional, digital-era health companies that aim to foster better health choices and overall physical and mental well-being.

Noom: Using Daily "Whispers" to Motivate Healthy Behavior

Noom started out as a weight-management program, providing daily, personalized support to individuals to help them change their mindset and to inspire them to adopt better diet, exercise, and mindfulness behaviors. Noom has extended its approach further into broader health-care support, for conditions such as hypertension and diabetes. Through daily engagement with content from its app, users develop habits that positively influence the many choices they make over the course of a day. Forty percent of the users who engage with Noom for four or more weeks lose at least 5 percent of their body weight. By reaching members daily with ten-minute content feeds—mostly just text—Noom has become an effective "whisperer" of ideas and motivation that can fundamentally change the user's mindset.

Every interaction is based on the constantly evolving insights Noom gathers about users' interests and actions. On their first visit to Noom's website, individuals are greeted with a question, such as "Do you have a weight loss goal? If so, what is it?"—a question that changes with each subsequent visit as Noom tests new possibilities. Based on their answers, users are gradually fed a series of questions that keep branching, depending on their previous answers. By going through the questions, potential users get an inkling of how Noom operates, how it will be tuned to their situation, and how they can envision changes in their lifestyle that will help them achieve their goals.

Every year, Noom tests hundreds of new content ideas, such as recipes, exercises, motivational tips, achievement badges, shared customer feedback, and discount incentives from partners. These amount to thousands of individual successes and failures, which have helped shape the product Noom is today. The company runs tests in short cycles, seeing within two days whether a new concept resonates. These tests focus not only on content but also on the target audience. They explore how to engage people who could be hitting a wall, or who tend to react only to certain kinds of content, or who may simply have lost interest, and so on. Noom found, for example, that some members will get back on track after seeing feedback from other members.

Kyle Smith, Noom's head of marketing for newer health offerings, describes how the company is building a formidable engine for personalization:

> [Every day should bring] a new surprise to the user, so we have to keep it fresh and varied. We literally see how showing different streams of content pull different kinds of people in—people who learn via multimedia versus text; people who want to share their progress with like-minded groups versus people who are more private; people who see exercise as a natural part of their day versus those who see it as an added activity which they would not otherwise do. The curriculum gets more tailored for each individual. More-engaged users, for example, might see more content for their specific challenges, such as careful snacking, or reminders to take the stairs at the office. We are essentially empowering someone to "retrain their brain" towards a healthier lifestyle.[2]

To augment the digital-app experience, Noom also offers an option for a personal coach. Coaches are supported by the data that flows through the app, while also adding their own personal style—humor, local references, motivational language. They are available for text interactions whenever a user wants motivation or particular advice on, say, the challenges of dining out with a group. Coaches also help test ideas for new offerings, providing immediate feedback so that effective ideas can be scaled in as little as a week.

As a startup, Noom didn't have much of a budget for specialized marketing talent, so it hired versatile talent, with basic skills in marketing, tech, copywriting, and analytics. This way, small teams were able to create the tests, write the copy, and roll the tests out. Noom's personnel were flexible and resourceful when faced with bigger challenges. For example, when Apple launched the iOS release that asked users to agree to cookies, Noom's teams promptly kicked into gear, developing new techniques for acquisition marketing that would not depend on third-party cookies.

"We learned to rebalance how we used different channels (text, email, search, social, and display ads), different kinds of content, and new targeting-selection criteria to find the right kinds of customers and keep them interested" as they explored Noom's services, Smith notes. As the company pursues more-clinical health-care opportunities, it can draw on its testing experience to develop new processes for incorporating the new messaging it will need. "While we want to continue our pace of experimentation and more-granular personalization, we know our business and our brand will be at stake if we are not very deliberate in how we adapt for more-regulated environments."

SonderMind: Guiding Psychotherapy toward Measurable Progress

The challenges of creating a personalized, data-driven approach to addressing mental health start from the moment an individual realizes they need help. Often, someone is not even sure what is wrong, what they need, or what their goals are. How do you find the right support when you can't easily describe your starting point, let alone understand the kinds of therapy or type of provider that could help you? Providers almost always do some form of intake assessment, but a patient's mental health context is often complex, and rarely does a provider get hard data that can be used to set a baseline and determine a treatment plan. Then, once they develop a plan, tracking progress is not easy; very few treatment protocols have quantifiable markers by which to gauge progress.

To address the gap in access to care, many new companies have stepped in. They are aiming to simplify access to treatment: for example, by using text and video, applying standardized approaches to specific common conditions (such as ADHD and anxiety), and engaging people in proven general wellness practices, such as meditation. Few, however, are using a personalized, data-driven approach to put individuals on a clear, continuously supported pathway to improvement.

SonderMind, a Colorado-based mental-wellness company, was founded in 2014 by Mark Frank, a former US Army captain who was concerned about the difficulty of treating veterans with mental health struggles. As he researched the problem, he discovered a broader opportunity to make mental health treatment more effective and scalable. It entailed collecting and activating new kinds of data that patients and therapists could both use to be better matched and to make measurable progress.

When a prospective SonderMind patient decides to seek help, they don't know whether their problems stem from a chemical imbalance, parental issues, specific experiences, or some other factor. SonderMind's support engine starts by helping the patient understand their situation through a series of fun, interactive experiences that assess twelve different brain functions, ranging from the predisposition to anxiety or compulsiveness to mental-processing speed. This assessment, or brain profile, provides the patient with a clearer picture of how their mind works. The results are then shared with a SonderMind therapist so that therapist and patient have a mutual understanding of the patient's starting point.

If a prospect isn't ready for therapy, SonderMind's algorithms suggest a self-guided program of exercises, and prompt the patient to take these actions. These exercises include keeping a diary of one's feelings or writing down one personal interaction each day that the patient thought they handled well. As the patient completes these exercises, the engine captures their activity and uses it to help the patient understand how they are responding to the support, whether they are making progress, and whether they should change course. For example, the program can use natural language processing to analyze the choice of words, grammar, and content noted in the patient's diary to get a sense of how the patient thinks and what's on their mind. The key to SonderMind's strategy is to create ways to quantify mental health attributes, capture data about the attributes, and then use that data to suggest next steps. Over time, its engine gathers more data about what works for each type of profile and uses it to refine its models. Says Frank:

> In genomics, medical scientists . . . map a person's DNA, and then correlate that with the millions of data points from other people to . . . see patterns. In personalizing mental health treatment, the approach is similar. By engaging the individual in a participatory data exchange and then stepping back to look at the bigger picture, we can better understand which variants in someone's profile [make them] more likely to respond to different treatment plans.[3]

This process becomes exceptionally powerful once a patient decides they want to work with a therapist. A second personalization engine matches therapist and patient. The underlying algorithms look at which matches led to second and third therapy sessions and which ones led to patients using the company's other tools. Most importantly, it examines patients' progress metrics over time. The tool also factors in a therapist's schedule, the modality of treatment types they are comfortable with, and their own demographics.

In other words, SonderMind's approach represents personalization not just for the patient but also for the therapist. Once a match is made and the patient is willing to share their profile data, a third AI engine uses that data to help the therapist develop a treatment plan. Most therapists lack access to such intelligence and instead must guess what kind of treatment protocols might work. With its treatment recommendation engine, SonderMind gives therapists predictive power, along with anonymized examples of patients with similar profiles and how their plans worked. It can then back up the therapist with another tool that helps deliver the plan by providing the patient videos, recorded exercises, prompts for between-session actions, backdrop sounds for meditation, templates for diaries, or suggestions for exposure therapy. Therapists can take the plan as is or adjust it accordingly. SonderMind then captures what transpires.

Frank notes that SonderMind's approach has helped attract and screen young therapists, enabling the company to build "a base of therapists who will match the trending profiles of the patients coming to us." The lower cost and better health outcomes that SonderMind's personalization approach is delivering to its payors allows the company to offer value-based economic models, where SonderMind takes on the cost and outcomes risk for the care of its patients. It's an appealing offering, and one that is accelerating the company's growth.

Personalization Makes "Patient Centricity" a Reality

Companies like Noom and SonderMind stand in stark contrast to the many companies for whom "customer centricity" is little more than a buzzword. They are determined to rapidly test new ideas, applying intelligence tools and new personalization techniques. They focus on constantly learning, building ever-larger databases of first-party data and insights on outcomes, thanks to a trusted exchange of data and experiences.

This approach raises a larger question about personalization at scale in health care: which brands will consumers trust to manage their data and their care? Can traditional medical providers—especially those affiliated with hospital systems—invest and build capabilities that can carry their patients in between visits? Can insurers, particularly in the United States, where the largest companies are also building in-house networks of clinicians, extend their data prowess to take on more management of their members' journeys? Or will specialists like SonderMind and Noom, built natively on AI, develop more-focused personalized solutions and assume the medical-cost risk for their members? Will they capitalize on their access to patients, and the trust they've already established with them, to become lead orchestrators?

We expect to see these players, and likely major tech players as well, compete for consumers' permission to use their health data. New mechanisms will evolve to help consumers manage those permissions. Outside the United States, the laws are stricter about getting permission and providing ways for consumers to control how their data is used. We sense that the upside from more, appropriately managed, health-information sharing will lead some to challenge regulations that restrict information sharing in order to protect privacy.

Chapter 7

Building Personalization through Smart Integration

Beyond the data components, it takes a lot of moving parts to create a personalization tech stack: targeting intelligence, experiment design and activation, orchestration, content management, experience delivery, testing, and measurement. But having first-rate point solutions for all these moving parts in itself won't give you advantage. What really counts is how you integrate these solutions into a well-oiled, intelligent engine, and how you make all of them smarter through your innovation, testing, and feedback loops. This involves a set of strategic choices.

So what should the technology and the systems underpinning the Five Promises of Personalization look like? Spotify—one of the highest-scoring companies in our Personalization Index—offers a great example.

Personalization Intelligence Cuts across All Five Promises

Every time you log on to Spotify, you are activating a fertile give-and-take. From the app to the customer data platform, from the targeting models and experimentation platform to the content management and generation—from Empower Me to Delight Me—Spotify's setup exemplifies the tech and data stack that is the cornerstone of a successful personalization program.

Let's look under the hood.

How Spotify Empowers Me. Everything is contained in the Spotify app, which delivers the experience and empowers the user to listen to whatever they like. When you open the app, you see the songs, artists, and playlists you are most likely to engage with. New features are added regularly, such as the ability to easily find and buy merchandise from your favorite artists. Any one of these options can be thought of as a potential action you might take in your music journey.

How Spotify Knows Me. To enable the Spotify experience, a very specific set of engagement data points must be ingested and tagged to each customer's identity. Among them:

- The songs you have listened to (and all their associated metadata), and for how much time

- What prompted you to listen to each song (a share, a message from Spotify, a link from somewhere else)

- The day of the week and time of day you listened to a particular song or artist

- Your friends on Spotify and songs you have shared with them

How Spotify Reaches Me. Each of the app's components are fed by intelligence that scores, ranks, and orchestrates the next best action for each user, and delivers it into the app. The inherent interest and engagement that people have with its app give Spotify powerful permission and access to reach its customers. The company notes your real-time location and context (say, commuting, working, or at home during dinnertime) and then reaches you through push notifications or by highlighting content when you open the app. It then displays new recordings, artists, or playlists; music that is trending more broadly for people like you; and upcoming concerts featuring artists you like, with a link to buy tickets.

How Spotify Shows Me. All of this data and intelligence would be useless without a content engine, which is Spotify's music library, its core product. But in addition, the content engine includes:

- **Content management AI,** which scans every song to document its musical characteristics, such as genre, era, tempo, and mood. It also analyzes and creates metadata about each song, including tags about the composer, producer, record label, and others involved in creating the song; when and where it was recorded; the other songs on the album; playlists it appears on; the song's popularity; and a slew of "embeddings" (data representations that are understood by AI algorithms) that are less discernible to humans.

- **Dynamic content matching,** the capability that creates fresh new daily mixes and genre-specific playlists. Spotify's AI builds out each list based on human ideas and then matches the myriad tags to each user based on who listens to the song, how far they get before skipping forward, and what other music those listeners enjoy. Ultimately, the AI predicts which unfamiliar song (and sequence of songs) will most effectively and uniquely delight each individual.

How Spotify Delights Me. Spotify is designed to get better and better, the more you use it. Spotify turns everything about the flow of discovering and enjoying music (and podcasts) into data that constantly enriches its engine. It then applies those insights to deliver progressively better experiences, predicting what you'll like, finding it, reaching out to you, delivering the songs best suited for you in a sequence you would likely enjoy. Moreover, Spotify lets the user feel in control; you can augment what the system automatically learns about your preferences through the direct feedback you give it about your likes and dislikes (e.g., every time you jump off an album to explore a similar artist or skip over a song). Spotify constantly designs and launches experiments, ranging from simple A/B tests, such as what to show in the app (and how to present it), to more-complex, multivariate approaches that test multiple variables at once, to so-called "multiarmed bandit" testing that allocates more and more of the audience to better-performing versions over time. At any given moment, every Spotify customer is either in a test, control, or business-as-usual mode, enabling Spotify to run hundreds of experiments simultaneously, all with automated reporting.

In thinking about the tech that powers personalization, many companies overlook one vital point: speed. What sets apart leaders like Spotify is the sheer velocity of feedback and learning that its tech stack enables. As you consider how to build your tech infrastructure, be ever mindful of the importance of slashing cycle times for experimentation and measurement.

Now: How should you think about your personalization tech stack and the best way to assemble its components?

Modularity Is the Mantra

Increasingly, software leaders are offering, and personalization leaders are adopting, open-source application programming interfaces (open APIs) that enable a more modular architecture and that allow interoperability—standardizing connections and data exchange even among closed platforms. Open APIs let developers pump and pull data into and out of proprietary software from different suppliers, through a simple, versatile standard. One simple example is an API that links a company's CRM system to a cloud-based phone system, thus allowing a call center agent to immediately phone a newly generated lead without having to exit the CRM software. With open APIs, information can be moved smoothly, models updated easily, and new capabilities added in a modular way.

Build versus Buy

With so many tools available and in development, and with the improving ease in linking them, executives rightly wonder: Which is the better strategy, build or buy? Over time, building your own proprietary solutions for a variety of tasks may become easier (thanks to gen AI), but maintaining that newly created code, and ensuring that it is scalable, secure, and reliable, will remain a constant challenge for companies without high-powered IT and data engineering teams. Creating competitive advantage from personalization does not require developing your own core tech systems. Masters of personalization—the likes of Spotify, Netflix, and Uber—build what they need for their particular operating environment. But most companies, including the masters, consistently start from open-source paradigms, integrating external tools for more-basic capabilities and developing niche components only when they need a unique application that's not available in the market. Many key components of the stack are widely available, which means companies can get to market more quickly and avoid all of the costs and headaches involved in maintaining one's own proprietary code.

One system cannot cover all aspects of the personalization stack across all channels—paid media, one's owned online channels, call centers, interactions in physical locations. But the larger providers, such as Adobe (with Experience Manager), Salesforce (Journey Builder), and HubSpot offer backbone experience-management platforms that other best-of-breed point solutions can append to. Despite their different capabilities, each of these platforms provides powerful new enablers for personalization: for example, interfaces with customizable models to visually lay out the rules for managing contacts, rules that set triggers based on customers' actions or other data. The platforms also establish rules to prioritize contacts if the same customer triggers multiple reasons for a contact simultaneously. AI monitors adherence to those rules in real time as the system captures response data.

Because these platforms are built with open APIs, other tools can plug into them to add even more capabilities. This means that companies can pull in data from sources not powered by the core platform (such as retail store interactions, billing data, or product-usage data), orchestrate contacts, interpret data, and render new experiences (such as personalized video). Smaller, more-focused platforms fill gaps, for example, by connecting all of the activities involved in paid media and managing the flow of ad exposures through an individual's buying journey.

A Hybrid Approach: Smart Integration

Personalization leaders invest the time and effort to learn and test new solutions for key parts of the stack before committing to one. The solutions you choose are consequential; they will affect not only what you'll be able to do and how data and systems will fit together but also how scalable and adaptable your stack will be. So personalization leaders start by articulating the most important use cases, not by identifying the tech features they think they'll need. They focus first on customer outcomes—considering experience improvement, automation, and optimization—and determine the points of greatest impact. Only then do they dig into the capabilities, the scalability, and the openness and interoperability of the solution (especially in terms of connecting with components in their stack), as well as the provider's record of support, security, and maintenance.

Two factors are most critical for advantage in personalization: how fast a company can launch a campaign, and the quality and extent of its experimentation. Faster and deeper learning, based on more impressions and more tests, leads to more insights that, in turn, foster a better customer experience. The ability to generate more content variants—setting up the cells for massive, multivariate testing—along with automated reporting to quickly draw insights and use these to refine one's models: this is the virtuous circle that powers competitive advantage. Powering this is an approach of strategically connecting point solutions with one's own proprietary systems and broader marketing platforms. This is what we call being a *smart integrator*:

- **Integrator,** because how well you integrate becomes a proprietary advantage: which tools you choose for aggregating and moving data to feed your AI and to capture the constant learning from tests and interactions from the systems that power frontline experiences; and

- **Smart,** because personalization is a process of ongoing improvement and refinement. It involves rethinking one's operations in order to use—and even more important, to feed—your intelligence so it can constantly learn within the context of your business.

Smart integration eschews the extremes of "build everything" or "buy everything" and instead focuses on modularity, allowing for the integration of ever-evolving technologies. Best-of-breed solutions are constantly in flux as providers add capabilities, and smart integration gives companies the latitude to treat data and tech ecosystems as propellants of constant learning. Fortunately, smart integration is a competitive leveler. You needn't be a tech leader to be a personalization leader. You don't need to be a big company, either.

For most companies outside of the tech world, the secret sauce is not necessarily their specific tools but, rather, how they assemble the stew. As technologies evolve and capabilities grow, it's likely you'll need to rely on several AI engines and software tools. That's why it's so crucial to design everything in a modular way: your data management and enrichment, analytics, orchestration, content management, experience delivery, and the feedback loops that will power faster learning and real-time tracking. By enabling flexibility, the modularity itself is another element that makes this approach "smart."

Let's look at how three very different companies implemented smart integration in practice.

Smart Integration and Automation at a Leading Bank

One of our clients, a leading global bank, provides a perfect example of smart integration at a legacy company. The bank wanted to become a personal financial partner to its customers, helping them to grow their savings and improve their financial health. To do this, marketers needed to dramatically improve the relevance and quality of their marketing outreach.

The bank's data infrastructure and processes, however, were major impediments to this goal. Hundreds of systems were involved in personalizing services across the enterprise. Even for something as simple as cross-selling credit cards, the necessary customer data was scattered throughout more than a dozen systems. Setting up a new trigger—such as using a customer's large deposit as an opportunity to follow up with them with ideas for investing the new money—took more than twelve weeks, thirty-five steps, and fifteen handoffs across teams. As a result, marketing teams were spending more than 70 percent of their time managing the process instead of improving the customer experience.

The bank recognized that it needed to integrate, harmonize, augment, and—not least—simplify its technology and its operations. Leadership knew it was critical to start with the data. Focusing on the most important use cases (such as promoting credit card use) and lines of business (moving high-value depositors into wealth management), it integrated several dozen data sources to assemble a single view of the customer. It did the same for prospects who had gone to the bank's website during their shopping journey but had not yet applied for a product. The integration was aimed at creating a new unified data model that spanned three key dimensions: customer, product, and campaign.

Consolidating the data in this way allowed the bank to begin uncovering more-advanced intelligence about its prospects and customers. For example, it was able to isolate those who had called into a service center with questions, or those who perused more content about specific credit cards before signing up, and then create segmentation schemes based on those insights.

Next, the bank decided to harmonize elements of the underlying tech infrastructure. It used a single cloud analytics environment, and consolidated its systems into a single platform to do triple duty: coordinate messages to the customer (or prospect) to move them forward in their journey; organize modular content; and enable more personalized interactions in major channels (e.g., branches, websites, email). The bank added selected experiential tools, such as SundaySky for personalized video and others for smart chatbots, along with tools for highly targeted digital ad placement.

Only a subset of the tech stack was custom built. Beyond the data model, the team customized aspects of a tool that could design and run advanced experimentation on a wide scale. They configured the tool to assign personalized content and offers to individuals and measure the results in real time with automated dashboards. To reduce setup time, the team used the experimentation module from BCG's Fabriq, which features prebuilt components made for automating aspects of the personalization workflow.

While the data and tech work was underway, the bank introduced cross-functional pod teams to streamline campaign creation. These teams of experts in customer experience, content creation, marketing activation, and data and analytics managed to reduce campaign development from thirty-five to eighteen steps, with no handoffs.

In as little as three months, the bank saw impressive results. Its credit card business was able to cut campaign creation times by two-thirds, with dramatic reductions of 50 to 75 percent in creative development time, approval time, build time and quality-control time. New tests could now be launched in days, rather than months. The bank gained hundreds of millions of dollars in potential incremental lifetime value from newly acquired customers. Equally—if not more—important was the more than 20 percent improvement in customer engagement and satisfaction scores. The multidimensional success of the effort convinced other lines of business to follow the smart-integration model for tech and adopt the agile-marketing approach of using cross-functional pods.

The bank chose to invest disproportionately in a few key elements to power its competitive advantage from personalization: experimentation design, the testing and measurement loop (including large-scale multivariate testing), and the next best action orchestration engine, which coordinates activities across channels. Unlike Spotify, the bank didn't need to invest as much in content management systems and sophisticated AI tools to analyze content. It was also able to use more off-the-shelf solutions that it could tailor in the remaining parts of its tech stack.

Next, let's turn to what the stack looks like for an established personalization leader seeking to take personalization to an even more sophisticated level.

Unlocking Sophisticated Personalization at Sephora

In 2017, senior executives at Sephora, a leading prestige beauty retailer decided to make personalization a strategic priority. The company's culture in the United States, says Juanita Osborn, vice president of personalization and orchestration, has always centered on rapid innovation and entrepreneurship to drive high growth.

With a large, highly engaged customer base in its loyalty program, Sephora was able to build on its already solid foundation of customer and purchase data and content management and testing capabilities. Through it, Sephora has established digital customer relationships on a massive scale; 95 percent of its transactions, both online and in its thousands of stores worldwide, are linked to loyalty program members. Nonetheless, the company's cross-functional personalization team identified four areas that needed upgrading:

- Using client and engagement data to create more-personalized, and eventually automated, journeys

- Using product data to refine recommendations and automate content

- Tagging creative content, which would enable the company to test more ways of versioning and personalizing messaging

- Increasing the volume of testing, especially for designing new engaging digital experiences

Like many personalization leaders, Sephora started with an agile test-and-learn approach. A scrum team quickly improved performance by developing personalized touches across a typical customer life cycle, such as a personalized welcome series; messages to entice an absentee customer to return or to win back an otherwise at-risk customer; and replenishment nudges. While building several capabilities (including a customer data platform) in-house, Sephora also adopted Monetate to run personalized product recommendations on the website and marketing channels, Bluecore to generate behavioral triggers, and Constructor.io to personalize how to display search results on a page. The company also introduced internal personalization machine learning models to improve campaign targeting and lay the decisioning groundwork for eventual personalization at scale—smart, automated, and relevant to consumers.

As the team began racking up successes, the company took note. Instead of gut instinct or "hindsighting," multivariate testing became the accepted approach. Sephora's executives, including retail merchants, started to see the value of scientific measurement and statistically valid control groups. The volume and quality of the tests increased rapidly. The team began working on more-sophisticated use cases, ones that would truly empower customers, such as personalizing content to educate them about products, and recognizing customers for their loyalty. For example, the "Beauty Offers" page on the site, once the place for mass promotions, now presented next best offers curated for each individual customer. The team relies steadfastly on the data from testing to identify changes that can eliminate friction from consumer experiences. It also looks to the data to decide how to better help customers, whether it's making customers aware that they can earn Sephora and Kohl's loyalty rewards simultaneously (Kohl's is a strategic partner), or providing quizzes to help consumers pick the right foundation shade or facial cleanser.

Although the numbers were clearly driving higher sales per customer, Sephora's leaders also recognized that their approach was hard work. Each marketing channel was still functioning independently, often relying on different martech tools. It wasn't long before the company saw the need for a more centralized approach, one that could take Sephora's personalization efforts to the next level of omnichannel insights, customer experiences, and efficient operations.

Recounts Osborn:

> We felt every channel had run about as far as it could on its own, building up separate tech capabilities, operating practices, and even sources of data. Every company that is not a digital-native startup, that has gone through this decade-long rush to build digital capabilities across all of its channels and lines of business, wishes they could just take a clean sheet and rebuild their now-sprawling martech from scratch. You have to step back, carefully think through what to build, what to buy centrally, and what is OK to keep separate by channel.[1]

Meanwhile, as customer expectations shift, she notes, the company is racing to keep up. "To build an orchestrated, cross-channel experience," Osborn says, "we are having to rearchitect and rethink some things from the ground up."

The team assessed where common tools were needed across the business. The first priority was to unify disparate content management systems. Sephora migrated to a "headless" content management system, which can access all creative and feed it to any channel. Building on the new CMS, the team is deploying a modular and dynamic content capability; this enables them to assemble components in real time to efficiently create personalized experiences for each customer across channels. The team is also looking to integrate an orchestration engine that decides who should get what messages, and that orchestrates a seamless, responsive beauty experience across channels. Any one of these actions would represent a big step forward, but integrating them will be a major leap. As these cross-channel capabilities are being put in place, the team is testing new customer experiences, such as personalized home pages, emails, and new-client and cross-selling journeys. Through such efforts, Sephora continuously tests where it can make its own improvements to the intelligence, experimentation-design, and customization components of its personalization tech stack—and where it would be best served with a vendor offering.

Now, with an understanding that integration and scaled experimentation are the catalysts to competitive advantage in personalization, Sephora can better distinguish between what is worth building (for customizations that could accelerate the testing and orchestration of customer interactions) and what makes more sense to buy off the shelf (content engines, site management, site search, channel delivery). This smart-integration approach will activate new capabilities in a harmonized way across Sephora's marketing channels.

"We still have a lot to do, and lots of ways we can continue to improve for our customers," says Osborn. Already, over the past five years, Sephora has added billions in revenue, nearly doubling in size. As a result, the company surpassed the top quartile in the BCG Personalization Index, and has remained a personalization leader among retailers since we started tracking results in 2017.

While the bank and Sephora had to evolve their existing tech stacks over the last decade to become leaders, a new generation of companies established in the last two decades is being built with personalization in mind from the start, showing how even startups and smaller companies outside of the tech industry can become personalization leaders.

Sweetgreen: Building a Company with Personalization in Mind

Established in 2007, Sweetgreen is a relative newcomer to the restaurant business, compared with the largest chains. Sweetgreen started with a clear vision, rooted in what customers wanted: to put wholesome, fresh food—tailored to their tastes and dietary needs—within reach. This required personalizing the three most critical aspects of the customer experience: the ability to choose the right item, to order through the most convenient channel, and to access the order in a convenient way. Right from the start, Sweetgreen was focused on building digital customer relationships in the communities it served and took a smart-integration approach, which allowed it to quickly match, and in some ways exceed, the personalization capabilities of the largest brands. So how did Sweetgreen do this?

First, it invested early into a connected digital experience. The restaurant chain launched a mobile app six years after its founding, before most large competitors even had one. At the time, the chain had only twenty-two locations. Sweetgreen soon followed the largest chains in adding order and pickup capability to its app (in 2013) and native delivery (in 2020)—the latter being a service that some large competitors fully outsourced to the likes of Uber Eats and other delivery platforms, thereby risking the loss of their owned digital customer relationships. (Customers using third-party providers see offerings from multiple brands side by side and can therefore more easily switch restaurants.) Sweetgreen promoted digital-only menu options, available only through its native delivery app, to spur customers into using the app, and in doing so grew sales from its most loyal customers. Sweetgreen was also one of the first restaurants to offer direct delivery to office building lobbies via its digital Outpost service, starting in 2018. Sweetgreen's early investment in digital channels and digital customer relationships paid off during the pandemic, when digital orders more than doubled. This allowed the company to recover from the loss of much of its in-store business in Manhattan, its biggest market.

Second, Sweetgreen architected the app with personalization in mind. The app—which won several awards as one of the top food-and-drink apps in the early 2020s—allows each customer to choose their preferred delivery channel.[2] Sweetgreen customers can also use the app to set dietary preferences and find curated recommendations to match. The company has considered expanding these capabilities with personalized nutrition and subscription plans to engage more users via its digital platform. Its acquisition of kitchen-robotics startup Spyce is giving Sweetgreen the ability to automate its customized salad production, so customers can choose a made-to-order salad and the company will be able to produce such orders at scale and at low cost.

Finally, the company invested early and heavily in technology; from the start, technology claimed the biggest chunk of Sweetgreen's G&A investment. It hired top talent from Amazon, Uber, and other digital natives. The company also applied the principles of smart integration: making use of off-the-shelf technology wherever possible, and swiftly adopting the innovations emerging from big-league players. For example, Sweetgreen used existing technology to rapidly launch personalized discounting in its app and issue gamified challenges and offers.

Despite its small size relative to the large chains, Sweetgreen ranks as one of the most digitized restaurant brands, with around 60 percent of its sales made via digital channels in 2023—even ahead of digital trailblazers such as Starbucks at the time.[3] The salad chain has reported greater visitation by its digital customers: in 2021 the company stated that customers who ordered in a digital channel visited Sweetgreen 1.5 times as often as customers who only patronized its physical locations, and those who ordered via two or more digital channels visited 2.5 times as often. More-over, the average value for digital orders was 21 percent higher.

The lessons from the companies in this chapter illustrate not just the power of smart integration and a personalization stack designed for flexibility and speed, but also how to apply many of the other lessons from the personalization playbook we have shared thus far. The companies also benefited from great leaders with the vision and foresight to make the case for the continuous advancements needed in their technology and people capabilities.

B2B Distribution
and Technology

n the B2B world, delivering on the Promises of Personalization comes
with added complexity. The purchase journey is typically circuitous,
involves many stakeholders, and calls for catering to one's salespeople
as well as one's customers.

The world's largest distributors serve hundreds of thousands of
customers globally—typically small businesses that could include offices,
convenience stores, restaurants, contractors, and maintenance providers,
depending on the distributor. Leading distributors have streamlined their
operations, but more importantly, they have begun personalizing their
management of each account to a degree that helps their clients stay stocked,
find new cost efficiencies, and successfully evolve their offerings (such as
menus in restaurants or planograms in convenience stores). During the
pandemic, some distributors built e-commerce platforms to enable their
customers to buy directly instead of having to order by phone. These systems remember standing orders and keep track of the rate at which customers consume products. For every order, they also generate a list of
adjacent items so that the distributor can suggest missing or complementary items that the customer might want to add.

One leading food service distributor goes a step further, tracking broader
trends in dining so it can source or create new menu components and promote them to appropriate buyers. For example, if a chef is buying rump
roasts or whole hams every month, the company might suggest they switch
to a precut or pre-prepared version to save time and cost. Another distributor, of office supplies serving small businesses, also applies this kind of
approach to customer engagement in its call centers. Instead of just taking

orders, reps now serve as "sales consultants." They have the information on their screens to understand any one of the different parties at a client company who may be calling in, and based on the caller's role (e.g., regional procurement manager, new business owner, office manager) can suggest new items and new replenishment tactics tailored to the individual customer. They can also proactively reach out to each individual to make valuable suggestions.

But the most advanced personalization capabilities in B2B are currently being built by the largest technology players. Microsoft has been an early mover.

How Microsoft's Global Demand Center Deepens B2B Account Relationships

In the early 2010s, Microsoft found itself facing competitors in a number of its key growth markets. Several forward-looking leaders came together to reimagine a new digital-engagement platform that marketers and salespeople could use across markets—a platform supporting new personalized approaches that would boost productivity and customer satisfaction.

Stephanie Ferguson, who leads Microsoft's Global Demand Center, the company's integrated digital marketing, tech, and analytics function, was one such leader. Shortly after Microsoft launched Azure, she recognized the challenges the business faced in trying to engage and sell directly online to thousands of corporate and independent developers around the globe.

Developers' priority, she notes, is often simply to try the product. And their experiences are vastly different. "We saw incredible variation," Ferguson says, "in the ways developers tried the service, wanted more information, got through purchasing the service, and then set up the full instance of Azure that they could start using." At the same time, Ferguson notes, every market had been creating its own way of managing its sales funnel.

> A marketer in Germany may do a fantastic job with an event and seek to prioritize all of those one-touch leads for sales to follow up on. Peers in France and Australia may do the same, but their customers may have had many other interactions with us and are

all at different stages, with different potential, needing different types of follow-up. We wanted to create an enterprise backbone that could enable moving each customer forward in the right way.[1]

In addition to supporting the Azure business with a new approach to trial and adoption early in the customer journey, Ferguson's team also saw an opportunity to apply a personalized customer journey approach to the company's more mature businesses, such as the subscription-based Microsoft 365 business (then, Office 365). Beyond the customer purchase, it personalized the post-sales approach to promoting customer engagement and product usage. The team built new capabilities for managing customers, from the initial marketing interaction through purchase and ongoing product usage, to ensure customers got value from their Microsoft investments. This was the start of Microsoft's Global Demand Center (GDC).

As they laid out their vision, the team realized that their existing tech capabilities would not be sufficient. Given Microsoft's global operations, the move to personalized customer management was complicated by having teams in many different markets that used many different tools and processes. Often these systems and approaches were developed organically as each market expanded. Instead of the patchwork of tools used in different markets, they needed a common digital-engagement platform. Applying the principles of smart integration, the team focused on building a central capability to manage data at both the account (corporate) and individual levels, while tracking every interaction within an account. Because of Microsoft's scale, Ferguson's team pushed the limits of most available software offerings. Over time, however, the insights they gained significantly shaped and accelerated product development for Microsoft's own suite of CRM tools. Ultimately, the team set up an integrated stack with a central data warehouse, a marketing and CRM platform, and a content management system that would become the standard architecture globally.

The GDC partnered with sales to create and train dedicated digital sellers who used customer insights and content from this platform to engage customers at the right moment in their buying journey and demonstrate the performance impact of connected sales and marketing. Seed money enabled the GDC to launch pilots without having to lobby the individual business units or markets for funding. The new connected sales and marketing approach created the first end-to-end view of the sales funnel, enabling the team to understand each customer's point in their journey, as well as to identify the next best action. It also—importantly—helped to scale best practices across markets.

The GDC could now start to personalize marketing programs to align with enterprise sales teams. They did this by building and fine-tuning AI models to synthesize millions of marketing interactions globally into seller recommendations for each account. "We started using AI to build analytic tools that could model the next best approach to a customer," says Ferguson. "This enabled our sales team to adapt their selling techniques and tailor content to best serve each customer." The team uncovered new, more-behavior-based customer segments, such as people who explore a lot of content on the site and in discussion forums and those who only want to start a trial. They also discovered different engagement preferences among segments: engineers crave highly technical content in social channels (not just detailed web content), while more-senior executives prefer thought leadership papers and events. Ferguson's team scaled orchestration capabilities that focused on coordinating touches at the account level for sales journeys (especially when the account had multiple customer contacts) and at the user level for post-sales engagement (e.g., encouraging users with a license who were not part of the original sales process to experiment with new use cases).

The team's early success caught the eye of then-CMO, Chris Capossela, and his successor, Takeshi Numoto, as they demonstrated the power of connected sales and marketing to surface rich customer interaction data that empowers sellers and improves customer experiences. They quickly supported a broader, rapid rollout. But the change management it required was by no means simple. For example, the team had to overhaul how the company tracked and measured value. "Historically, anyone might have built their own Excel spreadsheet of sales leads and then credited individual leads with the full value of closing a sale," says Ferguson.

> Now, with a much-more-sophisticated, longitudinal view, we could see that there were many people and actions contributing to a sale. Determining the value of any one interaction was no longer straightforward. A conversation at an event may have happened after an online trial, and a successful outbound phone discussion

may have occurred with someone who was referred by a colleague who had attended an event. Attribution was complex and conversion could happen in many ways.

To solve this challenge, the GDC team developed their Marketing Engagement Index (a measurement concept similar to the Engagement Ladder we introduce in chapter 9). The team used AI models based on their aggregate customer journey data to develop a score that showed the extent of a prospect's progress in their purchase journey. A recommendation of "highly engaged" was triggered when sales win rates were predicted to be four to seven times that of the average account. This new approach was quickly adopted by marketers and digital sellers to focus their efforts on the highest-value targets. Over time, Ferguson's team added further testing and analysis to suggest optimal timing to approach contacts in order to trigger higher engagement. The index produced specific next best action recommendations for field marketers and salespeople. In addition, both groups could get a longitudinal picture of the whole journey for an account at the corporate and individual level so they could build on the prospect's demonstrated interest.

One executive tour of the Dublin sales center proved to be a turning point at Microsoft. The GDC team had early adopters share their stories with attendees. Adoption quickly accelerated. Salespeople found they were able to successfully scale their account portfolios, and the data generated in the sales process helped them maintain momentum with their accounts—helping customers reap the very value that they sought at the outset.

The GDC also proved to be transformative for the marketing function. Instead of local marketing teams running fragmented marketing campaigns and collecting data locally, the GDC now provides a service to collect all the local insights from digital interactions with each customer, with local marketing activity aligned to global programs. The result is one view of each customer, enabling personalization of their journeys based on the patterns of engagement across the GDC's many individual stakeholders in the different geographies and divisions.

Today the Global Demand Center team is introducing more gen AI capabilities to create standardized, best-practice content—and cutting content creation cycle times by 20 percent to 25 percent. They are also getting increasingly granular in how they let people manage each account. Looking ahead, the team is excited to apply this personalized customer journey management approach to Microsoft's extensive ecosystem of partners and software vendors. Given Microsoft's customers' desire for integrated, end-to-end solutions, team members know that doing so can only deepen those partnerships.

The Future of Personalization in B2B

The Promises of Personalization at scale—Empower Me, Know Me, Reach Me, Show Me, Delight Me—are as relevant in B2B as they are in B2C. But delivering on them comes with added complexity: more routes to market, more layers of stakeholders to support, and more performance scrutiny from customers. To be sure, it's hard work getting salespeople to adopt new systems that require more data entry—systems whose more formal action recommendations might challenge their personal instincts. But as AI advances further, and the automatic data capture of every interaction is more widely adopted, the burden on the salesperson declines, and the value they see in the support increases.

In the race to decommoditize their products and alleviate the endless pressure from clients' procurement organizations, B2B personalizers are finding ways to add value from the experience of using their core products. Historically, any B2B company, especially one selling long-cycle products or services, keenly understood that the key to success was making its clients successful. But incentives were not always aligned. Often it was about pushing product, and sales targets reinforced that. Personalization done right strengthens the pursuit of mutual success by hitching the seller's success to the customer's success, helping clients achieve better performance, and building stronger relationships as a result. Looking ahead, as more B2B players configure more of their products to capture and activate data about their usage, the top players in each sector will want to differentiate themselves by shouldering more risk in their customers' pursuit of specific performance goals. Some may go as far as adopting performance-based pricing—pricing offerings according to their measurable impact, with bonuses and penalties built in.

PART TWO

LEADING THE TRANSFORMATION

Chapter 8

Expanding Roles in the C-Suite

Who leads the charge on personalization? Given the different types of organizational structures, and the fact that it takes a cross-functional, holistic effort to deliver end-to-end customer experiences, it's no surprise that various models are emerging. All, however, recognize the imperative for executive leadership, coordination across the business, and a shared agenda.

Early on, chief marketing officers were typically the prime movers of personalization. But that was when digital marketing focused on new-customer acquisition, and when personal data was seen as an instrument of segment-based advertising. As service companies (in particular financial services, telecoms, and health-care providers) began to see the value of managing customers throughout their entire life cycle, it became clear that personalization required integrating a broader set of capabilities.

This has led to the emergence of roles like the chief customer officer, who brings marketing, customer service, and responsibility for digital messaging and website experiences under one hat. Other companies opt instead for a chief growth officer, who combines responsibility for marketing and sales—a combination appropriate for transactional (nonsubscription) businesses like retailers, as well as many forms of B2B. In companies such as insurers, where data and analytical rigor are critical to driving personalization, chief digital, data, and analytics officers often lead the program. In addition, we would argue that most organizations need a dedicated head of personalization, typically at the SVP or VP level (sometimes also charged with broader responsibilities like loyalty or customer experience). That's because the extensive changes involved require a coordinating executive who sees how everything fits together from the customer experience and operational perspectives.

But instead of simply adding roles at the top, companies are balancing these new additions by reducing the number of senior leaders in traditional functions (e.g., marketing, operations, IT), especially as those functional teams need fewer midlevel spans of control once their members are dispersed across agile teams.

In reality, it takes a village to lead and manage personalization. Almost every C-suite member will be responsible for contributing to the personalization strategy. Most will also need to change their priorities, operating practices, and performance metrics to fuel progress, as will their extended circle of senior experts and advisers: the general counsel, data leaders, and board members. Let's examine these roles, clarifying their responsibilities and how they fit into the broader organizational context.

The CEO: Setting the mandate

CEOs must provide the rationale and the vision: how personalization will distinguish the brand's value proposition, how the company must rethink its investment priorities, and what new performance targets everyone should aim for.

Knowing that his company's future success lay in tapping its enormous store of customer information, William Niles, CEO of Brinks Home, set a clear vision for the future, proclaiming to his leadership team that "We are going to be a data-first, customer-focused brand that would stop investing in supporting legacy systems, and would create a roadmap for upgrading to open, cloud-based technologies."[1] Niles saw that automation could catapult the company's growth and efficiency to new heights. He felt Brinks could use its geographic diversity to build an advantage in experimentation. The company began by making renewals more personalized than ever, to boost performance without offering the same 25 percent discount to everyone. Quickly, the ROI of renewal activity more than doubled. Encouraged by these results, Niles's team decided to expand the program to other areas. As he says:

I also knew that my team would have to take more risks and move much faster in order to take advantage of the rapid learning-loop cycle that enables personalization. I gave them the license to do so, seeing every experiment that failed as a chance to learn. We energized the company dramatically.

Niles not only gave the company clear direction; he also gave people "air cover" as they innovated and experimented. He set a tone for iterative improvement and brought "oxygen" into the change process as Brinks scaled its personalization program. He talked to line managers, celebrated successes, recognized the learning from unsuccessful trials, and constantly questioned whether the investment budget was being spent appropriately to advance Brinks' progress.

The chief financial officer: Managing the return on enterprise-level investments

Personalization plays havoc with conventional ways of managing investments and expenses, in functional areas as well as product-area P&Ls. As the keepers of the capital budget, CFOs need to have a clear understanding both of the critical-path investments for putting the right enablers in place and of how they should be sequenced. Every department will have funding requests for new technology development or software licenses, or for new talent with new skills. The challenge CFOs face is how to allocate charges for investments (and even for operating expenses) that span functional areas, such as integrating customer data platforms or adding teams to implement new privacy guardrails. The new need to coordinate the flow of communications with customers means product groups should no longer pursue customers singlehandedly (at least not as readily), especially in companies where multiple groups are chasing the same segments. Performance targets will thus need to be adjusted. Certain product lines will now naturally be seen as foundational, and others as optional extensions, so their relative growth prospects may change.

One tech CFO we've worked with observed that while the company needed to maintain product P&Ls to manage the business, there were more and more tough conversations at the leadership level about how to rebalance them in order to fund enterprise-level investments in areas like AI, and on how to address strategic trade-offs to grow each customer's value. Having a "stand-alone" personalization P&L that measured progress against the overall business case, both in topline impact and costs, was an important tool for informing these discussions (see more on the personalization P&L in chapter 9).

The chief strategy officer: Championing the case for change

In their role as consultants to the executive leadership team, CSOs provide fresh perspectives on the threats and opportunities arising from market changes, competitors, technology, and regulation. Forward-thinking CSOs are challenging their organizations to add personalization as an explicit strategic pillar. Historically, personalization initiatives at many companies accrued organically as efficiency moves in marketing and sales, later expanding into improvements in customer service. CSOs are now bringing these efforts together, turning the direction into a coordinated strategy. With their longer-term and bigger-picture view, strategy leaders hunt for the tipping point, the place where it becomes patently clear that to achieve personalization at scale, the company will need a much-more-deliberate, coordinated program. They see the research and market data that shows when customers are switching to competitors that are doing a better job of giving them tailored, immediate, and often lower-cost experiences. In short, strategy leaders are the vanguard agents of personalization change, and they must champion its logic, financial implications, and urgency.

The strategy team at a leading financial services company explored different competitive scenarios based on adopting the personalization strategies of Uber, Netflix, and Amazon. This exercise sparked new ways of thinking about the company's business model, thinking that underscored the pressing need for customer data and a coordinated customer management approach. Customers, they reckoned, would increasingly value the brand if it helped them save money, manage their budget, or identify more tax-favorable investments, or if it helped guide them through the necessary financial steps when they lost a job or a parent died.

After some research, the team prioritized customer service use cases involving a rep or a chatbot. In this way, the company would save money (from a faster or digitized interaction), but more importantly, customers would perceive the brand to be helping them, rather than pitching to them.

The team then moved on to "advisory" use cases: those involving prompting customers with suggestions for helpful actions (such as opening an IRA upon making a large deposit). The strategy team established the sequence and the funding for new personalization initiatives. It then led discussions about capability- and resource-building: whether to buy versus build (e.g., for chatbot services), seek new partnerships (e.g., sharing data with key merchants to enrich loyalty program offerings), or pursue acquisitions.

Unit presidents and product P&L owners: Delivering a personalized offering

Having product responsibility means these executives have a direct and major role in personalization. They must coordinate more with their counterparts on other product teams to fulfill the customer's needs without stepping over one another and annoying the customer.

At one multiline business-software provider, these leaders know that their strategy requires building multiple product relationships with customers. But they also know that not every customer needs every product. Setting ever-higher targets across all product lines was simply too arbitrary; the different product teams ended up bombarding the same customers with pitches. The solution: establishing a central analytics team, under the auspices of the finance department, that regularly combs the customer base data, assessing the right upside potential for each account and assigning targets accordingly. Product teams are on the hook to enhance their product's value proposition, expand their potential market, and set reasonable prices—and must decide whether to fund investments in service support to keep customers engaged, costs low, and renewals high.

The chief operating officer: Optimizing the delivery system and its economics

COOs face a never-ending challenge: making sure that increasing the variation in customer experiences does not create diseconomies of scale. It's up to them to figure out how to use intelligence and automation to cut the costs of adding more complexity.

At one health-care company, the COO mounted an effort to cut more than $1 billion in costs from manual operations to fund investments in technology and AI. At regular check-ins the leadership team evaluated opportunities. For each customer segment, the team appointed a Digital Customer Experience leader who identified ways to become more streamlined (for example, getting paper out of the system, or using digital to speed up processes), while personalizing more. Every product and functional team was required to develop a strategy for delivering the target experience at a lower cost. Very few of the ideas put forth could be executed by a single team, and all had trade-offs to consider.

The chief information officer: Transforming the infrastructure

Along with having an increasingly critical duty to advance an organization's tech capabilities, the CIO must also be strategic, both in guiding tech choices and in architecting the best way to implement them. In many respects, CIOs are becoming more like product managers, responsible for partnering to deliver value with the lines of business and support functions—meeting their needs, at cost, while steadily increasing that value.

As it weighed its tech capabilities, financial services company Voya (featured in the Financial Services Industry Spotlight), like many companies, saw its customer information scattered about, in dedicated systems tied to each product and in different systems for marketing, sales, service, and claims. Most of these systems lived in older on-premise architectures, and in formats that were incompatible with each other. Identity resolution—the ability to link an individual's information across all company systems—became a top priority. As CIO Santosh Keshavan explains: "We simultaneously upgraded most of our systems to move into a much-more-flexible cloud infrastructure, while implementing tools that could help us match identity."[2] Voya extracted the key data needed about each customer and put it into a new customer data platform. It then had to ensure the system was sufficiently open to let the company overlay external information it had purchased and to connect with new operational systems that would run new experiences.

Some big decisions involved "biting the bullet to get rid of stranded costs in [our] outdated systems," Keshavan says. But Voya carefully managed its investments by starting with identity, enriching customer profiles with more data, adding intelligence, and then developing its web and mobile experiences to use that information. As CIOs navigate the shift from effectively managing a service group with a fixed budget for maintaining and upgrading established systems to becoming a driver of transformation, "They are proactively getting rid of legacy infrastructure and creating more-flexible systems that will enable users to do more themselves," Keshavan observes.

The chief digital and analytics officer: Activating the heart and brains of personalization

These relatively new roles (sometimes split between a chief digital officer and a chief data and analytics officer) are gaining ground as top executives and boards realize how critical data and analytics are to their businesses. These leaders must develop a practical (and funded) road map to elevate the value of data assets and build the talent and tools needed to amass real-time intelligence and insights. They also often design and deliver front-line digital experiences. Chief digital and analytics officers (CDAOs) can therefore have a dual function: supporting the entire business with data and analytics while also managing their own channels.

CDAOs need to act as product managers, where the "product" is the company's data and digital-interaction channels. These leaders must understand the needs of both their external customers and their internal business partners. They must translate the underlying requirements into development plans and use cases, manage the assets they deliver, oversee vendor relationships, and constantly stay on top of their performance from an operations and financial perspective.

One bank CDAO describes his role as a "constantly growing snowball" as the company becomes more data-driven and digitally automated. "We are essentially becoming the operations of the company," he says. Some teams serve the business units; others coordinate customer data at the enterprise level. The teams experiment constantly with new methods for setting up tests, analyzing results, creating predictive models, allocating investments, and so forth. Talent, he says, is a "huge challenge": his teams never seem to have enough data engineers to handle data management. The team routinely wrestles with build-versus-buy decisions, while recognizing that systems must conform to open standards so that customer data can flow all the way through. This CDAO has had "hard discussions" with many functional-area leaders about what they can automate, and the changes that automation would trigger in their organizations, processes, and performance metrics. He notes that his capital budget is "never enough. . . . We have to prioritize ruthlessly. I work closely with the CMO and the service-operations [team] to sequence new use cases and segments to address."[3]

The chief human resources officer: Designing the new operating model

The agile team structure so crucial to personalization creates immediate complexities for HR organizations. Organization charts don't adequately represent the cross-functional work structures that are essential for a personalization program. In matrix-type organization structures, people are simultaneously embedded in a project-based team and a functional area home base. HR leaders therefore need to guide decision-makers on incentive redesign and compensation. More broadly, they must prioritize how the training budget is spent, developing new technology, analytic, creative, and process management skills, and they must know when to lobby for more funds. CHROs are developing new job descriptions for roles involving advanced data management, complex customer experience, content design, and data-bias management. In parallel, they are supporting business leaders in hiring new talent and, as automation and AI supplant many manual processes, in making difficult personnel decisions.

One retailer elevated an "enterprise capability development" position to a level just below the CHRO. This person is responsible for budget expenditures for upskilling, making selective new hires, and headcount turnover. This individual is developing new rubrics for the skills needed for advancement, and is monitoring how other companies develop managerial profiles for hiring purposes.

The chief revenue officer and head of sales: Leading the front line

These roles are more prominent in B2B companies, which have sales forces, agent channels, account management, and multiple routes to market. Personalization has always been the secret sauce of the best account managers: they learn about, and stay on top of, their clients' details, tracking the economics of clients' businesses, their decision processes, and the impact their products are having. But as we saw in the Industry Spotlight preceding this chapter, scaling personalization in the B2B world means taking customer insights (of prospects and existing customers) to a deeper level and pulling in more real-time data across channels and geographies.

The head of European sales at an industrial-products company tells us that the company uses natural language processing tools to analyze all available digital communications related to a client and their competitors, and then distills the key points. "Our salespeople wake up every day with lists of the top 100 triggers coming out of their target customers, most of which also have suggestions for specific content to send or other action to take." By building data collection into more and more of its products, the company not only provides proactive maintenance services but also captures information about how clients use its products. "All of that informs the dialogue of our account managers," he says.[4] For smaller accounts, that same data triggers automatic messaging and is used to tailor the home page of the web for each client.

The chief marketing officer and chief customer officer: Orchestrating personalization

Historically, chief marketing and chief customer officers initiated personalization programs with use cases focused on near-term sales upside. Now, however, the mandate for personalization is moving well past the purchase part of a customer journey to extend throughout a company's relationship.

David Dintenfass of Fidelity Investments says, "One of the CMO's biggest responsibilities is getting everyone aligned around the lifetime value goal: how to measure it, and what it means for decisions. It requires constantly coming up with new use cases, designing experiments, and conducting tests." Dintenfass feels strongly about the importance of "showing the organization that we can do bold things."[5] But that doesn't require high-risk, large-scale tests. Adroit experimentation means marketing teams can pilot new innovations on small samples, and then apply the feedback to improve customer experiences even further. As we discussed in the Financial Services Industry Spotlight, Fidelity created a whole body of much simpler educational videos written in a tone tailored more for millennials than the company's standard content is. Says Dintenfass, "As we gradually automate more of the execution, it makes it much easier to focus on [that] creativity, rather than having to spend tons of time on manual delivery processes."

The general counsel: Managing the guardrails, spotting looming risks

The legal team is actively involved in managing compliance, privacy, and security risks, often prompted by the use and management of customer information. Governments around the world are beginning to grapple with the prospect of customers controlling their own data on a widespread basis. Worried about AI-based decision-making and its associated risks of misinformation and fraud, regulators are stepping up their scrutiny. Regulatory activity will no doubt intensify, and will continue to evolve, as technologies and practices evolve. General counsels will need to translate new requirements into guidelines or mandatory processes by which companies control their use of data and manage risk. Legal issues will likely be dynamic: for example, regulations that start in health care—say, about protecting privacy or mandating interoperability—could extend into other sectors as the expanding use of information affects consumer access, fairness, and safety more broadly. As always, the challenge for legal executives is to avoid imposing artificial constraints that could unduly suppress innovation. Instead, they should train their legal team to partner with business managers to find ways to accelerate speed to market while containing risk.

One telecom company formed a Reputation Council, which reviews new initiatives for potential risks and develops scenarios so the company is prepared to address problems swiftly. The council has also assigned compliance managers to work with the frontline teams that are using agile methodologies to develop new tests to eliminate bottlenecks in awaiting a legal opinion before bringing a new idea to market.

The board: Ensuring the strategic investments and safeguards for personalization

In addition to ensuring the funding for a company's personalization strategy, boards ensure that safeguards are in place to manage the compliance, security, and privacy risks associated with the broader use of personal data and AI. Board members should make clear to management that personalization strategy merits far more than a one-time presentation; instead, it is an active vector of engagement whose goal is to ensure the company is evolving its way of competing. To this end, we're seeing boards add new kinds of professionals to their rosters, such as former chief technology officers, chief marketing officers, security leaders, and analytics leaders.

The board of a large financial services company has established a special Tech, Innovation, and Operations committee to make sure that the strategy set by the CEO and the promises made to investors are being backed with the capital and change management activities needed to make the strategy and promises happen. Members of this committee are well versed in AI, agile ways of working, and cloud technology. They are challenging management to sharpen its investment road maps and its approach to slashing legacy stranded costs, so that it can fund the new capabilities (which, in many cases, can be high-risk efforts). Committee members press management to clearly articulate the new performance targets. They are also demanding more detail on how the company is protecting data, keeping it clean, and managing customer permissions. They want to look behind the curtain, both to understand how AI is driving decisions about customer offers and to mitigate potential biases in the data.

———————————

Appointing a single personalization leader may seem like a good way to prevent the program from getting lost in the perpetual corporate prioritization tug-of-war. But doing so would be insufficient. Given the many interdependencies, such a move by itself would inevitably result in failure. Across C-suites and boards, every role is being stretched, augmented, or reshaped. New ones are emerging as the personalization imperative takes root. Leaders are recognizing data's new position as the scarce resource, speed and integration as sources of capability advantage, and creativity as the fuel for growth. They are reimagining roles with this new reality in mind.

Chapter 9

Measuring Impact

Fundamentally, personalization is about serving the customer: giving them quality, value for money, and convenience—with the utmost speed. Customer satisfaction is, naturally, a true indicator of personalization success. And when properly nurtured, the customer satisfaction that a company generates translates into customer lifetime value—the other true (and ultimate) measure of personalization success.

Thus, given the substantial investments that personalization at scale requires, companies need to be sure they are indeed moving the needle on those two indicators. Investments should, of course, be prioritized based on their potential upside. Quick wins are crucial for securing the funding for further game-changing progress over the medium term. They not only prove the value, but in many cases make the personalization program mostly, and sometimes even fully, self-funding. As we explained in the previous chapter, meeting these requirements calls for a personalization head: someone whose job it is to wake up every day thinking about personalization across the enterprise. This person is accountable for delivering results, measured in customer outcomes and in return on investment.

A personalization P&L is an essential tool for any personalization program. It provides a 360-degree view of the costs and benefits of personalization to the business. In this way, it helps companies to continue investing in improving the customer experience, winning more customers, and making more customers for life.

Let's look at how to develop a personalization P&L, starting with the core metrics.

Customer Satisfaction and Loyalty: The Pivotal KPIs

Certainly, every company undertaking a personalization effort needs KPIs that show how the customer experience is improving. But although customer satisfaction is a universal goal, the KPIs that reflect it can differ substantially from sector to sector.

Retail, fashion, and consumer packaged-goods companies need to track new-product trial, traffic, transaction frequency, average order value, conversion, and repeat-purchase rates. Such companies should calculate the number of "one and done" customers they have had and estimate what percentage of them they could lure back—even just once. They should ask themselves: How might we boost the purchasing frequency of our loyalty program members, whom we know more about? What potential use cases could increase cross-selling and upselling—perhaps, for instance, personalizing add-to-cart recommendations or offers?

Companies in sectors that provide services and experiences, such as travel and tourism, telecom, and banking, need to pinpoint the main drivers of service satisfaction and loyalty. Service satisfaction comes down to "moments of truth": for an airline, how quickly lost baggage is returned or a flight delay resolved; for a telecom company, how fast service is restored after a disruption; and generally, for any enterprise, how promptly a complaint or special request is addressed. Loyalty is measured based on the components of customer lifetime value, including a customer cohort's frequency, switching behavior, and overall spend. Subscription-based businesses will track customer acquisition cost, spend-per-member over time, and churn rates.

Finally, businesses that sell outcomes, such as health insurers and care providers, will focus on measuring those outcomes. Spend per customer and churn rates still matter, of course, but for these businesses, customer goals—such as lowering one's blood pressure, improving one's diet, or maintaining overall health—are most important.

In addition to these hard metrics, softer (or leading) indicators, such as customer engagement, are useful, regardless of sector, for determining whether and where the inputs of personalization are generating enough interactions. These include the number of personalized impressions (e.g., the number of times customers interact with personalized content), website traffic, app downloads, monthly active users, email sign-ups and open rates, and store-visit frequency. The hard metrics validate whether those interactions are of the right quality, enabling executives to adapt their tactics accordingly. One large retailer worked to quantify the total number of interactions happening annually with customers across all channels and set explicit goals to eliminate low-value interactions (such as emails with low open rates) and increase the share of personalized interactions from 10 percent to 50 percent.

Measuring Customer Relationship Value with the Engagement Ladder

Customer satisfaction metrics tell you about an individual experience. But what about the *total* customer experience—the ongoing relationship? How do you know you're achieving the ultimate purpose of personalization? Which pathways do your loyal customers take over time—in other words, what actions do they take that solidify their loyalty more quickly? And how can you spur more customers to follow those pathways so that you create even more advocates for your company, with ever-better customer experiences?

The customer data you already have in hand provides a wealth of information from which to draw insights. One tool we developed to help brands organize and systematically assess these insights is the Engagement Ladder. It represents a hierarchy of customer status levels (rungs), from "lapsed" to "brand advocates," along with the company's goal for each level. While the actual rungs in the ladder will be different for every company, the Engagement Ladder concept can be applied equally to all companies, regardless of whether they sell products, services, subscriptions, or outcomes.

Every company has its own characteristic Engagement Ladder pattern in the evolution toward customer lifetime value. Figure 9-1 shows this pattern for a beauty retailer client, based on its CRM data. For each rung in the ladder, we mapped the company's annual spend, customer satisfaction scores, churn rates, and customer lifetime value. We also calculated the "headroom": the amount of incremental sales the company could potentially trigger from customers who were similar to the highest-value customers in their rung, but who were not yet engaging with the company to the same extent.

FIGURE 9-1

A beauty retailer's Engagement Ladder

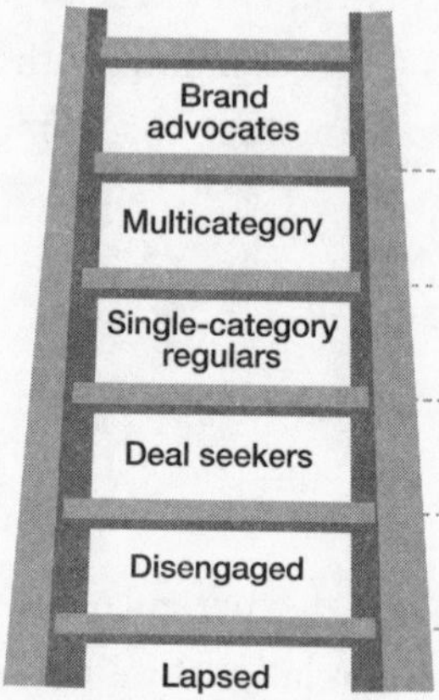

	Key insight about segment	Examples of tactics to pilot
Brand advocates	2x as valuable as next segment	Incentivize referrals to friends
Multicategory	Churn rate ½ of single-category	Drive loyalty program engagement
Single-category regulars	Trialing items in new categories is most likely to increase CLV	Incentivize trial in new categories
Deal seekers	Likely to shop at competitors	Reward regular purchase of replenishment items
Disengaged	New products drive engagement	Target content around new launches
Lapsed	Unlikely to return after 6 months	Invest drive to website in first 3 months after lapsing

This retailer in particular had an abundance of "one and done" customers in the middle of the ladder—the price-sensitive "deal seekers." Many were spending the bulk of their category dollars with competitors, and the somewhat loyal customers were essentially single-category replenishment buyers who were replacing items like shampoo. For such customers, personalization could be used to recommend an appropriate item from the company's wide assortment, while also catering to the needs of its more-frequent customers—multicategory buyers who were usually interested in hearing about the company's loyalty program, the latest new products, seasonal items, or exclusive limited-time-only items.

To create your own Engagement Ladder, start by analyzing your CRM data over the past three to five years. What main actions lead to customers increasing their spending over time? This might be downloading the app, buying in multiple categories, taking advantage of a promotion, coming in with their friends, and so on. Identify the most valuable triggers and define segments with progressively greater lifetime value. Analyze the key metrics for each segment, such as churn rates, satisfaction scores, engagement with new products, or digital channels, to derive insights that can be turned into personalization tactics. Laying out the data in this way enables a company to size the potential upside from personalization; revealing, for example, how much it is worth—in frequency, spend, and retention—to move 10 percent of customers up to the next level. It also suggests pragmatic actions to test.

The Personalization Top and Bottom Lines

Instituting these customer metrics is an important prerequisite for running personalization as a business. The next step is creating a bona fide personalization P&L to support executive decision-making. Your CFO and finance team should play an active role in setting up the P&L so that the metrics that justify your business case for added investments are deemed credible. This is especially important considering the many priorities competing for capital in every organization.

While lower-cost AI tools are removing barriers for smaller companies to adopt personalization, the investments are still significant and should be managed for measurable value creation in specific areas. At the same time, too many companies launch multimillion, three- to five-year Customer 360 initiatives to unify their customer data and solve all martech issues, only to pause the initiative after a year or so and be no closer to tangibly improving the customer experience. Most organizations, however, err in the opposite direction: they underinvest simply because they don't rigorously measure the total personalization P&L. That's why it is absolutely critical to have a robust means of tracking the value from personalization from the get-go, and to do so on a regular basis.

At the highest level, tracking the financials is deceptively simple. The personalization P&L statement needs only a few items: the capital cost of digital investments, net incremental revenue from personalization, operating margin, five categories of operating costs (people, data and analytics, ongoing technology, content, and digital customer acquisition), and personalization margin. (See figure 9-2.)

Creating these line items, however, is not always so simple. Most companies' existing financial reporting is not designed for personalization measurement. Determining each element underpinning the P&L requires deliberately setting up measurement systems and running programs in a way that allows you to keep track of the impact on the top and bottom lines.

First and foremost, you need to know how much net incremental revenue is being created by personalization across channels. Determining this figure can be challenging. It's one thing to measure the lift from individual

FIGURE 9-2

The personalization P&L

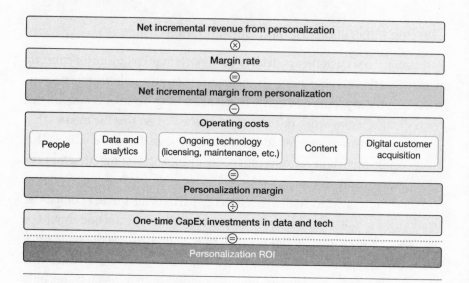

email campaigns or the click-throughs and conversion rates across different experiences on the website. It's quite another to ascertain the total revenue generated across the business.

There is a solution: building a universal control group (as we outlined in chapter 6). Here, you pull a group of customers out of the personalized-experiences pool for a short period of time. This is a straightforward exercise in email, text, and some parts of the app experience (e.g., in-app recommendations). In channels where this is impractical—for example, the call center, where customers are calling with complaints—you wouldn't want to "turn off" personalization. It would be more practical to compare the new personalized experience with the old approach in order to estimate the upside. In the case of the call center, for example, you might want to know to what extent the new personalized experience reduced churn rates for customers who called with complaints.

As personalization is extended across channels and different types of content (such as paid-media ads and email campaigns), it is easy to double-count the incremental revenue generation. This is why multitouch attribution and automated experimentation design are so important. These methods allow you to measure the total value of personalization across channels and then attribute the value created per channel. Suppose you are running a personalized ad campaign in search (a sponsored link at the top of a user's search results): you will see relatively higher response rates because customers who were searching for your brand were already likely to buy. What you need to know is which of these customers received a targeted ad campaign that led them to search in the first place. Because this kind of measurement is complex and extremely time-consuming to execute manually, it is critical to automate the analysis and reporting so the team can focus on drawing out the lessons and implications. This means that dashboards as well as the data pipelines that feed them should be automated so the information from different channels and platforms is pulled into one place without additional effort for each campaign.

Now, with an accurate view of net incremental revenue, you can estimate the margin rate on this lift to build a true personalization P&L.

Operating Costs

The key operating costs in a personalization program fall into five categories:

People and change management. Beyond marketers, personalization requires data scientists (to create the data models), data engineers (to design the data pipelines, clean the data, and create the data features that the data scientists need), IT experts, UI/UX specialists, creative-content designers, and legal and regulatory experts. Some of these resources can be borrowed or reallocated from other initiatives if they don't already have formal personalization responsibilities. But often, companies need to retrain or add personnel. As organizations mature and their personalization programs scale, their investments naturally shift from manual marketing activities and content creation to automation that requires more data scientists, engineers, and tech experts. Risk management costs will also increase, as companies add more roles, tools, and procedures for managing the compliance, privacy, and other growing risks associated with the increased use of customer data and AI. On balance, we find that the personalization team will typically need to grow even if automation saves costs in some areas.

In addition, it takes substantial change- and project-management efforts to adopt the new (agile) ways of working needed to support a cross-functional operation and rapid value creation. Personalization requires scrum masters and project managers with cross-functional and technical skill sets who are attentive to interdependencies and who can escalate and resolve issues promptly.

Data and analytics. This bucket includes costs for third-party data, licenses for data tools, and cloud-based computing costs. It can also include external expertise, such as the data scientists and engineers needed to augment internal teams. For larger companies, it is generally cost effective to staff the internal team that will conduct the ongoing analytics work (e.g., refreshing models, sustaining data tools), and rely on external resources for the one-time build work, which can be capitalized (more on this below). For smaller companies, which typically have little room for additional overhead or budget for outside resources, it is best to carve out a piece of the business—a segment, product line, geographic market—for personalization pilots, with a clear P&L that absorbs their costs and needed resources, while also accounting for the associated upside.

Ongoing technology. Typically this includes customer data platforms, content management systems, and digital asset management tools. This category also encompasses tech costs that are not capitalizable, such as everything from software licenses to hardware-maintenance costs. As companies fortify their architecture, adding more AI tools, cloud storage, cybersecurity, and so on, their licensing costs can quickly add up. As one CIO noted, "When we embed AI tools fully at scale, we do see the savings from automation. But the substantial expenditures on tech licenses can offset at least half of it."[1]

The personalization tech stack ties into the company's broader technology infrastructure and assets: namely, the call center (for customer service data) and point-of-sale systems (for transaction data). And while these broader overhead costs typically don't get treated as personalization costs, the substantial data-pipeline-maintenance costs involved in connecting these systems should in fact be included in the investment case and the budget.

Content. This category includes the costs of generating and managing new content and refreshing existing content, as well as continuously improving and launching new UI/UX and digital experiences. It also encompasses the cost of reengineering critical processes, which in addition to content generation includes campaign launch and measurement. Agency costs for developing creative content and digital ads will also come under this rubric. Companies can explore partnerships with content publishers to avoid generating all the content they themselves need (a grocery chain, for instance, might partner with a recipe website), or they can collect and use user-generated content that fits within established brand guardrails.

Digital customer acquisition. Finally, most companies looking to accelerate their personalization effort will need to invest in expanding their existing digital customer relationships. They also need to build customer awareness and promote usage of their digital experiences across these channels by encouraging app downloads, site traffic, email sign-ups, and so on, in order to gather valuable engagement data. It's important to personalize the onboarding journey for new digital customers to give them a reason to return; customers that download an app and don't use it again within three months typically leave. Even new customers can be segmented based on information collected at sign-up or based on their first few actions or third-party data, or both. Generally, digital customer acquisition costs will be substantial up front, but if managed well, will diminish over time as the company reaches critical scale.

For large *Fortune* 500 corporations (exceeding $5 billion in revenues, such as those in figure 9-3) with cross-channel personalization ambitions, the above costs could amount to tens of millions of dollars annually, depending on the scale they seek and the degree of change required in their operations. However, smaller companies that can move more nimbly are finding adroit ways to personalize their customer relationships cost effectively. As we noted earlier, Brinks Home is using a combination of AI adtech tools that optimize media spend and personalized landing pages that drive conversion and Sweetgreen is leveraging off-the-shelf martech tools to personalize games and challenges in its already popular app.

Capital Expenditures

Right from the start, personalization requires one-time capital expenditures (CapEx): up-front technology and AI investments in assets, as well as the cost of integrating them with existing systems, such as martech, the data warehouse, point-of-sale systems, and call center systems.

FIGURE 9-3

Investment benchmarks for *Fortune* 500 businesses ($5 billion+ sales)

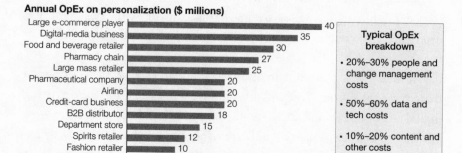

Annual OpEx on personalization ($ millions)

Large e-commerce player	40
Digital-media business	35
Food and beverage retailer	30
Pharmacy chain	27
Large mass retailer	25
Pharmaceutical company	20
Airline	20
Credit-card business	20
B2B distributor	18
Department store	15
Spirits retailer	12
Fashion retailer	10

Typical OpEx breakdown

- 20%–30% people and change management costs
- 50%–60% data and tech costs
- 10%–20% content and other costs

Note: Digital customer acquisitions vary significantly depending on the scale of the customer base and are therefore not included.

Source: BCG case experience and BCG Personalization Index research, 2023.

First, as noted in chapter 7, companies need to invest in smart integration across their systems and in converting their data into a much more usable structure: building the data pipelines and APIs to aggregate data in the right place, and establishing the data management systems to clean data and add the features (such as customer and product attributes) that will feed the models. They also need to build the models and algorithms that power personalization. Personalization leaders also build rules engines (such as a next best action decisioning engine that governs which customers get which communication in which channel). All of these are reusable, capitalizable assets.

Second, companies need to buy and integrate new systems (namely, content management tools and cloud-based analytics environments) and customize new martech and digital systems. Every company's specific needs will be different, but the core components should include the systems that compose the personalization tech stack:

- Data ingestion

- Customer 360

- Targeting intelligence

- Experiment design and activation

- Content creation, content management

- Next best action (cross-channel) orchestration

- Experience delivery

- Testing and measurement learning loop

Personalization leaders realize how critical it is to achieve performance gains from the get-go in order to sustain this level of investment. As our Personalization Index research shows, personalization leaders are growing 10 percentage points faster annually than laggards and they are gaining market share.

Building the Investment Case with Quick Wins

The key to making personalization affordable is making it largely self-funding. Many personalization leaders implement programs where up-front investments are fully funded by the margin from in-year revenue growth. From the start, your personalization program should be producing gains for both the business and your customers. That's what creates momentum and mobilizes the entire C-suite. But to make personalization self-funding, you need to achieve quick wins—the kind that generate value within the first three to six months. As Art Zeighami, former chief data and analytics officer at H&M, says, "It's important to rapidly put points on the board before you ask for more resources. Create a self-funding mechanism for the next set of use cases. Once the personalization team establishes a track record of value delivery, it becomes easy to secure resources."[2]

Achieving quick wins, of course, means committing your initial investments to building the foundation that will unlock these immediate sources of value.

Identifying the quick wins isn't the hard part. Most companies have an abundance of ideas but lack the cross-functional support necessary to launch them. And although the nature of the quick wins varies by industry, there are some clear all-around winners.

For retailers, personalized email offers can generate double to triple the ROI of mass discounts, enabling incremental growth and saving promotional dollars. Department stores, fashion brands, and grocers, which have historically spent 95 percent of their promotional dollars on mass offers, are now enjoying substantial success with this approach. Companies that are predominantly e-commerce players can quickly deploy personalized recommendations across their homepage, in carousels, on product pages, in their search function, and in the shopping cart to add several points of conversion (moves that, for large sites, can each be worth tens or even hundreds of millions of dollars). Amazon funded its personalization effort by extensively leveraging personalized recommendations on its site early on, and today, small, digitally native, direct-to-consumer brands are employing these same tactics.

For companies that cater to high-value customers and interact directly with them on-site, such as those in luxury retail or in high-end hospitality, in-person "personalized" selling is a reliable quick win. Every sales associate can provide effective personalized service with the right information at their fingertips. The Ritz-Carlton hotel chain, which prides itself on in-person personalization to achieve high customer satisfaction from check-in to check-out, significantly outperforms many high-end competitors. While chatting at check-in, associates know that a customer's most recent stay was, say, eleven months ago, or that she had recently complained to central reservations, or that she loves hunting antiques or going to Michelin-starred restaurants when in town.

In service industries with call centers, personalized recommendations for calls related to a purchase can contribute an additional 3 to 5 percentage points of sales from cross-selling. Putting personalized information at reps' fingertips shortens the call, thus pleasing the customer and saving money.

In industries such as financial services and health care, personalizing member acquisition and onboarding is often a source of quick wins. For example, we have seen personalized credit card acquisition campaigns lead to 30 percent to 40 percent higher ROI. At one major software company, personalizing the acquisition through onboarding phases led to a 30 percent drop in cost-per-new-user rates and a 25 percent drop in attrition rates. In B2B industries, two use cases stand out for their powerful, fast impact:

personalizing lead management (customizing the timing and type of outreach to coincide with when prospects are most likely to convert), and preventing churn. In both areas, companies have achieved double-digit percentage gains from personalization.

Second-Order Payoffs

A number of second-order benefits can help bolster the case for the investment necessary for personalization—among them improved marketing ROI and efficiency, which can be two to three times those of mass-marketing methods. Beyond the marketing efficiencies gained, the insights stemming from greater customer engagement are immensely valuable to many other parts of the business, from inventory management to new-product development.

Personalization can also generate insights that can be crucial in mitigating a serious business challenge. For example, when a major card issuer lost one of its co-branded retail credit card deals, customers flooded the call center with inquiries. By having personalization data and insights at hand, the call center reps were able to switch callers to alternative credit cards or immediately identify other ways to retain them. As a result, the issuer was able to stem customer defections.

Finally, investing in personalization is an opportunity to rethink customer satisfaction metrics and data-gathering methods. For example, instead of the occasional on-site customer survey or mystery shopper evaluations, traditional banks and brick-and-mortar retailers are following the lead of digital natives and embedding instant customer feedback into their apps and web experiences (e.g., a star rating, a thumbs-up or -down). Even moves as simple as these provide real-time data that can materially improve the customer experience. Such feedback metrics are even more valuable when injected into high-priority areas (such as the app features providing personalized recommendations), as they immediately reveal what engaged customers like. These metrics can also nip engagement problems in the bud. For instance, a pop-up or banner that annoys customers because it interrupts their experience will quickly get flagged, even if it generates incremental sales.

Drawing a Road Map to Value

Capturing your share of the $2 trillion personalization prize will take significant investment and a good few years. Having a well-defined road map with clear priorities is critical. Even companies that opt for mostly off-the-shelf tech solutions must undertake integration and customization work. They also need to maintain data pipelines and secure the in-house resources to continue designing, launching, and optimizing personalized experiences. While small companies can get started with a few hundred thousand to a few million dollars for licensing and integrating off-the-shelf point solutions, we have shown that many *Fortune* 500s typically spend between $10 million and $40 million each year in ongoing costs, over and above an equivalent (or greater) amount in one-time tech CapEx. It is therefore crucial that companies align the data, tech, and content road map with the use cases that will generate the most value early on.

Indeed, one of the biggest pitfalls we see in building personalization programs is the lack of alignment across functions. The data, intelligence models, and martech delivery pipelines might be in place, but if the content development or UI/UX is delayed, so is the value creation. Given the many moving parts and dependencies, infrastructure and capabilities must be in sync or companies will find it difficult to unlock the next phase of investment.

Chapter 10

Navigating Risk and Privacy

A consumer comment we cited in the very first chapter of this book bears repeating: "I may not have chosen to live in a world where brands have this much data about me, but they do. So now they need to put it to good use, responsibly, to make my life easier and better."[1] *Responsibly* is the operative word here. How do companies ensure they are acting responsibly? How do they navigate the risk landscape while they go about empowering and delighting their customers through personalization?

As technological innovation accelerates, the regulatory environment is rapidly evolving; witness the European Union's AI Act.[2] We're seeing growing publicity about the inappropriate uses of consumer data and mounting concerns about the opacity, potential for bias, and inaccuracies of AI outputs. It's no wonder that risk is invariably the first issue that comes up in our discussions with executives. So while we are confident that competing on personalization will become a critical basis of strategy across sectors, we can be equally confident that a parallel imperative—risk management—will also grow in importance.

Consumer attitudes about the use of personal data are mixed, reflecting uncertainty and often misconception. A recent BCG survey of one thousand US and Canadian consumers showed that 57 percent believed their data was being sold.[3] As we noted in chapter 1, two-thirds of the thousands of consumers surveyed worldwide for this book reported that in the past ninety days a company had communicated with them in ways that felt inappropriate. Other studies concur with our findings: a significant percentage of consumers believe they were victims of data misuse (defined as the use of personal data in ways unbeknownst to the customer and in ways they perceive as potentially harmful). The penalty for misuse can be significant. A well-known online mental health service and a drug discount app were fined millions for sharing and selling private customer information for advertising purposes without customers' permission, after promising to keep such data private. Research also shows that these incidents can do more than just affect revenues; they also—predictably—erode customer trust.

Given the stakes, leaders must understand the array of risks that ought to be on their radar, and the preventive actions they can take that will make it easier to limit those risks.

The first risk arises from the very act of personalization: using customers' information to anticipate their needs, guide their choices, and simplify their ability to take action. Therefore, the risks from pursuing a personalization strategy overlap considerably with the very same risks implicated in AI use: opacity, bias, and inaccuracy. With personalization, however, the risks are compounded by *how* companies are guiding their customers: Are they steering them toward outcomes that might not be in their best interests?

Certainly, personalization comes with basic executional risks. But as countless articles about AI have noted, there are broader risks to consider. It's helpful to think about them according to the Five Promises of Personalization. Starting with Know Me—a logical place, given that the data challenges represent the first and most obvious of the risks—we'll explore the types of management processes that personalization leaders are currently using, or are likely to be using, to mitigate the challenges, across all of the Promises. Then, we present a broader organizational system for managing personalization responsibly.

Know Me: The Risks Surrounding Data Collection and Use

Customer data is the lifeblood of personalization. Its misuse can not only cost a company the trust of its customers but can also lead to legal or financial penalties.

Regulators worldwide uniformly hold that consumers have a right to know that their data is being collected. The European Union's General Data Protection Regulation (GDPR) guidelines require companies serving EU customers to establish clear and transparent consent policies that are easy for consumers to understand, that state how customer data will be used, and that give consumers more control over their data—including the ability to opt out. China, India, Australia, and Singapore have similar requirements. Many US companies have adopted California's guidelines, including the California Consumer Privacy Act (CCPA) of 2018 and California Senate Bill 362 (also known as the Delete Act, passed in 2023), for all of their US customers. That's because customers share their data across states, and it is easier for companies to manage an across-the-board policy nationwide. Apart from giving customers the opportunity to opt out, these rules let customers remove themselves from a database and restrict the overall collection of data on children. Companies also face significant penalties for selling information without permission or insufficiently safeguarding it.

The leading internet browsers are also taking precautions: Apple's Safari blocks third-party cookies by default unless a user gives permission to provide them, and Google Chrome is phasing out third-party cookies, supplanting them with new privacy-preserving, open-standard mechanisms. The use of biometric data—such as facial recognition, eye scans, fingerprints, and even assessments of how people use their mobile phone—is growing, eliciting more calls for safeguards and regulation. Opportunities for consumers to remove themselves from databases and limit the collection, use, and sharing of all this data continue to grow. So does the requirement for companies to continually retrain their algorithms after removing the data.

The risk: Lack of permissioning. The big challenge now is getting customers' permission through the promise of greater value. Without an incentive, only 30 percent of US and Canadian consumers would be willing to share personally identifiable information, such as an email address, according to a 2021 joint BCG/Google study.[4] This share triples to 90 percent when customers are presented with the right value exchange (see figure 10-1). McDonald's, for example, reached forty million app downloads in 2022 by offering free burgers and other promotions.[5]

FIGURE 10-1

Incentivizing data sharing

Share of respondents who would share personal information for each of these incentives (%)

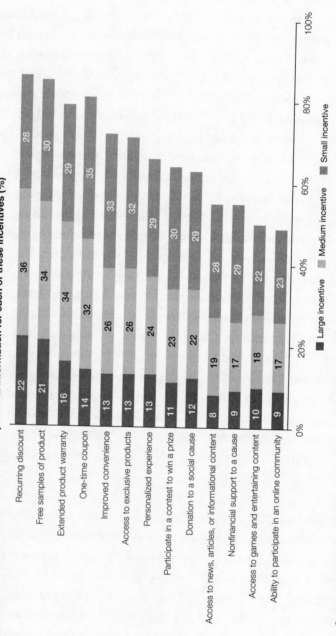

Source: 2021 BCG and Google joint survey on consumer privacy and preferences.

However, as companies learn the behavior of permission-givers, some are realizing that their marketing offers may not be attracting the most desirable segments. Customers who provide email addresses for incentives are most likely to opt out later. Moreover, the offer of greater convenience, exclusive products, and enhanced experiences can be a more-effective, and lower-cost, way to establish long-term customers. For example, findings from a 2023 BCG Customer Personalization Survey show that for wealthy and retired customers, greater convenience is the most compelling non-monetary value exchange. Recall that Lululemon (see the Industry Spotlight: Fashion and Beauty) offers customers emailed receipts, thereby obtaining their email address and permission at checkout. In return, the company allows the customer to return an item simply by providing their email.

A remedy: Design the right ask. The promise of value and the mechanisms by which permission is requested and value promised need to be simple and clear. Write the "ask" in plain language. Be candid about your reasons for collecting data, how the data will be used (and shared), and about the benefits the consumer will enjoy (such as a better experience, the opportunity to participate in incentive programs, advance notice of new promotions, and so on). Something as basic as clear language and tone in a cookie consent form can make a difference. Like any other marketing copy on a website, many options for permissions can be quickly tested. One company we work with saw a 20 percent increase in opt-in rates after testing different consent language, formats, and creative designs with different types of customers to find the right permissions approach.

The risk: Mishandling externally sourced data. Most companies obtain customer data from second- and third-party sources, and not just from direct interactions with consumers. A marketer's data supply can be a complex blend of many different inputs, with different levels of permissions and often varying degrees of accuracy. Data aggregators source from public records, demographic statistical bases, public health data, and other places. Data brokers and marketplaces selling ostensibly permissioned data are growing in number. As we explained in the Industry Spotlight: Retail, retailers now offer their vendors (primarily consumer packaged-goods companies) the opportunity to use data from retailers' media networks—data gathered through retailers' own direct interactions with consumers. More recently, loyalty program "ecosystems"—consortia of companies that ask participating consumers permission to share data—have begun cropping up.

In light of the potential risks, some companies are dramatically reducing or eliminating the use of third-party data sources and increasing the breadth and quality of their first-party data. When one Global 500 food and beverage company decided to phase out third-party cookies, it spent $10 million on the in-house technology and creative development needed to produce contextual advertising for consumers as they browsed. The move paid off: because of the successful interactions the ads inspired, the volume of the company's first-party data increased fivefold in a few years. The company was able to personalize 50 percent of its digital advertising, and per-household sales in key customer segments increased 50 percent to 100 percent.

A remedy: Keep track and simplify. Importantly, companies should tag their files with metadata that indicates which information can be used for what purpose. Some companies are sharing links with their customers so customers can see how their data was obtained and choose whether to edit or remove it. Organization leaders—chief privacy officers, chief data security officers, chief data privacy officers—can develop tools and processes for screening data sources and managing data for appropriate use. Another way to simplify data collection is to reduce the reliance on external sources and expand the use of zero- and first-party data.

The risk: Stranded data across the enterprise. Data assets of multiproduct companies, such as financial services, telecom, health care, and other providers, often burgeon across the many different lines of business or following an acquisition. As enterprises aggregate data at scale, they must reconcile the different levels of permission, the different data configurations, and the disparate processes for maintaining each dataset. Integrating databases is especially challenging. Customer data platform software companies offer a variety of tools to help manage these challenges. But that doesn't obviate companies' obligation to request permission explicitly. And as all of a company's customer data becomes more centralized and more widely tapped, cybersecurity will only become more important.

A remedy: Upgrade your data governance. Appoint a chief privacy officer or elevate your chief data officer to C-suite status to oversee the array of risks—accuracy, transparency, privacy, and security—associated with data collection and management. Working with data stewards across the company, this executive should be responsible for implementing tests and safeguards to determine the provenance of the data, audit its quality, manage access, and ensure mechanisms are in place to fix problems and give consumers appropriate legal rights of control if required in their jurisdiction. This executive should establish audit processes for tracking what data is collected and how it is used, so the company can be more transparent with customers. Most companies have appointed a chief information-security officer to encompass the company's full scope of digital assets and activities, well beyond personalization.

Reach Me (Securely): Targeting Accurately, Ensuring Privacy, and Preventing Bias

Whenever a company sends content out to a customer in an email or mentions personal information via a chatbot, it risks doing so in an insecure, inappropriate, or insufficiently private way. It also risks reaching the wrong person.

The risk: Not reaching the right person. Can a message be intercepted? Is there a risk that a message the recipient wanted to be private could be seen by someone else, even within the same family? Two-factor authentication, an authentication wall, and other established protocols can reduce the risk of exposing messages to the wrong party.

In financial services and, in particular, in health care and health-related services, the regulations surrounding content communication methods are strict. In the latter, for example, anything that might imply a person's health condition cannot be sent in a way that could be seen publicly. Emails can contain only limited information; usually, a link will take the recipient to a password-only, firewalled site. Health insurers approach these requirements with a zero-defect mindset, as any violation would not only jeopardize their reputation but also possibly cost them their license to sell in a given state. The misuse of information can trigger hugely expensive class-action lawsuits.

Other sectors are not nearly as restricted. It's not a problem to send an email to someone who visited your website looking for boots, and to try to lure them back with a targeted offer. However, consumers draw a line (although it varies) beyond which a company's outreach becomes annoying or even creepy: for instance, pushing the boots someone looked at after a few days, since they likely moved on or bought them elsewhere; sending seniors mortuary solicitations; or using information collected when someone uses an app (such as looking up a recipe for nachos) to then overload them with marketing related to their action (leading to a consumer being annoyed by an avalanche of ads for salsa). Because of this, regulation will no doubt continue to increase across industries.

A remedy: Use timely triggers and focus on quality control. The richer your first- and zero-party data, and the more timely it is, and the more balanced it is across the populations you serve, the higher the likelihood that your algorithms will flag the right person for the right outreach. Still, as your messages get more personalized, the likelihood of getting it wrong increases. AI analytics engines are getting better at spotting triggers that indicate someone is in-market, and at identity-matching to ensure continuity of communications with an individual. But these are far from flawless.

Human judgment still plays an important role in deciding what is appropriate. Beware of automated targeting systems with no one monitoring the outgoing messages. Sharp marketers invest in quality-assurance tools and dashboards that make it easy to review all manner of variants—including edge cases—before content goes live. One client who used these QA tools discovered that the algorithms for the company's personalized spend-get offers had set overly high spend hurdles for the most loyal customers; the client was able to avoid a mistake that would have upset its best customers.

The risk: Message bombardment. Perhaps the biggest risk in Reach Me is overwhelming customers with too much outreach—and losing their attention, if not their business, as a result. This is a particular problem for multiline or multiproduct companies whose various marketing teams are targeting many of the same customers. As an example, engagement plummeted for one company's customers who received more than four messages per month. Yet, the company was sending some of them more than twenty each month.

The bombardment problem is especially sticky for retailers who are experimenting with location-based text messages. These are intended to stimulate walk-in traffic when a customer (or prospect) is physically near a store, and then, once in the store, to highlight relevant deals. BCG research shows that location is one of the more-sensitive types of data for customers, although customers' willingness to share it has grown over the past six years, particularly among Gen Z customers.[6]

A remedy: Use orchestration tools and set frequency caps. The right frequency will vary by company and customer, but regular review and analysis are critical. Orchestration tools, backed with robust rules, can help companies prioritize messages among their different product lines and marketing teams, and raise the engagement rate for all. The client that discovered its customers' four messages-a-month threshold solved the drop-off rate by setting up its Salesforce Experience Manager tool with a hierarchy of messages organized by risk to the customer and value to the business. The impact was striking: by reducing the messages fivefold, average engagement doubled.

The risk: Inappropriate targeting. Targeting is an even bigger question. What rules do you use? Personalized marketing in financial services and health care has long been limited due to concerns about bias. Fair lending practices prohibit banks and other financial services organizations from offering different interest rates or offers to customers based on age, race, gender, religion, and other characteristics. Health-care companies cannot target their marketing for many products in such a way that avoids populations with higher health risks.

But the need to manage the many rules governing targeting is growing across sectors, as consumers become increasingly aware of how their data is being used. It's not enough to have some ad hoc guidelines for a privacy team to manage.

A remedy: Create rules engines. More companies are embedding explicit rules engines into their tech architecture. Such engines are built into the core of the algorithms that make triggering recommendations. As the algorithms are used over time, data accumulates on when and how these rules are being used. By extracting this data into a dashboard that analysts can track, you can see how the rules are working and whether the guidelines they represent need to be adjusted.

The risk: AI modeling bias. Algorithms are only as good as the data sets used to build them. Data models trained on limited, skewed samples risk neglecting populations relevant to your market or unfairly discriminating against certain customer segments. For example, companies that seek growth in key age or ethnic segments, but that lack relevant customer data about those segments, are at great risk when training their marketing models solely with data on existing customers' preferences. There's also optimization risk when algorithms meant to drive promotional offers, pricing, or product choice are based on narrow experiences with specific populations, which may result in actually penalizing those populations, considering them to be higher risk or less profitable.

A remedy: Test with underrepresented segments. First, companies should ensure that models are trained on the right data, and that there is a human in the loop. Many chief data officers, working alongside chief diversity officers, are also auditing their data to ensure that they have adequate depth of coverage for the diverse needs of their customer populations. Top marketers also routinely scour their databases to identify any demographic imbalances. Then they craft tests, focused on those populations, to build up their data on those segments' preferences to understand how those populations respond differently to offers and messaging. For example, an insurance company set up an agile pod specifically to run new ideas and marketing tests for different minority groups (e.g., Muslim communities outside Detroit, Brazilians outside Boston, and the growing number of Asian families settling around Atlanta). This enabled the company to gain a better understanding of the proclivities and values of these groups, leading to programs that dramatically increased the insurers' market share.

Show Me: Erroneous, Inappropriate, or Misused Content

The volume and variety of content today is exploding: from social media posts and PR to website material, texts, and emails; from salesperson prompts to customer and product information directed to a call center rep. It's being assembled in many different ways, and goes beyond proactive marketing materials to include interactive experiences such as chatbots, website Q&As, and other tools.

But do you know what your individual customers are actually seeing and experiencing? The risks that content is inaccurate, inappropriate, or misused will only escalate as the use of gen AI grows. Just as marketers need to explicitly manage their data supply chains, so too must they secure their content supply chains. Consider the following questions:

- **Where did the content come from?** Especially if from an AI system, how was it sourced? Do you have permission to use it? Did any of it require usage licenses? Is the source up to date? Is it trustworthy and authoritative (for content that is making claims)? Are you promoting views that come from biased or automated sources?

- **Is the content accurate?** Is it providing the right information to your particular audience?

- **Is it still timely?** How often does each type of content need to be refreshed or screened? When should it be retired?

- **Is it consistent?** Does a landing page match the message and the link that brought the customer there? Is it promoting the same offer the customer received?

- **Is it on-brand?** Were the brand guardrails and voice followed? Does it contain offensive language or images? From the photography to the fonts and language used, content (whether sourced or generated) could confuse customers or, worse, put the brand directly at risk.

We tackled these questions from an operational and cost-efficiency perspective in chapter 6. From a risk management perspective, however, there are additional considerations.

Content is issued by so many areas of a company that it would be impossible to completely centralize it. Many companies are appointing a chief customer experience officer or a content leader to formally manage content-related risks.

The risk: Outdated content. Most companies' websites have tons of buried content that hasn't been screened in years. Consumers could easily stumble upon outdated content, thinking an obsolete product is still available, or they could see incorrect pricing or promotional information or, even worse, access inaccurate advice related to areas like health care. With all the microsites, and with product-specific and geo-specific experiences launched over time, most companies have far more than they realize, and the digital detritus they leave behind is confusing for customers. Our enterprise clients typically discover several hundred such sites and apps floating around, a situation that not only makes it impossible for them to manage their content but that also means they are quite likely competing against themselves in their company's search rankings.

A remedy: Audit digital content. Personalization leaders create rules for when different types of content need to be screened and refreshed and for when they expire. They also launch ongoing initiatives to whittle down the number of sites, shutting them down, consolidating them, or converting them into a templated version within an existing site. One financial services client, for example, reduced its points of presence from more than four hundred to fewer than fifty in just over a year.

The risk: Valuable content locked in inaccessible formats. A significant volume of worthwhile content exists in PDFs and other inflexible formats. Locked content is also problematic when rules change or content otherwise needs updating.

A remedy: Shift to modular, templatized microcontent. Converting content into templatized microcontent allows the individual components to be independently developed, kept up-to-date, and tracked for customer interaction. This way, the same offer gets sent to the same customer, regardless of interaction channel. Most health companies, for instance, have now put their required disclosures and disclaimers into modular pieces that can be easily updated and automatically plugged into relevant content, ensuring that the latest messaging is always available.

The risk: Copyright infringement, inaccuracy. Both of these risks can come at a high cost—legal, financial, and reputational. Inaccurate information can even cause harm to customers.

A remedy: Use AI tools that allow for source transparency, guardrails, and content tracking. In implementing gen AI approaches for content creation, it is critical to design the architecture in a way that provides a clear audit trail for content sources. This should include the type of permissions the company has secured for reuse as well as any applicable restrictions that limit the types of content you would consider using. If you are using a gen AI model to assemble or create new content, you need to tie it to your content management system via "embeddings," so the content it actually generates is assembled safely from your own body of content. (Embeddings are direct plugs-ins that retrieve content assets from outside of a gen AI model's memory, thus enabling source verification.)

The risk: AI content bias. This can include inadvertent stereotyping, acts of omission, or lack of inclusivity in imagery and messaging. The ability of gen AI systems to automatically create content and variations doesn't preclude the need for human oversight. We have all heard about facial recognition software that could not adequately acknowledge people of color, for example. Such bias is especially an issue for companies that rely on algorithms developed by other companies; their marketers don't know the original data set used by their supplier. It is also an issue for companies that want to expand their reach to audiences they have not adequately served in the past; for example, speakers of a non-native language who didn't respond to earlier outreach because of language issues.

A remedy: Keep humans in the content development and usage loops. As we have already noted, personalization leaders embed review checkpoints and leverage quality-assurance tools in their content processes. Teams preemptively assess major chunks of content produced by the AI system and inspect random samples of content prior to publication. Ensuring copy is translated into the full set of languages needed for the intended audiences is key. Another wise tactic is putting employees first on the list to receive content so you can more easily catch it as an added safeguard.

Up-front prevention of mistakes is crucial. Those designing creative material should focus on developing appropriate new content that is tailor-made for new markets even before letting AI optimize that content. Content developers should be especially wary of letting a gen AI system create new concepts from scratch without supervision. A beauty brand found that targeting ads to customers with models that looked like them (in age and in skin or hair type) significantly improved response rates, especially for younger customers and those from ethnic minorities. But AI systems, lacking sufficient examples of ethnically diverse models, could not generate the images they needed without significant prompt engineering.

Delight Me: Constant Learning as New Risks Emerge

To keep delighting customers, companies need to continuously learn from all the concerns they identify and remedies they implement along the way. The bar only keeps rising in all the areas we've covered so far.

A further highly complex area to manage is the configuration of the algorithms that power personalized experiences. These algorithms can have unintended consequences that do the opposite of delighting the customer. Stories abound of people pushing gen AI systems, such as ChatGPT, to extremes and getting back "hallucinations"—bizarre responses, offensive language or images, or responses solidly asserting recommendations that are obviously wrong. No customer would be delighted by a head-spinning interaction.

The risk: Edge cases. Here, an individual's situation (e.g., an outlier problem) or way of interacting with a system (e.g., asking strange, uncommon, or inappropriate questions) leads to inaccurate outcomes. This is a particular problem when AI systems are the intermediary between the customer and the company—where such systems' lack of transparency can be dangerous. Gen AI providers are opening up more ways for corporate users to manage the inputs used by the system and to create rules by which these systems interpret data. Nonetheless, we believe users of gen AI systems will always need to supplement the capabilities of their tools with active, ongoing testing and frequent intervention.

A remedy: Focus on prevention and root-cause analysis. Companies must preempt such problems as much as possible. Part of the solution is engineering the system appropriately; for example, clearly limiting what types of questions a gen AI assistant will answer and providing transparency into where information was sourced from. Implementing preventative measures also helps. A financial services company established a small "red team" to test all of its systems for unusual scenarios. The team culls odd comments from social media and outliers from the company's own customer data analysis (e.g., customers who call customer service repeatedly over minor issues), and then develops new ideas to test or guardrails to help mitigate these scenarios. A telecom company has established a rapid-feedback team that uses data from a natural language processing system called DataOrb to identify uncommon issues that customers are raising in the company's call centers, or that escalate there. The team hunts down the root causes, tests the systems involved to understand why the event occurred, and institutes new capabilities, whether guidelines, new data, or new processes, to prevent a recurrence.

Empower Me: Risks from Sharing Data on the Customer's Behalf

The fundamental goal of personalization is to empower customers to get what they want—better, faster, cheaper, and more easily. This means providing a solution based on the purposeful use of information about them. One obstacle to this goal is the automation that sits between a company and its customer—often clunky, limited, and sometimes inaccurate interfaces that do little more than frustrate the customer. Just think of all the times you've encountered an interactive voice response (IVR) system over the phone that forced you to go through several levels, held you back from getting to a human, and in the end prevented you from accomplishing an action you thought would be rather simple.

The risk: Mismanaging data sharing within the company. Personalization leaders are keenly aware of the IVR problem, and are testing more-advanced AI systems to enhance their capabilities and get customers to the right place faster. But they are also empowering their reps with more customer information. Call center systems providers are adding intelligence to stitch together a customer's journey across all points of contact, sending the resulting information to a rep, together with recommended prompts for handling the customer's call. At the same time, however, in an AI world, the rich detail in the customer's request also becomes data *about* them, and will need appropriate protection.

A remedy: Training and data access safeguards. Because many agents now have access to more customer data than ever, they need to be trained on how to use it appropriately. In addition, companies must carefully manage access to data that is not germane to the discussion and that the customer would regard as private. Companies with reps who work remotely need to implement additional safeguards that keep data secure and that control what customer information shows up on reps' screens.

The risk: Inappropriate data sharing with other companies. Increasingly, empowering customers will mean creating a connection between them and multiple parties behind the scenes: a travel company coordinating air, hotel, and ground travel; an event planner orchestrating catering, furniture rental, and decorations; a home remodeling company coordinating multiple contractors. Apart from the operational and brand risks of any one of these parties not doing the right thing, there are information-flow risks. Who gets customer data, and at what level of detail? Who is tracking the activities of each party to know the parties are coordinating properly? Does the customer have a single point of contact from beginning to end, to be assured that everything is progressing as planned? The Sungevity solar panels story at the beginning of this book showed that personalization can mean using customer information to create a coherent multiparty experience. Sungevity coordinated the panel installer, the lease financier, the power company controlling the electrical grid, and its own customer service team—all available to the consumer through an app, and all orchestrated through a well-designed experience powered by customer data. With gen AI systems able to create code that can better connect databases, including those from multiple parties, companies can make sure that customers get solutions to more-complex goals. And brands will be able to coordinate the response to a customer's prompt, such as: "Here's a snapshot and the dimensions of my front yard, along with ideas about the kinds of plants and landscaping I would like. Show me three yard plans that I would like, the budget for the materials, and the cost of a gardener."

A remedy: Tracking and managing data flows. To make this possible, leading chief data officers are already putting in place the tools to monitor how data is moving through their ecosystems. They are creating APIs to organize how data is communicated, while putting rules in place regarding what can be shared and what operations data needs to be captured, so the ecosystem can track how data is moving across the systems of its many participants.

Extending Corporate Risk Management to the Challenges of Personalization

The long list of potential perils we've outlined here raises the question: Is personalization worth it? The cost of creating the mechanisms to manage these risks is undeniable. We've only begun to figure out how to manage accuracy, privacy, bias, manipulation, and copyright risks at scale. Personalization leaders are already building audit streams into their data files and algorithms to avoid "black boxes," as they see the importance of being able to track down how an outcome occurred. Of course, the risks from personalization and AI more broadly are completely intertwined. While we describe how to manage them from the perspective of pursuing a personalization strategy, many will already be covered if a company takes a holistic approach to managing AI responsibly.

Boards will expect to see risk-monitoring dashboards. And external watchdogs, including lawyers representing legal challenges, will demand them. Public pressure also demands it. So how might corporate risk management operations extend to cover personalization? We've developed a framework based on our experience with several client companies, to manage what we call Responsible Personalization (see figure 10-2). It provides a blueprint for how operating teams and the highest levels of company leadership can work together to manage risk, resolve issues, and protect customer trust. But clarity on roles and responsibilities is not enough. What matters most is embedding into the everyday work of your cross-functional teams an awareness of the risks and an understanding of the prevention tactics shared throughout this chapter. That is just as much a part of the Responsible Personalization agenda.

Guiding risk management priorities: The C-suite and the board. Responsible Personalization starts at the top, with the CEO and the board recognizing the primacy of earning customers' trust so that customers grant you stewardship and use of their information. (See the sidebar "Five Questions for Your Next Board or Corporate Leadership Meeting.") The reputational risks alone are high, and as we've noted, companies face a number of financial and legal risks, as well. Putting customer trust high on the C-suite's list of priorities means giving a C-level officer or team the charter, budget, and seat at the executive table to put appropriate safeguards and processes in place, especially setting up an ethics and risk committee, consisting of the chief data officer, a privacy officer, and an information security officer. It's rare that all or any of them would report directly to the CEO, but at least some would be positioned under a top leader who oversees data, digital, security, and privacy.

FIGURE 10-2

An organizational model for Responsible Personalization

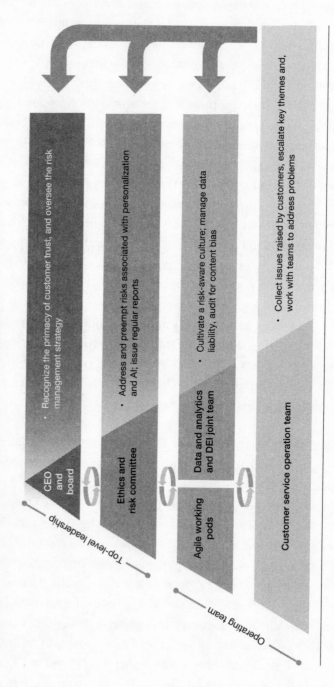

Top-level leadership

- **CEO and board** — Recognize the primacy of customer trust, and oversee the risk management strategy

- **Ethics and risk committee** — Address and preempt risks associated with personalization and AI; issue regular reports

Operating team

- **Agile working pods / Data and analytics and DEI joint team** — Cultivate a risk-aware culture; manage data liability, audit for content bias

- **Customer service operation team** — Collect issues raised by customers, escalate key themes and, work with teams to address problems

Five Questions for Your Next Board or Corporate Leadership Meeting

1. Looking at our personalization strategy, how will we prioritize the risks from customer data, targeting, content, operations, and especially new uses of AI?

2. Can our current corporate risk management processes be adapted to cover personalization? Or do we need to extend them, add resources, and establish new guidelines?

3. Which metrics can we establish in a dashboard to track operations, bias, and security on as near a real-time basis as possible?

4. If we add new elements or approaches to our personalization program, do we have in place a rigorous method for assessing any new risks we may be incurring?

5. What external parties can we look to for ongoing ideas, warnings, remedies, and possibly talent to keep vigilant about risks we need to address?

Boards should refine the agenda of the risk management committee to address all of the risks involved with personalization and AI and issue a regular report from the C-suite executive in charge. Companies will need dashboards (shareable with the board) on such metrics as permission coverage, opt outs, open rates, and the outcomes of ongoing audits. Overall risk management will likely also include being affiliated with a broader group of industry leaders who regularly share their experiences, incident responses, learnings from specific vendors, and efforts to improve data transparency. Teams, working under the chief data officer or the chief customer officer, will need to constantly test personalization engines with atypical use cases, seeding employee names into databases to learn what they experience, and develop rapid-response protocols for scenarios involving sudden challenges.

One powerful means of ensuring diverse perspectives is setting up a multidisciplinary committee to help steer the overall personalization program and resolve complex ethical issues, such as bias and unintended consequences. The committee should include representatives from various business functions (business units, public relations, legal, compliance, and the AI team) and from different regions and backgrounds. BCG research confirms that increasing diversity on leadership teams leads to more and better innovation and improved financial performance.[7] We believe the same holds true for personalization and AI oversight teams. Navigating the complex issues that will inevitably arise as companies deploy AI systems and implement personalization at scale requires equally diverse leadership.

The customer service–C-suite loop. Beneath these top-level structures, leaders build a feedback loop from customer service operations to all of the C-suite leaders associated with personalization. This ensures that issues raised by customers get to the teams assigned to address the underlying problems so those teams can test solutions, and use that as fodder for devising scenarios of new challenges that could arise. Given the risks from using third-party tools and data, personalization leaders engage their own procurement teams to set contractual parameters for managing liability. For example, these teams help them define appropriately permissioned data and set procedures for content acquisition. They also review risks from outside algorithms the company licenses. Chief data officers and chief diversity officers set up joint teams to audit data and content systems for potentially inappropriate biases and for offensive content. And perhaps most importantly, they nurture a risk-aware culture on the agile working pods through training, rules, and managed protocols. Such protocols would limit access to customer data where not needed and prohibit inappropriate data sharing or any uses of customer data that could violate the trust implied when a customer grants permission.

The AI and other tools that power today's personalization engines are the fastest-growing class of applications ever. Their accuracy will improve as the pool of tapped data increases and as parallel AI systems, along with humans in the loop, work to find and remedy biases and "hallucinations." This progress will pull many established brands into creating new AI-forward operating models to manage more-personalized customer interactions. But as AI and customer data management open up a whole new level of opportunity between companies and customers, companies need to rigorously implement guidelines and controls to manage the privacy, security, and appropriateness required to build and maintain customer trust.

Chapter 11

Competing on Personalization

Throughout these pages, we have demonstrated the quantitative link between personalization and customer satisfaction, growth, and value creation. We have presented examples of how companies are finally achieving the kind of personalization that so many have only aspired to. We have also examined how, by fulfilling the Five Promises of Personalization, companies across the industry spectrum can compete on personalization. But as the BCG Personalization Index shows, too few companies are pursuing personalization with the necessary commitment and urgency. And the bar keeps rising. Even the leaders have considerably more work ahead of them.

In this chapter, we offer four pragmatic steps any organization can take right away to accelerate its personalization efforts.

Clarify Your Objective

Your personalization goal should always be framed from the customer's point of view. As we've said from the start, personalization should empower customers in the most critical steps of their journey. In order to define the overall ambition, you have to do some foundational work.

Most organizations have no shortage of ideas about how to use personalization to give customers more of what they want. If anything, companies tend to have too many ideas, with no process to prioritize and coordinate them. As a first step, dig into your data and understand which customer journeys lead them up the Engagement Ladder (as described in chapter 9) to become loyal fans.

How to set your company's personalization ambition

In a half-day workshop with twenty to thirty experts from across the organization, you can readily articulate your company's personalization objective. Include professionals from marketing, operations, product areas, digital experience and technology, data and analytics, and customer service. In preparation, collect use case ideas, determine what analysis has already been done about unmet consumer needs, and gauge the size of the personalization prize. Share a common set of consumer insights with participants, including a view of your Engagement Ladder.

During the session, inspire the group with examples of personalization leaders' efforts and the latest thinking on the topic. Conduct interactive exercises using both the foundational work your teams have already done and ideas raised in the group discussion. For example:

- **Define your organizational goal.** Ask "How far do we want to go to fulfill each of the Five Promises of Personalization?" Discuss what it would take to be best in class in your industry or across industries and whether that should be the ambition. Strive for a consensus.

- **Brainstorm use cases.** Have the group ideate additional use cases. Develop an exhaustive inventory of the big ideas, grouped into themes corresponding to the stages of the customer journey: for example, "personalized clienteling" or "personalized offers" for use cases at the conversion stage.

- **Prioritize use cases.** Organize the use cases based on value and feasibility, using an interactive online tool (such as a Miro whiteboard). Aim to have a first-pass list that can later be refined offline by a working team.

- **Create a rallying cry.** Define the ultimate goal of personalization with a short statement. Examples include "become the most personalized brand in the world" (a large retailer), "create the right offers for every customer" (a major grocer), "make health care . . . all about you" (a large health insurer). Beyond the long-term ambition, consider what would constitute a realistic leap forward to aim for over the next twelve to eighteen months. Maybe scaling a subset of personalized experiences that could transform the customer experience? Applying personalization to generate massive value in one or two channels that could fund your next-stage personalization investments? At this stage, don't let feasibility limit you; challenge everyone to imagine what it would take to leapfrog your competitors.

While setting a clear vision is important to scaling personalization, it is not a prerequisite to getting started. We firmly believe that interacting with customers is still the best way to understand what they want. Traditional consumer research and surveys are useful, but rapidly testing minimum viable use cases will give you direct, actionable consumer input. It will also give everyone in the organization a clearer idea both of what it takes to deliver personalization at scale and of which enablers need to be strengthened (more on this below). Personalization entails considerable organizational complexity, so trying to perfect the strategy before testing it with customers will only bog down your effort with endless cycles of alignment. Of the hundreds of personalization efforts we've guided, the most successful ones were those that we started by challenging a small team to launch a new personalized experience within a few months, even before convening the ambition-setting workshop we describe above. This created tangible early wins and learnings to talk about as we set the strategy.

Secure Your Personalization Foundation

While you are formulating a clear ambition, it's important to evaluate your existing foundation—the state of your data platform, automated systems, and people capabilities—and your ability to deliver on each of the Promises of Personalization. The assessment criteria we discussed in chapter 1 for the Personalization Index provide a handy guide for this review (see table 11-1).

Competing effectively on personalization also requires formulating a strategy that lets you leapfrog competitors. Here it's worth referencing the

TABLE 11-1

Assessment criteria for your personalization foundation

Empower Me	Know Me	Reach Me	Show Me	Delight Me
• Level of personalization by channel and step in the customer journey • Personalization efforts focused on the most important channels/journey steps • Overall impact of personalization on customer experience	• Number and depth of digital customer relationships • Retention and growth in digital customer relationships • Integrated 360-degree view of each customer and quality of data	• Data is used to target each customer based on their needs • Experiments designed at scale using automation • Next best action orchestration across channels, sequence of messages, timing	• Ability to create content that speaks to each customer at scale • Ability to rapidly launch personalized experiences • Sophistication of content management capabilities	• Ability to run rapid test-and-learn process at scale, with iteration cycles measured in days • Clear, rapid measurement with actionable KPIs • Personalization has clear ownership and committed funding • Cross-functional teams work in agile ways

"experience curve," one of BCG's most seminal business concepts, developed by founder Bruce Henderson nearly sixty years ago.[1] The experience curve showed how the act of producing more and more of a good would, over time, lead to smarter ways of producing that good and build simple economies of scale. By accelerating the volume of production, a company's costs would fall, theoretically faster than those of its competitors. The concept is predicated on a strategy of taking risks to secure a greater volume of sales—even at prices lower than profitable at the start—in order to win the race to a competitively lower cost position.

In our era, growth at the expense of profitability—growing the customer base and data assets faster than your competitors can—has long been the chief tenet of information-based businesses. Unfortunately, being the fastest-growing new brand doesn't automatically confer advantage, as many businesses have learned the hard way.

However, by applying the principles of the experience curve to the promises of Know Me, Reach Me, and Show Me in businesses where value can legitimately spring from ongoing, personalized customer relationships, you can indeed create competitive advantage. With more-direct customer relationships, you can glean insights to make smarter decisions about new-product innovation, inventory allocation, and marketing investments. With more interactions with those customers, and more owned channels through which to reach them, you'll increase your ability to anticipate their next purchase and capture a higher share of their category spend. And with more-personalized content, you have more ways to inspire customers, make recommendations, and move customers along the journey, ultimately expanding the category itself by unlocking new customer "occasions" that spur sales growth.

Personalization leaders understand the value of speed in pursuing personalization. They are hurrying to amass more and more interactions with customers in their category, and not just during the transaction, but throughout the customer journey. They know that every such interaction begets new insights on personalizing the next interactions for millions of other customers—and doing so better than the competition can. Personalization leaders in long-purchase-cycle industries are gathering engagement data at every point of the customer journey to learn about purchase intent and likelihood to convert, which financing options are appealing, channel preferences, maintenance events, and of course, customer satisfaction. Industries with multiyear purchase cycles, such as automotive and insurance, are finding ways to instrument the customer journey with a plethora of touchpoints that create signals for personalization. The resulting knowledge they are accumulating about customers is creating a hard-to-replicate competitive advantage for these companies. In contrast, fast-moving consumer goods companies, with fewer direct consumer interactions, are finding it much harder to build up such data arsenals.

In order to understand their relative standing in this race, executives must assess the people, data, and technology capabilities needed for carrying out the Five Promises of Personalization. They will then be able to establish priorities and develop plans and budgets that support their ambition.

How do you assess your personalization foundation?

Start by ranking your company on the Personalization Index. You can generate a high-level qualitative view by assessing each of the criteria listed in table 11-1, or by taking the Index survey, available at www.personalizedthe book.com. Review the results with a cross-functional team, examining the key areas in play: data, tech, content, marketing, operations, and so forth. Conduct interactive exercises. For example:

- **Explore capability gaps.** Identify the major gaps, in particular those that must be addressed in order to deliver the most promising use cases. Discuss what is needed to close them.

- **Evaluate current plans and budgets.** Most large companies are not starting from scratch. They have existing plans, if not initiatives under way, to close capability gaps. Review your current initiatives and their budgets and identify what to start, stop, and add in those plans to accelerate your progress.

- **Develop a personalization road map.** Prioritize the key activities involved in launching use cases and building the personalization foundation. Iterate on and refine this first-pass view with a working team.

Cultivate Agility to Compete with Speed

As we've been saying, competing on personalization is all about speed. If you cannot run hundreds of experiments with the push of a button, you are falling behind. We've talked repeatedly about the need for agile processes and automated tools that enable companies to continuously ideate, test, capture feedback, hone their intelligence, and strive for ever-increasing granularity and prediction accuracy over time. But it is not just the organizational and technology enablers that make this happen. Agile is as much about mindset as it is about process and tools.

An ingenious way to think about it was laid out many years ago by John Clarkeson, then CEO of BCG, in his classical-versus-jazz music analogy. Clarkeson wrote:

> In the world of classical music, the symphony is regarded by many as its most complex creation, requiring the integration of a large assembly of highly talented individuals for its performance. Some

suggest that CEOs need to resemble the great conductors. But there is one major flaw in this analogy: no one gives a CEO the music he should play.

The recent history of American music suggests another possible answer. Duke Ellington was not an unusually gifted individual or musical theorist. It is disputed how well he could read musical notation. But he created an astounding number of original compositions and many would regard him as a dominant figure in twentieth century music. How is his prodigious creativity to be explained? From people who worked with him it appears he learned how to forge the divergent personalities of his jazz group into a single, highly creative instrument. Members of his band have described how he learned to create on the run: he would offer up a scrap of an idea, suggest in general what he wanted, and then rely on his players to take cues from each other and to fill in their parts as they thought best.

His players were good but not without equal. He knew their quirks, their gifts, their problems, and he encouraged them to learn to do things they didn't think they could do. Some players came and went, but many stayed for years. They developed through their membership in the group, and they learned from each other. Most of all, their capacity for innovation grew as they built on their cumulative experience. Finally, by performing live in the close atmosphere of a jazz club, audience reaction was immediately visible to all, and refinement of new ideas came fast. On piano, Ellington was in the middle of the process, and communication was instantaneous. The results were astonishing.

The winning organization of the future will look more like a collection of jazz ensembles than a symphony orchestra. Functional barriers will be reduced. Different specialties will work in more permanent teams around specific customer opportunities. Customer contact will be continuous. Information will be current, rich, and available to all.[2]

Sound familiar? We think this analogy is a perfect way to view the role of the CEO, or any team leader, in fostering the agile culture so essential to personalization.

Challenge your teams to learn ten times faster

In most organizations today, the pace of learning and the sense of urgency about learning fast are simply inadequate. Get the doers in the room—for example, everyone involved in executing your last personalized marketing campaign. Mapping what it takes to run a personalization experiment is a powerful exercise that can help you find ways to exponentially increase the pace of learning.

- **Sketch out the steps and handoffs.** Delineate what's involved in creating, launching, measuring, and adjusting a personalized marketing campaign, a new personalized digital experience on the website or in the app, or a new customer service process with personalization embedded.

- **Talk through each step of the current process.** Take stock of the manual processes you still rely on, which may involve many handoffs. Figure out how long your learning cycle is; for many organizations, it can be anywhere from eight to sixteen weeks.

- **Assemble a cross-functional team and challenge them to reduce the end-to-end cycle time.** Review every step of the current process and ask: Can it be removed, automated, or simplified? Look at every handoff point and discuss what it would take to eliminate it. Estimate the time saved from each of these changes. By cutting the cycle time down to three to five days, a company can run hundreds of tests in the same amount of time it takes the average organization to run a dozen.

The list that results from this interactive exercise will not only inform your personalization road map but can also show the art of the possible—and galvanize your execution teams to change.

Embed Personalization in Your Corporate Development Agenda

Dozens of major companies have explicitly made personalization a top strategic goal, including the likes of Kroger, Starbucks, and Alibaba. Some companies are also making personalization a key impetus of their corporate development agenda. From its purchase of TurboTax (in 1993) to its acquisition of Mailchimp, the marketing-automation and email platform (in 2021), Intuit's corporate strategy has reflected the company's pursuit of personalization as a means of growing with its customers, as well as helping them grow.

Indeed, over the past decade, there has been a growing wave of corporate development activity among leading companies in which personalization figured prominently in their strategy as an industry-shaping move. One example is CVS's acquisitions since 2018, which include Aetna, the health insurer; Signify Health, a home-health-care provider; and Oak Street Health, a primary care provider. Through these acquisitions, CVS has expanded the base of its customer relationships (especially in the Medicare space), learned more about those customers' needs from the broader range of services it offers, and is setting the stage to manage more of those customers' health needs. Starbucks's partnership with Alibaba in China to launch personalization and digital capabilities in its mobile app is yet another example of personalization's growing importance in corporate development strategies.[3]

How do you elevate personalization as a pillar of your corporate strategy?

First, take the steps we already described in previous chapters to ensure that personalization becomes an enterprise-wide initiative:

- **Choose the right leader** to own the end-to-end personalization agenda.

- **Challenge leaders throughout the organization** to devise ways to embed personalization initiatives as priorities across key functional areas, including operations, product areas and lines of business, and customer service.

- **Set shared goals and align on targets (and embed them across functions),** including sales lift, customer lifetime value, overall customer satisfaction, the number of digital customer relationships, and customer engagement, as well as specific KPIs that the relevant leaders can rally around.

Next, think beyond the present, and beyond your corporate boundaries. Consider the following:

- Is personalization high enough on your corporate strategic agenda?

- What if you took a different tack to fast-track your personalization program? You could try partnerships, mergers and acquisitions, or ecosystem plays, such as data sharing and connected loyalty programs, where you build loyalty experiences that cut across companies (e.g., Delta and Starbucks's connected loyalty program)?

- What game-changing moves are possible for your company—and the industry as a whole? How likely is it that any of these will become a reality in the next three to five years, and thus warrant scenario-planning within your current corporate strategy process?

- Finally, what are the implications for your primary and home markets? Your international and secondary markets? Given the technology and people costs, whatever you choose to build in your largest markets may be better accomplished through partnerships or vendor relationships in those markets.

Now that we have shared with you what "good" looks like in personalization and armed you with practical to-dos, we want to leave you with an impassioned plea as you begin to bring—or continue to bring—personalization to life in your company.

Take a day to immerse yourself in your own customers' experience. What does your typical customer experience online, in your store/branch/office, or when they call your call center? Could you make the experience more personalized in order to make it more convenient, faster, of better value, or more helpful for customers?

In your quest for speed, do not settle for mediocrity or expedience. Given the complexity of personalization and the high stakes involved, rally the organization around a common goal with urgency. Create scale by growing the number of digital customer relationships and the volume of interactions with customers. Train your teams to seize the challenge to "learn ten times faster." That is how personalization becomes a true source of competitive advantage.

As we argued in our chapter on risk, consumers are increasingly noticing the effects of personalization gone wrong and are voting with their wallets, while regulators tighten rules and leading companies raise the bar for Responsible Personalization. Never step out of the customer's shoes or forget their mindset. Relive their journey with your teams. Continue challenging your company to find more and better ways to empower the customer. And then use all that to prioritize the investments needed to know your customers, to reach them, show them, and delight them—more and more, in ever-better ways. That is what the personalization leaders of tomorrow are doing today.

Chapter 12

Personalization of the Future

What might personalization look like in the coming years? Consider your future family vacation.

On departure day, your rideshare app syncs with your personal calendar and traffic data to suggest when to schedule your ride to the airport. It recommends when to pick you up, based on your location, traffic data, and your gate location. Coffee and breakfast sandwiches await you in the car—your favorites, recommended by the restaurant's app (which recognizes that you are traveling) and ordered with one click. The car drops off your barcoded baggage at a specially designated area of the terminal so you don't have to hassle with bag check. You made all of these steps happen through the airline app in which you've linked the loyalty programs of these other providers. Your family breezes through security in a contact-less manner and boards without your ever needing to take out your phone, thanks to the biometric data you provided the airline. When your flight is delayed and it's clear you won't make your connection, you receive an automated text informing you that you've been rebooked. Along with the text are scannable coupons for food in the airport, so you don't have to wander around searching for a place to eat when you land. The text also assures you that your bags will arrive with you.

Upon arrival, your EV rental car's sound system syncs with your music streaming account. The directions to your hotel are preloaded in the car's GPS system, and as you drive off, the music from your vacation playlist kicks in. On the way to your hotel, a quick-serve restaurant app pops up, identifying you and your family as loyal customers who will be passing by one of their stores in thirty minutes. The app recommends a healthful and convenient lunch option the whole family will enjoy. Once at the hotel, you bypass the front desk and head straight to your room, where you discover an AI-powered portal, accessible on the TV and your mobile devices, that's tailored to your family's preferences. With it, you can make reservations for local attractions and restaurants, access loyalty program perks, see reviews from families like yours, and get an itinerary that feeds back into the car's GPS system to make navigation seamless. The portal's recommendations are so helpful you don't even realize that some of them are ads paid for by local businesses.

Personalization has taken the fuss and stress out of your trip, so the vacation you and your family are actually having is even better than the one you dreamed of.

Such a scenario is close to being a reality: the experiences described here are either already happening or are being tested or developed by well-known companies and some partnerships. With gen AI, it will become easier for customers to navigate experiences across companies. Companies themselves are finding ways to share data in a secure, permissioned way; for example, by making it easy for customers to link loyalty programs.

Over the next several years, the differences between the personalization "haves" and the "have nots," already apparent in our Personalization Index, will grow only more pronounced as leaders expand the volume of their high-quality personalized interactions. The "haves" are today's personalization leaders, companies that have firmly established digital customer relationships and adopted some of the requisite AI capabilities. Yet, there is no guarantee that all of them will maintain their leadership position. Indeed, even as some of the leaders pull farther ahead, we expect significant changes in the rankings, thanks to three powerful trends that are enabling companies to leapfrog their competitors: speed, as cycle times and processes accelerate; AI's continued evolution; and the rise of ecosystems and the end-to-end solutions they make possible.

We believe these trends are not just here to stay. They are actual game changers. Already they are starting to reshape business strategies, alter the balance of power between consumers and companies, and hasten the spread of personalization throughout the economy.

Speed as advantage

Competing on personalization, as we noted in chapter 1, boils down to competing on speed. As leaders build scale in the volume of engagement touchpoints and gather learnings even faster, the size of their competitive advantage derived from personalization will grow. Some companies are already able to run hundreds of simultaneous experiments involving millions of customers, extract the insights in days, and incorporate them into the next round of interactions. Many of those companies, however, are going about this haphazardly. They may have adopted agile ways of working, but they haven't invested adequately in automation, so they are essentially throwing headcount at the problem. Or else they've built great systems, but can't fully leverage them because functional silos get in the way.

In the near future, more companies will be combining smart integration and automation with new ways of working. This will further compress cycle times. The next generation of leaders in digital, marketing, data and analytics, tech, and operations will have grown up operating in agile pods, accustomed to collaborating across functional silos. The personalization leaders of the future will continue to shrink the test-and-learn timelines to hours and grow the number of monthly experiments to thousands, and they will do so with a fraction of the effort required today.

Customer relationships will be increasingly managed on the basis of customer triggers rather than through campaigns. Millions of tailored interactions will be happening simultaneously. In parallel, companies will constantly be running complex multivariate tests. Small, cross-functional teams will become the norm—to enhance data, uncover new insights, design innovative experiences, develop the atomic content for real-time assembly for each interaction, set up the rules and tests for interactions, oversee the AI engines powering personalization, and embed the necessary safeguards and compliance filters that keep a company out of trouble. Teams will be incentivized on how much and how fast they are learning as well as on their results—yet another motivation to slash testing cycles from weeks to days to hours.

The need for speed will also mainstream two important organizational changes we have advocated in this book. For one, companies that haven't already done so will designate a senior leader for personalization. This executive will set the priorities and road map based on customer needs, not on the needs of the individual business units or functions. Companies will establish clusters of agile pods, each focused on a customer segment or use case. Over time, companies will regularly reevaluate both their pod structure—the personnel, assignments, capacity, coordination, and resources—and how to raise their game through new capabilities. In addition, functional groups will act as centers of excellence that serve as affiliations for pod members. Functional leaders will be responsible for hiring, evaluating, and training and for augmenting the core capabilities of pod members with skills such as personalized creative development, gen AI, data engineering, and technology.

AI with a heart?

While the evolution of AI presents new risks (as we describe later in this chapter), it also presents tremendous opportunity. As traditional machine learning approaches mature and gen AI solutions are fully scaled, personalization will evolve to individualization, where every piece of content and every action is tailored in real time to the individual customer, and no two customers are likely to receive the exact same experience. Advanced AI capabilities will allow companies to automate experimentation at gargantuan volumes and to continuously hone their predictive models, freeing companies from relying solely on historically based propensity models. Gen AI will continue to enhance traditional machine learning techniques with powerful large-language models (those trained on vast amounts of data to enable effective two-way dialogue), streamlining the customer's experience and enabling companies to generate exponentially more content better suited to each customer's context. As manual tasks are automated away, human-centered designers can focus on setting the right guardrails within which machine learning can optimize, as well as on the right prompts for gen AI. We don't claim that they will get it perfectly right at first: inaccuracies and biases will persist (and there is a very real risk of content overload if guardrails are not set well), but we believe that customers will nevertheless feel significant improvements in their experience and that they will reward companies that get it right.

What, specifically, does this mean?

Content creation accelerates, regulatory scrutiny grows. With gen AI, component creation—the many variations of a call to action—will explode in volume and speed, and will grow far more precise. When combined with machine learning, gen AI will serve up just the right content from a massively expanded pool to just the right customer. Personalized social media campaigns will be launched in minutes instead of days. Messages will be translated into multiple languages and adapted to new segments in a heartbeat, although humans will still need to check that they are appropriate and that they make sense for each new population (a process that will be done with the help of easy-to-use tools).

We also expect an enormous leap in content delivery productivity over the next several years. Gen AI solutions specifically designed for rapid content creation (such as Jasper and Cohere) will turbocharge the test-and-learn programs of companies that have built robust content libraries with modular, tagged content. Designs that were once prohibitively expensive for companies with smaller budgets—for instance, movie-set animations, the same character placed in myriad different backdrops, inanimate objects brought convincingly to life—will be feasible at scale. Computer-generated imagery software will become more affordable, and the speed of production will foster even more experimentation, as designers can test many more variations.

Meanwhile, as gen AI becomes more embedded in digital interactions, regulators will be watching its evolution more closely. Copyright infringement claims will grow, and some companies will suffer reputational damage from their missteps. In both the public and private sectors, significant efforts will be directed toward understanding and protecting against gen AI bias.

Machine learning leaps forward. Creating all this content will require the more widespread use of machine learning techniques, along with thoughtful design principles, to ensure relevancy for the customer. Predictive models and machine learning will be more deeply embedded in targeted pricing, contextual search, recommendations, and assistive capabilities (such as home energy management, meal planning, and extended-family calendar management). Interfaces in "smart tools" will make it easy for consumers to access helper bots: by providing the bots more information, consumers will help the bots help them find what they need. Meanwhile, AI-enabled automated content tagging solutions will help marketers organize the vast amount of content they already have so it can be more easily discovered by consumers who are looking for something specific.

Recommendation engines will become significantly more accurate. Machine learning, in combination with gen AI, will produce better information for customers seeking to manage more-complex planning, such as their educational course load, health treatment plan, or travel itinerary. Between the data accumulating from ongoing interactions, and the ability to access broader pools of data from connected partners, algorithms will have massive data sets to draw from. These can be combined with even more (zero-party) feedback from individuals about their activities or goals. For example, a spur-of-the-moment traveler who prefers spontaneity on long weekend trips to new cities could get a daily text message with ideas for dinner, sightseeing, and off-the-beaten-track attractions for their next trip. The AI can be designed to improve over time by asking for and incorporating feedback (a capability known as reinforcement learning from human feedback).

At the same time, we can expect missteps, as companies rush new solutions to market and biases creep into their recommendations as a result of imperfect data sets used to train the systems. AI biases in facial recognition of gender and race are well documented, and more types of bias will emerge. This, in turn, will spark a wave of consumer concerns, and inevitably more regulation.

The customer gets more empowered. We talked about gen AI's ability to produce personalized content to an unprecedented degree. But as we've noted, its power also lies in its ability to generate code. As they expand their use of gen AI, companies will be able to tailor every aspect of a digital interaction to the customer's preferred flow, rather than requiring them to navigate more menus and feature choices on apps and websites. Drawing on the customer's real-time data feed and everything the AI already knows about their context, the software becomes personalized, facilitating a shortcut that takes the user from command directly to tailored action in milliseconds.

Forerunners of this capability include Expedia's integration of OpenAI into its website to enable more-complex travel planning; Adobe's Photoshop, with its more-complex editing features, such as finding and removing a construction crane from a cityscape with a simple text command instead of multiple clicks; and OpenTable's ability to allow users to find a restaurant and make dinner reservations via chat. Companies will need a tech architecture that enables gen AI to pull facts from a database while making sure precision, not just general accuracy, is a critical priority; for example, identifying restaurants within a ten-minute drive in heavy traffic that offer vegan and gluten-free menu items and have openings tonight at 7:00 p.m. for five people.

Inspired by examples like these, companies will increasingly provide proprietary tools that tap into their content and data and enable customers to simply ask for what they want. Mistakes will be made along the way, both by the AI and the human designers of the experience, but the trend will endure. Personalization leaders will not question whether AI and gen AI should be deployed, but rather how best to use them safely to most empower the customer. As we observed in chapter 10, many personalization leaders will embed Responsible Personalization principles in their teams' daily work approach to preserve customer trust.

The rise of personalized ecosystems

Personalization leaders recognize that their company may not be able to fulfill the customer's end-to-end need, but that they can own the customer relationship if they act as a gateway to integrated solutions, offered via partnerships and smart digital tools. With connected loyalty and blockchain technology, companies can build ecosystem solutions without giving up control of their digital customer relationships. Within this decade, we foresee ecosystems emerging in more markets around many more of consumers' key needs.

Airlines, hotels, rental car companies, rideshare companies, and connected-car manufacturers will offer connected experiences around travel. Banks, payment providers, and merchants will collaborate to provide easy, rewarding shopping and checkout experiences. Health-care providers, physicians, wellness apps, and insurers will collaborate in order to provide patients with better health outcomes. Loyalty-based ecosystems will attempt to form even broader coalitions spanning everything from travel and fashion to grocery and credit cards.

Ecosystems will get "smarter" as the number of customer signals grows exponentially. Wearables will become more widespread and be able to collect even more insightful data on things like a person's health. Near-field communication—wireless personal-area-network technology that lets phones and other devices in close proximity connect with each other to transfer data—will become more prevalent and more powerful, as it already is in many Asian countries. Such targetable access provides endless opportunities for interaction where permissioned user data is available and where the media can selectively deliver different messages at the right time to different people. In retail environments, for example, shoppers themselves, using an accumulation of tokens, can actively share information about themselves that they want the store to have. The retailer can share this information with a store salesperson, or simply use it to send the shopper texts with discount offers, paid for by one of the brands the retailer sells. The physical store will thus become yet another fully addressable media environment for marketers. While much of this practice is already under way today, it will become more enhanced and widely adopted.

Now, let's consider how these game changers will reshape the overall landscape, looking first at what is less likely to happen and then at developments we can more confidently predict.

Doubtful Scenarios

Many prognosticators tout three personalization scenarios that we believe are overhyped and unlikely to transpire.

"Precision targeting will stanch the flood of marketing messaging"

There's no question that massive volumes of customer data, together with continuously improving orchestrating technologies, will lead to more-relevant marketing outreach. But the very ability to create these messages at exponentially greater volumes and speeds makes consumer bombardment inevitable. Consumers will be even more awash in content: from all of the testing, from companies' cross-channel messaging hitting them from multiple angles, and from content transmitted in the many more addressable interfaces that will surround us. And because interaction data, such as behavioral data, is even more valuable than simple customer profile data, marketers will be incentivized to push for more interactions so they can run more tests. Consumers will be overwhelmed. Channels will get "burned," as customers delete apps and unsubscribe en masse from email and text notifications. In a world of increasing overload, the premium for true relevance will go up, as useful interactions stand out.

So how can you be heard amidst the cacophony? The brands that will get noticed will have set up a permissioned exchange of information with consumers, a transparent request for data that gets translated into useful offers or services that the consumer recognizes, or into content that fits the user's expectations. We've described these various steps throughout this book; in the future, companies will need to abide by them relentlessly in order to maintain trust and uphold standards.

"Consumers will control much of their data"

Many believe that the heightened awareness of data collection and use, and the growing prospect of regulation, will mean that consumers will gain greater control of their personal data. Not likely, we say. Permissions will remain sufficiently broad to preclude this. Only a minority of consumers will be rigorous about who they grant permission to, and few companies are making it consistently easy for consumers to understand how they can take more control.

We predict that the major platform players, such as Apple and Google, along with specialty startups, will extend the capabilities of their existing "wallets" to let consumers store all of the codes for their blockchain tokens, and other personal information (such as sensitive health data). With such tools, consumers could selectively grant data access to certain brands, possibly in exchange for a better deal or special service.

Nonetheless, considering the thousands of marketers, information services, and data brokers that have already accumulated substantial volumes of information on individuals, it is unlikely that those wallets will be able to gather the totality of an individual's data that is spread across the digital landscape. Data collection and exchange is far too decentralized, and the economic incentives for businesses to hoard and use data are too great to allow for a significant rebalancing of data ownership.

But the pressure will still be high for marketers to be transparent and to offer consumers more control over the data the individual marketers already have and how it is used. Marketers will need to remind customers routinely about the data they have and offer opportunities for updating, removing, or managing permissions.

"All customers will benefit from personalization"

Many people believe that the sheer awareness of the potential for bias in AI datasets will ensure that all consumers always benefit from personalization. Indeed, marketers will try to mitigate the problem by amassing broader data pools. But even if they achieve a more-balanced view, companies will still optimize for business outcomes. And because different customers hold different value to a company, and the costs to engage them differ, business strategies will inherently be biased toward segments that represent the greatest upside.

Already, companies offer different prices and promotions to different individual customers, based on their buying behavior, price sensitivity, and other variables considered predictors of lifetime value. As companies shift their marketing spend away from mass promotions, there will inevitably be more discounts for some and fewer for others. Already, those who have an app, are members of a loyalty program, or engage more digitally are getting offers that others are not. We believe this practice will proliferate, as personalized offers in stores, on travel sites, in restaurants, and on e-commerce sites become the norm. It will produce winners and losers among customers. Savvy companies will need to build in safeguards to ensure this is done in a way that is consistent with their brand. For example, some large mass retailers today are prioritizing personalized offers with deeper discounts to highly price-sensitive, lower-income households that show a propensity to become more-loyal customers.

Companies should also challenge whether their sense of a customer's value is based on limited data, limited experimentation, or preconceived notions. As noted earlier, leaders are always trying new ways to learn about populations that may not be in their core.

Prepare for the Likely Scenarios

Now, let's explore three pivotal actions companies should prepare to take, based on trends we see unfolding.

Position to play in the data exchanges

Consumers will use some form of "data wallet" to accumulate and share their own information about their purchases, profiles, and interests. These wallets, moreover, won't be offered only by the likes of Apple, Google, and others that dominate the transaction infrastructure; big banks, credit card companies, and platform retailers will also probably get in on the action. The market potential for these wallets is significant, given demographics.

Younger customers are already demonstrating a willingness to share more of their personal data. Our global 2023 survey found that the younger the customer, the more of their personal social media and shopping data they are willing to share for a better customer experience (see figure 12-1). Younger customers—those who will shape the future landscape—understand the value proposition: a personalized experience offers benefits that make it worthwhile to share one's information about hobbies and interests, friends and followers on social media, past purchases, and browsing history.

The data exchange paradigm is already unfolding in the US health-care system. Federal regulations, issued in May 2020, require hospitals and doctors as well as insurers to make their data accessible in a standardized format (with a government-mandated API), so that consumers can access, accumulate, and share their health information as they see fit. Google and many startups are already pursuing this opportunity to serve as the trusted manager of a consumer's health data, helping the consumer move their data

FIGURE 12-1

Willingness to share information by age group

Average number of data types each customer is willing to share, by age group[1]

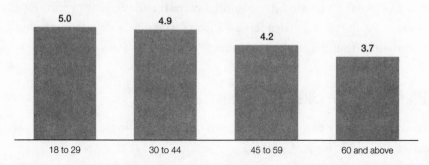

1. Survey question: What types of personal social media and shopping data are you comfortable sharing with a company you like in exchange for a better customer experience? Select all that apply.

Source: 2023 BCG Customer Personalization Survey (n = 5,000).

around as they seek care and making it immediately available for emergencies or to get better pricing.

We expect this same capability to extend to property and casualty insurers (covering data on homes, cars, and other possessions), banks (with lockboxes for financial and estate information), and other sectors, such as travel. Already some fintechs, like Voya (see Industry Spotlight: Financial Services), are asking customers for access to information across their accounts in exchange for providing them a consolidated view of their finances along with tools to help them manage those finances. These services will expand beyond their original sector, and consumers will find themselves overwhelmed by competitive offers to manage their data.

To be among the winners, you will need to build and maintain brand trust, and offer value beyond your core products or services via partnerships, while also securing permission to access information shared in data wallets.

Empower your customers by using gen AI tools

Gen AI's ability to create code from simple text prompts will enable customers to carry out commands in the moment, with increasingly complex

FIGURE 12-2

Perceptions of virtual assistants

Percentage of customers with a recent positive interaction that they knew was not with a real person, by age group[1]

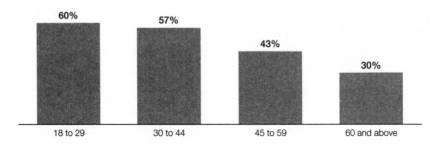

60%	57%	43%	30%
18 to 29	30 to 44	45 to 59	60 and above

1. Survey question: Have you had a positive experience with a customer service agent lately (via phone or chat) where you knew it was not a real person?

Source: 2023 BCG Customer Personalization Survey (n = 5,000).

parameters. "Show me your best deal for a frequent flyer who is looking to build points for a European holiday in two years"; or "Show me the best dresses for a summer cocktail party at my colleague's house that go with the shoes I just bought and can be delivered tomorrow by 3 p.m."; or "Create a playlist for a weekend gathering of my college buddies that excludes grunge and slow ballads, in which all the tracks seamlessly mix." We see younger generations driving this trend, too. Our global 2023 survey found that younger consumers viewed virtual assistants more positively (see figure 12-2).

Many skeptics wonder, Will companies open up their data, content, and systems to empower the customer? The answer, we believe, is yes. Personalization leaders will indeed enhance their software platforms so that customers can essentially spin up an automated agent in an instant to coordinate all aspects of a wedding, a home renovation, a mortgage application, and on and on. Companies will strategically tap all of a customer's information in order to prefill forms, prequalify the customer, and know the customer's context (such as the year the customer graduated from college as they generate the playlist for that weekend get-together). B2B personalization will evolve similarly, as suppliers and customers share more data, as suppliers apply more intelligence to help customers achieve greater efficiencies, and as customers access information more quickly by posing simple questions to the supplier's interface.

Create the trusted ecosystem to deliver end-to-end solutions

Inspired by many apps already in use in China, leaders will roll out broad-purpose, multifaceted apps that feature their own ecosystems of partners, becoming gateways to whole categories of customer needs. Leading brands that are already making rapid progress in managing customer data in their categories—the likes of Marriott, Whole Foods/Amazon, and Home Depot—will aim to become the go-to solution for achieving a customer's goal. They'll use their gen AI coding ability, open APIs (to connect with other entities), multibrand loyalty programs, data pools, and next best action orchestration to guide customers through coordinated pathways, from text prompt to follow-up questions, from content to customer goal. Startups will emerge to compete with established companies that don't build these capabilities fast enough.

Uber and Airbnb are already expanding into new adjacencies, and it's highly likely that fintech and health-care players will also soon seek to position themselves as gateways and managers of valuable personal data. Connected vehicles are yet another area we expect to become gateways, as a greater share of the global installed base of vehicles is equipped with a wide variety of sensors and digital screens that collect and deliver data. Those competing to own the ecosystem will try to keep a tight rein on their customer relationships in order to capture advantage through the snowball effect: the more data they gather and the more connections they amass, the more valuable they become to their partners and customers alike. But the power of these ecosystem owners will depend critically on trust: on how information is used, who gets to use it, and whether it leads to a great outcome.

The Ultimate Differentiator: Trust

In a world where companies are increasingly able to know and reach customers and show them something personalized, people will become more discerning about the brands that strive to empower and delight them. Trust will increasingly become a determinant of brand preference, as consumers ask: Who knows what about me, who can reach me—and who is bombarding me? Can I believe what they show me, and is it pertinent? Are they delighting me with something truly valuable? Can I trust their partners to coordinate, use, and safeguard my information appropriately and responsibly? And most of all: Are they empowering me to get done what I need to? These are big questions. Earning and sustaining customer trust will get more challenging. As more breaches occur and more high-profile court cases arise, consumers' radar will become even more sensitized.

Corporate oversight will also get more stringent. Companies will need to conform to—and stay ahead of—regulations governing permissions and transparency on the data they collect and how it is used to influence policies that affect peoples' lives (e.g., selective access, loan and insurance underwriting, health-care coverage). At the same time, advances in machine learning will improve marketers' ability to find and match individuals' identities, so companies must therefore set clear policies regarding data use, permissions, and transparency. The need for such policy-setting becomes even more apparent as tech vendors pitch the value of their "identity stacks"—tools that help marketers track unidentified customers across their digital touchpoints.

Service, not just selling, is what builds relationships. Companies that recognize their value as a destination won't bombard their customers just because they can. Their appeal will come from the functionality and breadth of execution they offer, and their judicious use of customer data. Wise strategists will challenge their companies to step back and think through solutions that will motivate customers to invest their data, time, access, and spending with them.

The personalization leaders of the future will open up a new dialogue between companies and their customers, not like the hoped-for exchanges on social media twenty years ago. This time, it will literally be a dialogue: information and permissions given and used, questions posed and answered, requests made and personalized delivery accomplished. This dialogue will directly create value for customers and companies alike. Winning companies will empower, know, reach, show, and delight their customers as they accomplish more together, and laggards will fall farther behind. The race to shape that future is well under way, as personalization leaders are well aware. By the end of this decade, the information bonds between companies and their customers will determine how every business competes.

Seize the Opportunity

Presumably, throughout these pages we've convinced you that personalization is poised to shape the future of competition. As you prepare for an increasingly personalized future, consider this straightforward advice.

Grow your base of customer relationships and knowledge. Accelerate the velocity of your testing and learning efforts. Look for opportunities to streamline handoffs and automate manual work and unlock the potential of new digital and AI tools. Mobilize to build trust through better experiences, and then challenge your teams to constantly improve those experiences through continuous experimentation. Instead of saying "we are already doing personalization," ask your teams how you could be doing even more of it.

We look forward to the day when we'll be able to report that a company— yours, perhaps?—managed to achieve a score of 100 on the Personalization Index. However, even that accomplishment will prove to be fleeting, because as customer expectations rise, so too does the bar for fulfilling the Promises of Personalization. Still, winners will emerge, companies that emphasize the volume of engagement touchpoints and the speed of learning. The $2 trillion prize in growth and an even greater prize—brand love and shareholder value—await.

The time for personalization is now.

Notes

Preface

1. "Takt, Inc. Raises $30 Million in Series A Funding Led by BCG Digital Ventures," *Business Wire*, July 25, 2016, https://www.businesswire.com/news/home/20160725006071/en /Takt-Inc.-Raises-30-Million-in-Series-A-Funding-Led-by-BCG-Digital-Ventures; "The Home Depot Doubles Down on Data Science," Wired Brand Lab, https://www.wired.com /sponsored/story/the-home-depot-doubles-down-on-data-science/; Mark Abraham, Robert Archacki, Josep Esteve González, and Stefano Fanfarillo, "The Next Level of Personalization in Retail," BCG, June 4, 2019, https://www.bcg.com/publications/2019/next-level-personalization -retail.

Chapter 1

1. "Home Depot Engagement Up 238% with Personalization Data," *BrainStation*, January 27, 2020, https://brainstation.io/magazine/home-depot-engagement-up-238-with -personalization-data; "Visit a World of Personalized Commerce," J.P. Morgan, https://www .jpmorgan.com/payments/commerce-solutions/personalized-commerce; "How Starbucks Is Transforming Customer Engagement with AI-Powered Personalization," pizzamarketplace .com, September 20, 2022, https://www.pizzamarketplace.com/news/how-starbucks-is -transforming-customer-engagement-with-ai-powered-personalization/; Jamie Grill-Goodman, "How Kroger's Personalization Science Impacts Digital Carts," Retail Info Systems, September 13, 2021, https://risnews.com/how-krogers-personalization-science -impacts-digital-carts; Lisa Johnston, "Nike's Record Quarter Fueled by 300 Million Members and Their Consumer Insights," Consumer Goods Technology, June 25, 2021, https://consumergoods.com/nikes-record-quarter-fueled-300-million-members-and-their -consumer-insights.

2. 2023 BCG Customer Personalization Survey.

Chapter 2

1. Interview with Arti Zeighami by Mark Abraham, August 22, 2023.

2. See Howard Schultz's remarks in the Management Discussion Section of the Starbucks Corp. Q3 2016 Earnings Call, July 21, 2016, FactSet: callstreet, https://s22.q4cdn .com/869488222/files/doc_financials/quarterly/2017/transcripts/SBUX_Q3-2016-Earnings -Call-Transcript.pdf.

3. See Kevin R. Johnson's remarks in the Management Discussion Section of the Starbucks Corp. Q2 2017 Earnings Call, April 27, 2017, FactSet: callstreet, https://s22.q4cdn .com/869488222/files/doc_financials/quarterly/2017/transcripts/SBUX_Q2-2017-Earnings -Call-Transcript.pdf. See also Sarah Whitten, "Restaurant Industry Ends 2016 on a Sour

Note," CNBC, January 4, 2017, https://www.cnbc.com/2017/01/04/restaurant-industry-ends-2016-on-a-sour-note.html.

4. Starbucks, "Our Mission," https://archive.starbucks.com/record/our-mission.

5. Matt Ryan and Gerri Martin-Flickinger, "The Digital Flywheel: Strategy and Impact," Presentation at 2016 Biennial Investor Day, December 7, 2016, https://s22.q4cdn.com/869488222/files/doc_presentations/2016/SID16_1206_MattR_GerriMF.pdf.

6. Ryan and Martin-Flickinger, "The Digital Flywheel."

7. See Howard Schultz's remarks in the Question and Answer Section of the Starbucks Corp. Q4 2022 Earnings Call, November 3, 2022, https://s22.q4cdn.com/869488222/files/doc_downloads/2022/11/SBUX_Corrected_Transcript.pdf.

8. Interview with Aimee Johnson by Mark Abraham and David Edelman, August 2023.

9. Heidi O'Neill and Adam Sussman, 2017 Nike, Inc. Investor Day, October 25, 2017, https://s1.q4cdn.com/806093406/files/images/irday/Heidi-Adam-Transcript-with-slides.pdf.

10. Basir Mustaghni et al., "Building Bionic Capabilities for B2B Marketing," BCG, March 8, 2021, https://www.bcg.com/publications/2021/building-bionic-capabilities-to-improve-b2b-marketing.

11. Laurie Sullivan, "Google Shares Exclusive Data on How B2B Buyers Changed, Adapted during COVID-19," MediaPost, September 14, 2020, https://www.mediapost.com/publications/article/355690/google-shares-exclusive-data-on-how-b2b-buyers-cha.html.

Industry Spotlight: Travel

1. Interview with Peggy Roe by Mark Abraham and David Edelman, August 31, 2023.

2. Ben Wade et al., "Seven Trends That Will Reshape the Airline Industry," BCG, January 9, 2020, https://www.bcg.com/publications/2020/seven-trends-reshape-airline-industry.

3. Bernard Marr, "The Amazing Ways Expedia Is Using ChatGPT to Simplify Travel Arrangements," *Forbes*, May 1, 2023, https://www.forbes.com/sites/bernardmarr/2023/05/01/the-amazing-ways-expedia-is-using-chatgpt-to-simplify-travel-arrangements/?sh=3d8417603e7b.

Chapter 3

1. General Data Protection Regulation, Regulation 2016/679 of the European Parliament and of the Council, April 5, 2016, https://gdpr-info.eu/. The California Consumer Privacy Act of 2018, https://oag.ca.gov/privacy/ccpa.

2. Peter Dewey et al., "B2B Marketing in a World without Cookies," BCG, March 24, 2022, https://www.bcg.com/publications/2022/planning-for-cookieless-marketing.

3. Creating look-alike audiences, a decades-old practice, involves uploading an email list to a social media platform with instructions to find more customers like those in the list—with the goal of getting a higher return.

4. Elizabeth Hearne et al., "Loyalty Programs Need Next-Generation Design," BCG, May 30, 2023, https://www.bcg.com/publications/2023/loyalty-programs-need-to-continue-to-evolve.

5. "Rakuten and SQREEM Launch Rakuten SQREEM, Inc.," Rakuten press release, February 3, 2020, https://global.rakuten.com/corp/news/press/2020/0203_04.html.

6. William Brangham and Sarah Clune Hartman, "Personal User Data from Mental Health Apps Being Sold, Report Finds," PBS, February 19, 2023, https://www.pbs.org/newshour/show/personal-user-data-from-mental-health-apps-being-sold-report-finds.

Industry Spotlight: Financial Services

1. Steve Thogmartin et al., "How Bank CMOs Can Do More with Less," BCG, June 6, 2023, https://www.bcg.com/publications/2023/how-bank-cmos-can-do-more-with-less.
2. Interview with David Dintenfass by David Edelman, July 21, 2023.
3. Interview with Santosh Keshavan by David Edelman, August 27, 2023.
4. "IBD's Fourth Annual Survey of the Most Trusted Financial Companies," Investor's Business Daily, September 25, 2023, https://www.investors.com/news/financial-companies-vie-for-consumer-trust-in-ibd-annual-survey/; "Most Trustworthy Companies in America," Newsweek, 2023, https://www.newsweek.com/rankings/most-trustworthy-companies-america-2023.
5. Declan Harty, "BlackRock's Fink: Customization Will Be a 'Revolution' in Sustainable Investing," S&P Global, February 3, 2021, https://www.spglobal.com/marketintelligence/en/news-insights/latest-news-headlines/blackrock-s-fink-customization-will-be-a-revolution-in-sustainable-investing-62446263.
6. "Vanguard Completes Acquisition of Just Invest," Vanguard press release, October 1, 2021, https://corporate.vanguard.com/content/corporatesite/us/en/corp/who-we-are/pressroom/Press-Release-Vanguard-Completes-Acquisition-of-Just-Invest-10121.html.

Chapter 4

1. "How AI Will Help Build Personalized Health Engagement Strategies," Icario blog, June 19, 2018, https://icariohealth.com/blog/how-ai-will-help-build-personalized-health-engagement-strategies/.
2. Interview with Peter Eliason by David Edelman, August 24, 2023.

Industry Spotlight: Retail

1. "Customer Success Stories: The Home Depot," business.adobe.com, accessed July 27, 2023, https://business.adobe.com/be_nl/customer-success-stories/the-home-depot-case-study.html.
2. Interview with Melanie Babcock by Mark Abraham, September 7, 2023.
3. Wired Brand Lab, "The Home Depot Doubles Down on Data Science," Wired, March 28, 2022, https://www.wired.com/sponsored/story/the-home-depot-doubles-down-on-data-science/.

Chapter 5

1. Interview with airline CMO by Mark Abraham, September 2023.
2. "Video Marketing Statistics 2022," Wyzowl, https://wyzowl.s3.eu-west-2.amazonaws.com/pdfs/Wyzowl-Video-Survey-2022.pdf/.
3. "Site Merchandising Solution for Fashion E-commerce," vue.ai, https://vue.ai/solutions/site-merchandising/.
4. Nathaniel Rounds, "Five Surprising Insights Brinks Home Learned through Automated Experimentation," OfferFit blog, December 16, 2022, https://www.offerfit.ai/content/blog-post/five-surprising-insights-brinks-home-learned-through-automated.

Industry Spotlight: Fashion and Beauty

1. Pandora Annual Report 2021, https://www.pandoragroup.com/-/media/files/investor
-relations/emtn-programme/3-2021-annual-report.pdf.
2. Interview with Jesper Damsgaard by Mark Abraham, July 21, 2023.
3. Pandora Annual Report 2022, https://www.pandoragroup.com/-/media/files/investor
-relations/emtn-programme/4-2022-annual-report.pdf.
4. Interview with Jesper Damsgaard by Mark Abraham, July 21, 2023.

Chapter 6

1. Interview with Arti Zeighami by Mark Abraham, August 22, 2023.

Industry Spotlight: Health Care

1. Howard J. Bolnick et al., "Health-Care Spending Attributable to Modifiable Risk
Factors in the USA: An Economic Attribution Analysis," *The Lancet*, October 2020,
https://www.thelancet.com/journals/lanpub/article/PIIS2468-2667(20)30203-6/fulltext.
2. Interview with Kyle Smith by David Edelman, July 14, 2023.
3. Interview with Mark Frank by David Edelman, July 11, 2023.

Chapter 7

1. Interview with Juanita Osborn by Mark Abraham, August 30, 2023.
2. United States Securities and Exchange Commission, Form S-1 2021, Sweetgreen, Inc.,
2021, p. 4, https://d18rn0p25nwr6d.cloudfront.net/CIK-0001477815/24da3782-69f6-4401-bc43
-144ba5a8afc7.pdf.
3. Emma Liem Beckett, "Sweetgreen's Digital Sales Made Up 67% of Q4 2021 Revenue,"
Restaurant Dive, March 7, 2022, https://www.restaurantdive.com/news/sweetgreens-digital
-sales-made-up-67-of-q4-2021-revenue/619858/.

Industry Spotlight: B2B Distribution and Technology

1. Interview with Stephanie Ferguson by Mark Abraham and David Edelman,
September 18, 2023.

Chapter 8

1. Interview with Williams Niles by David Edelman, August 20, 2023.
2. Interview with Santosh Keshavan by David Edelman, February 1, 2023.
3. Interview with a bank chief digital and analytics officer by David Edelman,
September 2023.
4. Interview with a head of sales by David Edelman, September 2023.
5. Interview with David Dintenfass by David Edelman, July 24, 2023.

Chapter 9

1. Interview with CIO by David Edelman, September 2023.
2. Interview with Arti Zeighami by Mark Abraham, December 19, 2022.

Chapter 10

1. 2023 BCG Customer Personalization Survey.
2. The EU Artificial Intelligence Act; https://artificialintelligenceact.eu/.
3. Derek Rodenhausen et al., "Consumers Want Privacy. Marketers Can Deliver," January 21, 2022, BCG, https://www.bcg.com/publications/2022/consumers-want-data-privacy-and-marketers-can-deliver.
4. Rodenhausen et al., "Consumers Want Privacy. Marketers Can Deliver."
5. "40 Million People Downloaded McDonald's App in 2022," OmniTalk blog, January 24, 2023, https://omnitalk.blog/2023/01/24/40-million-people-downloaded-mcdonalds-app-in-2022/.
6. 2023 BCG Customer Personalization Survey.
7. Rocío Lorenzo et al., "How Diverse Leadership Teams Boost Innovation," BCG, January 23, 2018, https://www.bcg.com/publications/2018/how-diverse-leadership-teams-boost-innovation.

Chapter 11

1. Bruce Henderson, "The Experience Curve," BCG, January 1, 1968, https://www.bcg.com/publications/1968/business-unit-strategy-growth-experience-curve.
2. John Clarkeson, "Jazz vs. Symphony," BCG, January 1, 1990, https://www.bcg.com/publications/1990/strategy-jazz-vs-symphony.
3. "Starbucks and Alibaba Group Announce Partnership to Transform the Coffee Experience in China," Starbucks Stories & News, August 1, 2018, https://stories.starbucks.com/press/2018/starbucks-and-alibaba-announce-partnership-to-transform-coffee-experience/.

Index

Acknowledgments

Mark Abraham: I would like to express my gratitude to the long line of mentors who have guided me throughout my two decades at BCG, starting with Michael J. Silverstein, the founder of BCG's Consumer Practice, and more recently, Joe Davis and Jean-Manuel Izaret. I would also like to extend an extra-special acknowledgment to my incredible chief of staff, Stephanie Hujet, for working magic to make time on my calendar for this project.

David Edelman: I would like to pay tribute to the late John Clarkeson, former CEO of BCG, and to George Stalk, a BCG living legend, for their mentorship through my years "growing up" at BCG. I also want to thank Richard Winger, the BCG partner who in the late 1980s (and pre-internet) encouraged me to pursue segment-of-one marketing as a topic area for BCG. I also want to give special thanks to my terrific BCG assistant, Kelli Hortman, for managing my crazy calendar.

Special thanks to the amazing Jan Koch for her tirelessness, for the many hours she has devoted to this project, and for her expert editing of this book. Her thought partnership was critical in bringing clarity to our ideas.

To our project manager, Jason Coleman, for always keeping us on task and on schedule—or at least trying to!

We also extend our gratitude to the following experts, practitioners, and colleagues who contributed their knowledge, experiences, and support.

To the inspirational personalization pioneers we interviewed for this book and those who gave wise counsel along the way: Katya Andresen, Melanie Babcock, Seraj Bharwani, Scott Brinker, David Carrel, Ian Chapman-Banks, Andreas Combuechen, Abhishek Dalmia, Jesper Demsgaard, Jim Dicso, David Dintenfass, Peter Eliason, Gerri Elliott, Sarah Fay, Stephanie Ferguson, Jon Francis, Mark Frank, Ben Howell, Aimee Johnson, Santosh Keshavan, George Khachatryan, Julie Kim, Priya Krishnan, Mark Levy, Max Lightowlers, Amitabh Mall, Andrew McInnes, Vineet Mehra, Jonathan

Neman, William Niles, Rebecca Nounou, Juanita Osborn, Marc Ossinger, Sue Page, Richelle Parham, Rene Raiss, Alok Ramsisaria, Peggy Roe, Paul Roetzler, Vish Sastry, Stephen Schwartz, Neil Shah, Kyle Smith, Steve Wigginton, Arti Zeighami, and Joey Zwillinger.

To the amazing Chris Lynes who leads our Personalization knowledge team and the hard-working BCG team that supported the ground-breaking research for this book: Marlin Bottex, Sam Falcone, Khushi Gandhi, Karan Jagtiani, Emma Kessler, Sam Kittross-Schnell, Max Schaefer, Preston Swasey, Sarah Tarta, and Kathleen Tong.

To Florian Kogler for his diligence in making sure the whole world knows about this book and to Laurent Acharian, Russell Batra, Ann Charles, Mark Fortier, Danielle Gerard, Lori Lepler, Marcus Liem, Joe Linginfelter, Heather Nowaczyk, Eric Passarelli, Nidhi Sinha, Joanna Stringer, Glenda Toma and Dan Wolf for their support of our marketing efforts.

To the industry experts who contributed to making the Industry Spotlights relevant: Raakhi Agrawal, Nitasha Anusvi, José Francisco Arias Miguel, Ryan Barbaccia, Kate Bell, Ipshita Bhattacharya, Marika Bigler, Matt Birch, Pavlo Borovyk, Aaron Brown, Riley Brown, Sumit Chandra, Harsha Chandra Shekar, Warren Chetty, Will Chung, Matt Cooper, Tijsbert Creemers, Ed Crouch, Austin Davis, Ben DeStein, Shirish Dhar, Mike Engel, Vicki Escarra, Giovanni Fassio, Saul Flores, Becky Frederick, Japjit Ghai, Valerie Gong, Jason Guggenheim, Yasmine Hamri-Donnedieu de Vabres, Ali Harcourt, Elizabeth Hearne, Julie Hess, Pia Holdsworth, Takuya Ikemachi, Caroline Israel, Xiao Jiang, Therese Jordal, Jaison Justin, Marcela Keramidas, Julian King, Clara Lachmann, Matt Langione, Gilbert Lemieux, Eduardo Leone, Andy Levine, Richard Lewis, Dimitri Limberopoulos, Kevin Lowe, Franck Luisada, Amanda Luther, Maddie Macks, Andreas Malby, Mary Martin, Dima Martirosyan, Simonas Matulionis, Ciara Maynard, Joen Moller, Nadine Moore, Johannes Nordqvist, Andrea Orfeo, Leandro Paez, Peter Pessoa, Jackie Post, Harsha Ramalingam, Vaishali Rastogi, Barric Reed, Romney Resney, Guia Ricci, Jon Roberts, Alyssa Rosenbaum, Andres Ruiz, Dan Saacks, Suchi Sastri, Gonzalo Scaglia, Marc Schelenz, Michael Schniering, Martin Segerberg, Phillip Shinall, Joe Simon, Jeremy Sporn, Emily Sunderland, Khaled Tawfik, Elodie Teboul, Steve Thogmartin, Kyle Trahair, Laura van den Bergh, Manaswi Veligatla, Justin Vincent, Bodo von Hülsen, Josh von Zeil-Singer, Jerry Wang, Drake Watten, Monica Wegner, David Welch, John Wenstrup, Marco Werner, Erin

White, Alpha Wong, Haytham Yassine, Kazuaki Yuba, Allen Zhang, and Changan Zhang.

To Paul Michelman, BCG's global head of content, and to the team at the Bruce Henderson Institute, led by Martin Reeves, for their coaching and advice: Amanda Wikman and Brigitta Pristyak.

To the team at BrightHouse, led by Ashley Grice, for their design and creative support: Cally Bybee and Sarai Wingate.

To our Personalization and Marketing, Sales & Pricing Leadership teams for their enthusiastic support and ideas: Phillip Andersen, Jessica Apotheker, Aaron Arnoldsen, Alex Barocas, Nicolas de Bellefonds, Mitch Colgan, Olof Darpo, Rob Derow, Ben DeStein, Peter Dewey, Dharmendra Dubey, Rob Fagnani, Leo Fascione, Shane Fisher, Bryan Gauch, Betsy Heckenbach, Kale Hungerson, Dwight Hutchins, Ben Jacobsen, Karl Johnson, Nirav Kathrani, John Keezell, Leora Kelman, Lara Koslow, Fred Lam, Karen Lellouche, Haoran Li, Yun Lim, Justin McBride, John Mulliken, Steven Mills, Brian Nadres, Silvio Palumbo, Megha Ramanuja, Sanjeev Reddy, Scott Rhodes, Adil Riaz, Derek Rodenhausen, Christian Sandberg, Stephanie Schoen, Shilpa Sharma, Rachael Stein, Sohum Talreja, Cathy Taylor, Lauren Taylor, Alejandra Torres, Adam Whybrew, Michael Widowitz, Lauren Wiener, and Ray Yu.

To Juan Martinez, our *Harvard Business Review* editor, who supported our foundational and follow-up articles in 2022, 2023, and 2024 and who encouraged us to write this book.

Finally, we are so grateful to Courtney Cashman, our editor at Harvard Business Review Press, for challenging us to make this book better with each review. We also thank Sally Ashworth, Jordan Concannon, Julie Devoll, Lindsey Dietrich, Stephani Finks, Alexandra Kephart, Cheyenne Paterson, Jon Shipley, Felicia Sinusas, and Jennifer Waring for their ongoing support in bringing this work to fruition.

About the Authors

MARK ABRAHAM is a senior partner at BCG and the founder of the firm's Personalization business, which he has built into a global team of more than a thousand agile marketers, data scientists, engineers, and martech experts. Mark's passion is bringing together disparate capabilities across different parts of an organization to drive innovation and results. It is how he and his team have accelerated the personalization, retail media, and AI efforts of more than a hundred iconic brands (including Starbucks, Home Depot, and Google) and built some of BCG's largest ventures and AI platforms, including Fabriq, for personalization. In his everyday interactions, Mark saw the urgent need for a book that would address the many questions business executives face in their efforts to deliver on the Promises of Personalization. Currently, Mark leads BCG's North American Marketing, Sales & Pricing practice and is reenergizing the growth and development of talent in what is one of the firm's largest regional practices. A dedicated father of two, Mark lives with his boys and his partner, Jason, in the Pacific Northwest. His stories and photographs from their off-the-grid treks speak to his love of adventure, the outdoors, and special family time.

DAVID C. EDELMAN has a long history of personalization work stretching back more than three decades. In 1989, he wrote the BCG Classic article "Segment-of-One Marketing," in which he predicted the possibilities of personalization. Since then, he has chronicled the evolution of the field, offering the visionary ideas he's developed as a practitioner and a consultant. David worked with dozens of companies on personalization, AI, and agile marketing at BCG and Digitas before transforming Aetna's approach to customer experience while serving as the company's chief marketing officer. Today, he is a senior lecturer at Harvard Business School, an executive advisor and board member to brands and technology providers, and an advisor to BCG. *Forbes* has repeatedly named him one of the Top

20 Most Influential Voices in Marketing, and *Ad Age* has named him a Top 20 Chief Marketing and Technology Officer. Together with Mark, David wrote the March–April 2022 *Harvard Business Review* article "Customer Experience in the Age of AI," which was the germ of this book. A music fanatic and avid tenor sax player, David lives with his wife, Miriam, and their two labradoodles in the Boston area, where they periodically host their three grown children.